Zainichi (Koreans in Japan)

Diasporic Nationalism and Postcolonial Identity

JOHN LIE

Global, Area, and International Archive
University of California Press

BERKELEY   LOS ANGELES   LONDON

Frontispiece: Y. David Chung, *Satisfaction* (detail), 1993, graphite and watercolor.

The Global, Area, and International Archive (GAIA) is an initiative of International and Area Studies, University of California, Berkeley, in partnership with the University of California Press, the California Digital Library, and international research programs across the UC system. GAIA volumes, which are published in both print and open-access digital editions, represent the best traditions of regional studies, reconfigured through fresh global, transnational, and thematic perspectives.

University of California Press, one of the most distinguished university presses in the United States, enriches lives around the world by advancing scholarship in the humanities, social sciences, and natural sciences. Its activities are supported by the UC Press Foundation and by philanthropic contributions from individuals and institutions. For more information, visit www.ucpress.edu.

University of California Press
Berkeley and Los Angeles, California

University of California Press, Ltd.
London, England

Library of Congress Cataloging-in-Publication Data
Lie, John.
    Zainichi (Koreans in Japan) : diasporic nationalism and postcolonial identity / John Lie.
        p.   cm. — (Global, area, and international archive)
    Includes bibliographical references and index.
    ISBN: 978-0-520-25820-4 (pbk. : alk. paper)
    1. Koreans—Japan.   2. Japan—Ethnic relations.   I. Title.
DS832.7.K6L54   2008
305.895'7052—dc22   2008019409

Manufactured in the United States of America

17   16   15   14   13   12   11   10
10   9   8   7   6   5   4   3

The paper used in this publication meets the minimum requirements of ANSI/NISO Z39.48–1992 (R 1997) *(Permanence of Paper).*

Zainichi *(Koreans in Japan)*

For Charis and Charlotte

Contents

Preface

Human beings may very well have a nesting instinct—a deep desire to settle down—but they have also uprooted themselves out of necessity or volition. These two impulses clashed mightily in the twentieth century. Governments frequently sought to enhance allegiance by fostering nationalism—with its attendant beliefs in shared genealogy and geography, history, and culture—but they also deployed soldiers and banished dissidents. Even as nationalism became a potent political ideology and at times a redemptive religion, people deracinated themselves in order to avoid danger, pursue profit, seek adventure, or follow kin. Korean nationalism flourished when its largely rural population was profoundly and repeatedly unsettled by the looming threat of colonial subjection, the collapse of a long-lasting dynasty, the nascent but turbulent development of capitalist industrialization, the discipline and violence of Japanese colonialism, the murder and mayhem of a fratricidal war and the ensuing division of the putative homeland, and the consequent churnings of urbanization and modernization. Perhaps it is not surprising that people who live in interesting times should express heartfelt beliefs in their solidarity born of blood and soil, custom and tradition. Contradictory to the core, to be sure, but somehow complementary are the reality of change and difference and the ideology of stasis and commonality.

This book focuses on a population (Koreans in Japan) and delineates the birth and transformation of a peoplehood identity (*Zainichi*). It is neither a comprehensive history of the Korean minority in Japan nor a systematic study of ethnogenesis and ethnic relations (there exist, even in English, many books on these topics: see for instance Mitchell 1967, Lee and De Vos 1981, Weiner 1989, Ryang 1997, Hicks 1998, Lie 2001, Chapman 2008, Ryang and Lie 2008). Instead, I stress the instability and complexity of a

postcolonial, diasporic identity in Japan called *Zainichi*, the literal transla-
tion of which would be "residing in Japan," with an inevitable inflection on
its impermanence. One may very well be Zainichi Chinese or Zainichi
American, but the term refers almost always—by ethnic Japanese and ethnic Koreans alike—to a population of colonial-era migrants from the
Korean peninsula that settled in the Japanese archipelago and their
descendants.

Nationalist discourse often asserts the chasm between Korea and Japan
and the essential homogeneity of each population. This line of thinking
minimizes or ignores connections, differences, and changes; thus there are
Japanese in Japan and Koreans in Korea, but not Koreans in Japan or
Japanese in Korea except as short-term sojourners. Ontologically speaking,
Zainichi should somehow not exist. Reality is more complicated, confus-
ing, confounding. Consider only the basic facts of nationality and name.
During the colonial period (1910–45), Koreans living on both the Japanese
archipelago and the Korean peninsula were Japanese imperial subjects. In
spite of colonial racism, Japanese law and official discourse decreed ethnic
Koreans as Japanese nationals and the Emperor's children. The 1952 San
Francisco Peace Treaty restored Japanese sovereignty but rescinded Japanese
citizenship for ethnic Koreans remaining in Japan. Overnight, imperial
subjects became resident foreigners; Japanese citizens became Koreans
[*Chōsenjin*] when there was no Korea, only two warring states claiming
the mantle of Korea.

By the end of the Korean War in 1953, the political division in the peninsula rendered difficult what in English is an uncomplicated assertion of
being "Korean." Partisan politics, with more than an innuendo of racial
discrimination, plagued the seemingly simple act of appellation. In Japan,
the very name *Korea* became contested: *Chōsen*—the common colonial-
era appellation—came to refer to North Korea (*Kita Chōsen* for North
Korea, and *Chōsenjin* for Koreans affiliated with North Korea).
Simultaneously, *Chōsen*—inflected by both colonial-era domination and
postwar anticommunism—was a racial epithet. In the 1950s, the term for
ethnic Koreans in Japan was *Zainichi Chōsenjin*, reflecting in part the
population's overwhelming allegiance to North Korea (often called the
"Republic" [*Kyōwakoku*]). Later, waning allegiance to the North, especially after the 1965 Normalization Treaty between Japan and South Korea,
required an explicit reference to the divided Korea: *Kankoku* was the preferred South Korean term for (South) Korea and *Kankokujin* for Koreans
affiliated with South Korea. Hence, the normative nomenclature in the
1970s and 1980s for the totality of ethnic Koreans in Japan was the rather
cumbersome *Zainichi Kankoku Chōsenjin* [resident South Koreans and

North Koreans in Japan]—though those strongly allied with one of the two Koreas would prefer either *Zainichi Kankokujin* or *Zainichi Chōsenjin*. When NHK—Japan's national broadcasting service—aired a course on the Korean language in 1984, it avoided both renditions in Japanese [*Chōsengo* or *Kankokugo*] and instead opted for the name of the script *(han'gŭl)* (Ōmura 2003:267–84). By the 1980s, some used the English term "Korean" to neutralize the split between the two Koreas—*Zainichi Korians* [resident Koreans in Japan] (Ōnuma 2004:iv–v). Others preferred the Sinified equivalent, *Zainichi Kanjin* (Yoon 1992:204). The ideology of Japanese cultural and ethnic homogeneity had effectively barred the plausibility in Japan of the term *Korean Japanese [Kankokukei* or *Chōsenkei Nihonjin,* or *Nihonseki Chōsenjin* or *Kankokujin* or *Korian]* (cf. Kishida 1999:61–62; Kim Yondal 2003b:21–23). By 1995, however, a popular Zainichi singer, Arai Eiichi, would identify himself as "Korean Japanese" in his autobiographical song, "Chonhā e no michi" (The road to Chonhā). No wonder most people were confused (Miyauchi 1999), even though shifts of ethnic appellation are generic, as we can see in the serially acceptable terms *Colored, Negro, Black,* and *African American* in the twentieth-century United States. This multiplicity and instability in nomenclature suggests the conundrum of a population stubbornly struggling for recognition while being denied—and at times denying themselves—their place in Japanese society.

My portrait of Zainichi history resists the received narratives that are at once tragic (vilifying Japanese colonialism and racism) and triumphant (praising the heroic struggles of the Korean minority). Rather, and without denying the reality of both moments, I see it as both more nuanced and more humdrum. I also don't assume a well-formed and widely held common consciousness and ethnonational identity among ethnic Koreans in Japan at any point, and certainly not a coherent and popular national identity among people living on the Korean peninsula at the turn of the nineteenth century. Although we can employ the category *Koreans* to refer to a population, we should not assume the existence of Koreans as a peoplehood, a self-conscious group identity. The divides of social status, regional origins, gender, and generation, among many others, almost always imperil the attempt to depict a group as a coherent body. The persistent flaw of essentialism—seeking the least common denominator, or essence, of a group—is that its presumption often turns out to be empty. It is frequently difficult to generate useful predicates about a subject group beyond the nominal definition: colonial-era Korean migrants to Japan and their descendants. What may seem solid and permanent, moreover, turns out to be effervescent and ephemeral. On reading some accounts the reader may conclude that every Zainichi has felt a profound sense of belonging to the Korean people and wanted passionately to return to her or his homeland. Alas, neither proposition can charitably be called correct today. The brute passage of time wreaks its grinding havoc on fervently espoused ideologies and identities. Be that as it may, the focus of the book is very much on the vicissitudes of and fractures within Zainichi identity. I seek to sketch the population and the people: its history, culture, experience, and understanding. In exploring the complexities of Zainichi experience and identity, I hope to shed some light on the vexing topics of diaspora and population movement, identity and group formation.

Somewhat grandiosely I had called my trio of books on Korea and the Korean diaspora—*Blue Dreams: Korean Americans and the Los Angeles Riots* (Abelmann and Lie 1995), *Han Unbound: The Political Economy of South Korea* (Lie 1998), and *Multiethnic Japan* (Lie 2001)—the "sociological imagination trilogy." I suppose that this book makes it the sociological imagination tetralogy. C. Wright Mills's idea of the sociological imagination—to make sense of the biographical against the larger contexts of history and social structure—strikes me as a powerful way to link the personal and the political, the past and the present, the concrete and the abstract. It is a mode of science in which one may express life as freely and as wholly as one can. At times, however, some readers—or nonreaders—took it to mean that these books are all about *me*. This is exceedingly unfortunate. Personal anecdotes can illuminate larger historical, structural, or theoretical points, which in turn cannot possibly exist without them. It also slights a fundamental motivation of the human sciences and human thinking: inevitable queries about where we have come from, who we are, and where we are going. The Delphic injunction to "know thyself" is merely one of the earliest expressions of this all-too-human desire. As much as we wish to avoid particularism, ethnocentrism, and other limitations of our cognitive capacity, we cannot transcend our finitude—contextualized in a particular place and time—as we struggle with questions that inevitably emanate from these essential human conditions.

My observations are drawn primarily from the Tokyo metropolitan area, including my extended stays in Shibuya in the 1960s, Tsukishima and Kawasaki in 1985, and Mita and Hiyoshi in 1993, as well as sporadic sojourns from 2003 to 2007. Regional diversity—such as the distinct role of Osaka in Zainichi experience and imaginary—is crucial but this book remains undoubtedly Tokyo-centric. Because I don't discuss—and certainly don't cite—much of my "data" ranging from casual conversations to television shows, this book may seem excessively bookish. I may write as though everything exists to end up in a book, but I struggled to follow Joubert's anti-Mallarméan insight that many things should be left in life, not put into books. In any case, the stuff of human life—experience—is amorphous and ephemeral, resisting any sustained (and probably successful) attempt to categorize and conceptualize it. It is a truism that experience is theory dependent, but we should not forget that experience also resists and supersedes every effort to theorize it. The tangible and the theoretical are co-dependent as they are contradictory. This is one of the fundamental challenges of the human sciences for which, I am fairly certain, there are no perfect answers.

I have sought to minimize the use of local locutions and references but I have not expunged all of them. The colonial period began tentatively in 1905 when Korea became a Japanese protectorate and decisively in 1910 when it was annexed outright. The war in this book refers inevitably to World War II, or the Pacific War, which ended with Japan's unconditional surrender on 15 August 1945. Prewar and postwar periods are therefore divided by that fateful day in 1945 (cf. Dower 1999:559; Yomota 2007:10–14). While the end of the colonial period is clear, there is no consensus on the end of the postwar period: already by summer 1956, the post-Korean War economic boom made "no longer postwar" a catchphrase; for others the ending came in the early 1970s with a series of shocking events such as Nixon's 1972 visit to China and the 1973 oil crisis; for Japan-centric people, it came with the end of the Shōwa period, or the death of Emperor Hirohito, in 1989; and for yet others it came with the end of the Cold War in 1989–92. For the Korean peninsula, given its continued division, perhaps neither the postwar period nor the Cold War has really ended. For Japan, however, the postwar period effectively did end in 1989 with the profound symbolism of Hirohito's passing and the beginning of the end of the Cold War. In particular, the three decades between 1955 and 1985 constitute a coherent period not only of the centrality of the Cold War and conservative politics in Japan but also the dominance of monoethnic ideology.

At the risk of courting confusion and controversy, I have transliterated Zainichi names into English as the Japanese pronunciation of the Korean reading of the Chinese characters that constitute their Korean names. As discombobulated as this may seem, it captures some of the confusions and contradictions of Zainichi existence. The representative Zainichi writer Kin Kakuei (2006b:553) uses the Japanese reading of his Korean name because "it somehow symbolizes the inner truth about myself." I have made exceptions when someone has a preferred transliteration or when the received practice is deviant. Thus, for example, the Korean surname "Kim" is rendered as it is, rather than as "Kimu," as a phonetic Japanese reading would have it. As futile as it may be, I hope to convey to the Anglophone reader how Zainichi people who use their Korean names and their Korean readings call themselves. In the same spirit, I present East Asian names in their customary order: surnames first. I have also by and large adopted the received western transliteration of well-known place names, such as Seoul or Tokyo. Otherwise I have followed the McCune-Reischauer system for Korean and the modified Hepburn system for Japanese. All translations, unless otherwise noted in the reference section, are mine.

The statistics cited in the book, unless referred otherwise, are from the Japanese government, conveniently available on the Web. I have drawn on the Ministry of Justice (http://www.moj.go.jp/) for population figures, and the Ministry of Health, Labor, and Welfare (http://www.mhlw.go.jp/) for marriage-related data. Because of monoethnic ideology, there are no systematic sources of numerical data on Zainichi.

I have written about Zainichi on and off for over two decades and I have incurred far too many debts—intellectual and personal, however unacknowledged most of them remain—and this book expresses but a mere token of my gratitude. For constructive criticisms and superb suggestions, I thank Nathan MacBrien, Mark Selden, and an anonymous reviewer. For logistical and social support in Stephens Hall, I am very grateful to Monica Allen, Sharon Lyons Butler, and Joan Kask. And without the love and companionship of Charis and Charlotte I am sure that this book, and most certainly the author, would have been worse off.

1. Silence

Peter Carey's self-conscious search for the Real Japan ends with an elderly, Kabuki-loving Japanese woman kissing the cheek of his son, who remarks: "Must be the Real Japan. . . . Let's get out of here before we learn we're wrong" (Carey 2005:158). What drew the novelist's son to Japan was neither Kabuki nor the Kabuki-loving woman but rather *manga*, the *Japonisme* of his generation. Manga has long antecedents in Japan and elsewhere, as Carey and many others are wont to pontificate, but modern manga in Japan emerged in the postwar period. Far from only producing pap, the genre has generated such masterpieces as the dialectical-materialist historical epics of Shirato Sanpei and the dystopian scientific fantasies of Ōtomo Katsuhiro. Periodicals, such as *Shōnen magajin* and *Shōnen janpu*, garnered mass readership and engendered the "manga generation" in the 1960s. Its artistic conscience was the periodical *Garo* and the work of Tsuge Yoshiharu.

Among Tsuge's *oeuvre* is "Ri-san ikka" [The Lee family], a 1967 portrait of a Korean family in Japan. The narrator one day discovers a family occupying the second floor of his dilapidated house: a family of four named Ri (a Japanese rendering of the surname usually transliterated into English as "Lee," though it is pronounced as "Yi" in Korean). The parents are unemployed, the children don't do much, and the family gets by on almost nothing. Indeed, nothing much happens in the short piece—the Ris are in equal measure impudent and inscrutable—but in the end, they are still there, all four family members staring silently and blankly at the narrator (or the reader), their baffling stubbornness worthy of Bartleby. It would not be difficult to read Tsuge's short piece as an allegory of ethnic Koreans in Japan. To put it as pithily as possible, one day they came and they are still here. They are Zainichi, "residing in Japan."

Despite the ubiquity of ethnic Koreans in postwar Japanese life, many

Japanese almost instinctively denied their legitimacy and at times their very presence. Yet this persistent repression of ethnic existence faces the recalcitrant reality of a multiethnic Japan.

MULTIETHNIC JAPAN

The beguiling temptation of history writing is to begin with the original couple, whether Eve and Adam or, in the case of Japan, the creator deities Izanami and Izanagi. From this couple, a narrative of pure descent flows that naturalizes and justifies all claims of contemporary homogeneity. Postwar Japanese historiography followed "hermit historiography" *[sakoku shikan]* in limning a lineage of homogeneous Japanese people. Marxism, dominant in the historiography of the immediate postwar decades, symptomatically served to promote this nationalist and essentialist frame. Consequently, a monoethnic history effaced both the Korean peninsular origin of the imperial household and the transnational movements of people over the centuries. But there is nothing natural about such tales of descent. We may just as well flip over the ancestral tree, replacing the original ancestral pair with geometric growth in the number of ancestors (two parents, four grandparents, eight great-grandparents, and so on). Such a genealogical perspective promotes a polymorphous parentage that accentuates hybridity and heterogeneity, and thus would encourage the investigation of exogenous influences and influxes (e.g., Denoon, Hudson, McCormack, and Morris-Suzuki 1997). It would, in short, be non-nationalist. Whether we consider the earliest period of Japanese history (the Jōmon Period) or the critical era of state building *(ritsurei kokka)*, the impact of people from the Korean peninsula was profound. Even during the Tokugawa period, when Japan was officially "closed" *[sakoku]* to foreign contact, non-Japanese peoples, commodities, and cultures circulated around the archipelago (Arano 1988).

In a multiethnic historiography, Japanese people today would trace their ancestry beyond the current Japanese borders. To the best of our knowledge, the global dispersion of the first modern human beings from Africa occurred between 100,000 and 10,000 years ago: a mere flicker in geological time (Cavalli-Sforza and Cavalli-Sforza 1995:158). From the perspective of the *longue durée*, we are all part of the African diaspora.

Against the commonsense presupposition that people who live in present-day Japan have always regarded themselves as Japanese, the dissemination of a popular national identity was a signature feat of modernity (Lie 2004b:chap. 3). State institutions, ranging from military conscription to mass schooling, relayed and reproduced the message of national identity, and state-led infrastructural developments, such as nationwide circuits of transportation and communication, constructed the media to disseminate it. Equally significant was an ideological transformation. Recall Ernest Gellner's (1983:x) influential definition of nationalism as "a theory of political legitimacy, which requires that ethnic boundaries should not cut across political ones, and . . . ethnic boundaries . . . should not separate the power-holders from the rest." Premodern polities rejected such a bond between the rulers and the ruled; the former were, whether because of divinity or lineage, superior to the latter. In contrast, modern polities accentuated the bond. In part because of the heightened demand of political legitimacy—necessitated in turn by mass conscription, for example—modern polities, whether democratic or authoritarian, promoted one or another form of nationalism, often asserting ethnoracial isomorphism among the populace. This is not surprising in a country, such as modern Japan, that fought wars virtually continuously and relied on citizen conscripts. Modern state making, with its infrastructural development and inclusionary ideology, promoted and propagated national identity and patriotic nationalism.

The development of popular nationalism occurred in tandem with the making of multiethnic Japan (Lie 2001:chap. 4). Precisely when popular national identity surfaced, the modern nation-state became irrefutably multiethnic. The fundamental mechanism was colonialism. The modern Japanese state conquered Hokkaidō and its indigenous Ainu population. In the 1870s, Ryūkyū, or Okinawa—a southern group of islands, which had been an independent kingdom, albeit with tributary relations to both the Qing and Tokugawa—was absorbed into the ever-expanding Japanese empire. Beginning with Taiwan in 1895, Japan annexed Korea, Manchuria and other parts of the Chinese mainland, and the southern Pacific islands. Not only did Japanese territory expand fourfold, but the Japanese polity also became irreducibly multiethnic. This was not only because of the empire, but also because the empire, so to speak, came home. A massive influx of colonial labor transmogrified Japan into a multiethnic society. Hence, its dominant self-conception was not in reality monoethnic—Japan as a monoethnic nation is a postwar idea. Imperial Japan occasionally sang paeans to monoethnic nationalism, but the leitmotif accentuated its multiethnic meter. Koreans, both within and without the Japanese archipelago, were imperial subjects [*shinmin*]. Japan may have been a family-state, but Koreans and Chinese were also the Emperor's children [*tennō no sekishi*].

THE ORIGINS OF THE KOREAN POPULATION
IN MODERN JAPAN

As the Japanese imperial ideology suggested, people from the Korean peninsula had been sailing to the Japanese archipelago and shaping Japanese
history and society at least from the beginning of surviving documents
(cf. Kim D. 1990). Yet these past influxes and influences have little direct
bearing on the contemporary Zainichi population. Neither should we focus
on students, merchants, and workers who entered Japan in the first four
decades or so after the Meiji Restoration (1868): only several thousand
Koreans were in the main Japanese islands at the time of Korean annexation in 1910. Rather, the proximate cause of a significant Korean presence
was the labor shortage of the 1920s. Between 1920 and 1930 the number of
Koreans in the main Japanese islands—usually referred to contemporane-
ously as *naichi* or inland—expanded over tenfold to 419,000; by 1945,
there were about 2 million Koreans (Kim Yondal 2003b:87–89).

The received Zainichi historiography depicts the Korean population in
colonial Japan as poor peasants from southern Korea who were forcibly
brought to Japan. Expropriated by Japanese colonialism and exploited by
Japanese capitalism, they faced relentless racial discrimination, exemplified
by the Japanese massacre after the 1923 Great Kantō Earthquake (e.g., Pak
Kyongsik 1965; Zainichi Kankoku 1970). That is, Japanese imperialism and
capitalism created and crafted the unwilling population who had to endure
and struggle against racist Japanese society. As the protagonist in Kin
Kakuei's (2004:34) iconic Zainichi story, "Kogoeru kuchi" [The frozen
mouth, 1966], summarizes: "Inevitably books on Korea touch on the tragic
history of the Korean people . . . and [how] they still live amidst pathos and
suffering" (cf. Ko 1986:22–23).

Most ethnic Koreans in prewar Japan were farmers from three southern
provinces (North and South Kyongsang and South Cholla, including
Chejudo). In a 1932 survey of Korean residents in Osaka, 87 percent were
agricultural workers and 92 percent hailed from the three southern provinces (Osaka-fu 1982:44–47, 69). In a 1936 survey of the neighboring Hyōgo
Prefecture, the picture is roughly the same: 92 percent came from the same
three provinces where 87 percent were farmers (Hyōgo-ken 1982:36, 33).
Many of them were ill-educated and illiterate. In Osaka, 62 percent had no
schooling, whereas the figure was 34 percent for Hyōgo (Osaka-fu 1982:69;
Hyōgo-ken 1982:125). They therefore engaged in manual and menial work,
occupying—along with Burakumin (descendants of premodern outcastes)
and Okinawans—the lowest tier in the urban labor market (Nishinarita

1997:74–75). In particular, construction and mining came to be dominated by Korean workers; by 1930 nearly half of Koreans in Japan were construction workers, constituting over 35 percent of the country's construction workers (Kim Chanjung 1979:12–14). Similarly, over 30 percent of coal-miners in the 1940s were ethnic Koreans (Totsuka 1977:191; Kim Chanjung 1980:98–100). They often received much lower wages than ethnic Japanese; in the 1920s, for example, Korean construction workers earned 70 percent of what their Japanese counterparts made (Ishizaka 1993:193; cf. Iwamura 1972:35–36). Because of poverty and discrimination, migrants congregated in Korean ghettoes, which were often contiguous to Burakumin and Okinawan neighborhoods (Sasaki 1986:211–12; Nishinarita 1997:67–69). Already by the early 1900s, the earliest Korean ghetto *[buraku]* appeared in Ikaino, Osaka (Higuchi 1978:550).

Ethnic Koreans were enmeshed in, as well as suffered from, the Japanese war effort. Wartime labor shortages led to enforced migration *[kyōsei renkō]*. In the name of eliciting "volunteers," ethnic Japanese and Koreans colluded in the conscription of Koreans to work in factories and mines. Between 1939 and 1945, 700,000–800,000 Koreans were made to work in Japan (Unno 1993:120–21). The notorious *teishintai* (*chongsindae* in Korean) was initially designed not to produce sexual serfs for Japanese soldiers, but rather to recruit Korean women workers into ammunition, textile, and other factories. Beginning in 1944, 110,000 ethnic Koreans were conscripted by the Japanese military (Kim Yondal 2003a:59). Many Koreans in Japan suffered war-related injuries and deaths: 239,320 Koreans, according to Higuchi (1979:44–46). Up to 30,000 ethnic Koreans died in the atomic bomb explosion in Hiroshima (Yoneyama 1999:152).

If low regard for Korean culture was a pretext to colonize Korea, then actual colonization confirmed it, conferring disreputable characteristics, such as poverty and turpitude, *pudeur* and acedia (cf. Duus 1995:404). After the 1923 earthquake, racial prejudice mixed with racial fear (cf. Ryang 2003:738). A rumor that Koreans were poisoning the water supply unleashed a massive pogrom, resulting in perhaps thousands of deaths of not only Koreans but also Okinawans and Chinese (Yamagishi 2002:112–14). Along with enforced migration *[kyōsei renkō]*, the earthquake and the ensuing mass murder became an enduring memory and source of identity for the Korean population in Japan, the equivalent of slavery for African Americans and the Shoah for Jewish Americans (O 1971:71–75). The post-earthquake massacre became something of a literary tattoo or an ethnic meme (e.g. Yū 2007a:418–21). As the naturalized Zainichi protagonist in Lee Hoesung's 1975 novel *Tsuihō to jiyū* [Exile and freedom] expatiates: "What crimes

Japanese have committed against Koreans. . . . Do you know why Koreans
are afraid of an earthquake? They are afraid that they would be massacred
again. . . . We suffered enforced migration *[kyōsei renkō]"* (Lee H.
1975:32–33).

Ethnic Koreans were not silent subjects to Japanese domination; there
were repeated manifestations of Korean resistance and Korean-Japanese
conflicts. As I elaborate in chapter 6, Japanese colonialism unwittingly
enhanced Korean nationalism. The concentration of Korean workers in
mining and construction at times led to mass mobilization (Ishizaka
1993:209–13). Koreans denoted violent agitators, and prewar Zainichi history can be narrated as a chronicle of resistance and struggle (Pak Kyongsik
1979; Ko 1985). In more mundane ways, manifold tensions flared between
Japanese and Koreans based on landlord-tenant conflicts, cultural misunderstandings, and employment competition (Mitchell 1967:32–38, 92–99).
The ubiquity of the epithet *"Futei Senjin"* [Korean malcontents] suggests
not only the Japanese presumption of Korean insolence and treachery but
also the fact of Korean resistance and struggle (Morris-Suzuki 1998:105):
at times they committed garden-variety crimes; at others, political resistance. It was not simply paranoia that prompted Japanese authorities to
institute extensive surveillance of ethnic Koreans within and without the
Japanese archipelago (Pak Kyongsik 1973 2:chap. 5).

Thus, the received Zainichi historiography delineates a tragic arc of
expropriation, exploitation, discrimination, and resistance. It would be a
moral solecism to justify Japanese colonialism, but this unremittingly
tragic (though heroic) picture misrecognizes the character of the Korean
influx. Given the preponderantly rural and impoverished nature of colonial-era Korea, it should not be surprising that many Koreans were
unschooled. Yet barriers of information, resources, and will to travel and
seek employment minimized the abysmally poor from the ranks of Japan-
bound Koreans (cf. Kim Chanjung and Ban 1997:43–45), who came more
commonly from the middle strata, with correspondingly higher educational attainment (Higuchi 1995:55). Although Korean migrants are often
described—and identified themselves—as farmers, some of them had been
engaged in urban employment in Korea (Nishinarita 1997:47–48). Perhaps
10 percent of Koreans in Tokyo were there for educational purposes
(Tonomura 2004:76).

The fundamental fact is that Korean immigration to the Japanese archipelago was more or less voluntary until wartime mobilization generated
involuntary recruitment in the 1940s. Motives are almost always murky,
but the pragmatist insight that action generates belief, much more than

belief spawning action, helps us order the kaleidoscope of recollected, and frequently justificatory, Zainichi memories of the sojourn from the peninsula to the archipelago. The received Zainichi historiography exaggerates the elements of constraint and force. The Japanese empire—including the economic transformation that uprooted the peasantry—is certainly a condition of possibility for the Korean diaspora in Japan. But it should be seen, at least in the 1920s and 1930s, as facilitating opportunities in Japan as much as destroying livelihoods in Korea. *Kyōsei renkō* [enforced migration] is not synonymous with Zainichi origins (Kim Yondal 2003a:35–37). Chong Jaejung (2006:6) recalls the popular refrain in the southern Korean countryside in the 1920s: "Tokyo in Japan / What a wonderful place / If you go once / You will never come home." Born in 1909, Chan Jonsu (1989:38) "escaped" his parents in 1926 in order to continue his studies in Japan. That is, Japan was a land of opportunity and promise for many Koreans in the 1920s and 1930s (cf. Osaka-shi 1975:352). It would be equally problematic, however, to absolve the prewar Japanese government and employers, as coercion did escalate during wartime (Weiner 1994:195–203). Even in the case of voluntary recruitment, as recalled by Pae Hakpo, fraudulent promises and horrid conditions turned Koreans into virtual "slaves" (Tsubouchi 1998:55, 161). The emotional resonance of *kyōsei renkō* rests much less on the fact of involuntary recruitment as the reality of horrible working situations that goaded so many ethnic Koreans to escape or resist (cf. Kim Munson 1991:117–18). Historical injustices—what is history but a chronicle of wrongs?—tempt victims to rehearse and magnify their sufferings and seduce perpetrators and their descendants to convenient amnesia or self-justificatory ratiocination. We should take a leaf from the self-identified "enforced migrant" worker Jon Chonjon (1984:6), who bemoans at once the plight of Korean workers who died like insects, and the erasure of numerous, nameless Japanese who defended them.

By 1930, ethnic Koreans constituted a recognizable social group in major Japanese cities. Until the late 1920s, most of them were male migrant workers who shifted rapidly from one job and place to another (Hōmu Kenshūjo 1975:7–10), but thereafter some Koreans settled down in *naichi* (Kimura 1997:118–19). The changing orientation can be seen, for example, in the rising number of Korean women and children (Nishinarita 1997:52–58). The greatest concentration of ethnic Koreans was in Osaka and the surrounding area (Pak Cheil 1957:41). By the mid-1930s, nearly a third of Koreans were born in Japan, which explains the rising number of Koreans who spoke Japanese as their primary language and their aspiration for permanent residency in Japan (Tonomura 2004:96). In the aforementioned surveys from the 1930s, 66 percent in Osaka and 60 percent in Hyōgo expressed their intention to reside permanently [*eijū*] in Japan (Osaka-fu 1982:77; Hyōgo-ken 1982:141). By 1933 there were already 984 ethnic organizations boasting some 130,000 members (Tonomura 2004:153). The existence of stable communities in many major cities accounts in part for the rapid organization and mobilization of Koreans in the immediate postwar years. As the appellation *buraku* [ghetto] suggests, the ethnic communities existed in relative isolation from mainstream society. Koreans formed an enclave economy—from Korean food markets and restaurants to Korean shamans and doctors—which was largely operated by and for co-ethnics (Tonomura 2004:148–59, 168–71). Language, food, and clothing (especially for women) readily distinguished most ethnic Koreans from ethnic Japanese (Tonomura 2004:176–79). Because of inequality, discrimination, and segregation, the interethnic liaison was something of a taboo, one that nonetheless held tremendous temptation and constituted a major literary theme in the second half of the colonial period (Nan 2006:7–9). The rate of intermarriage hovered around 1–2 percent of all Korean marriages in Japan in the 1930s (Tonomura 2004:168–71) but increased steadily thereafter. Interestingly, regional differences that had hitherto separated people from the Korean peninsula began to dissolve once they settled in Japan. Peasants from southern Korea and fishing villagers from Chejudo alike became "Korean" (cf. Sugihara 1998:96–98), yet not only were regional differences profound, but class differentiation was also a well-recognized fact by the late 1930s (Sugihara 1998:167–69). Generational difference—with the attendant linguistic gulf and all that implied—also became an enduring cleavage.

After Korea's formal annexation in 1910, ethnic Koreans became Japanese imperial subjects, but the Japanese state rigidly enforced the distinction between "inland" [*naichi*] and "outland" [*gaichi*], especially in the early phase of colonial rule, making ethnic hierarchy a structural feature of the Japanese empire. Taunts and bullying in schools and neighborhoods, exclusion and discrimination in education and employment, and the general Japanese presumption of Korean inferiority weighed like a nightmare on ethnic Korean consciousness (Chan 1966:32, 86). Paradoxically but symptomatically, the very act of ethnic identification and appellation—to be called "Korean" [*Chōsenjin*]—was the ultimate epithet from the colonial period well into the postwar period (Chan 1966:32; Nomura 1996:25). As the poet Lee Chongja (1994:39–40) rhapsodizes: "My encounter with ethnicity was in the spring when I was six, teased as Korean [*Chōsenjin* in *katakana*, a script to denote things foreign] . . . I passed my adolescence listening to the teasing refrain of 'Korean, return to Korea.'" Painful memories of rejection by Japanese peers—because of their national origins or their "smelly" food—were, however, redeemed by the grace of "good" Japanese (Chan 1966:86–88). That is, ethnic Koreans did not face a uniformly racist society but a mixture of "discrimination and sympathy" (Kim Munson 1991:15). The contemptible almost invariably elicits compassion from some—the sense of pity may in fact be enhanced by the ferocity of the hatred—but racism-free regions existed in the realm of darkness and sorrow: "There was no discrimination in the world of construction workers" (Chan 1966:21).

The imperial ideology of formal integration, or assimilation from above, intensified after the 1930s, and Japanese policy thereafter insistently sought to extirpate Korean culture, to transform Koreans into the Emperor's people [kōminka] and achieve Japanese-Korean unity [naisen ittai]. By 1940 Koreans were forced to be part of the Japanese educational system and to use Japanese names [sōshi kaimei] (Pak Kyongsik 1973 2:61–65; Miyata 1985:175–76): yet another potent source of postcolonial trauma encapsulated in Richard Kim's 1970 novel *Lost Names*. Japanese leaders asserted the harmony and unity between Japan and Korea. As Nomura Kōsuke (1982:9) phrased it in 1943: "There is no doubt that 24 million comrades in the peninsula are imperial subjects. There may be differences in wealth, wisdom, and beauty but they are the Emperor's children. We must be one family, one body." The policy of Japanization reached its apogee in the idea of Japanese and Korean isogeny—at least a third of Japanese was said to be "mixed blood" (Kayama 1978:358)—and the promotion of isogamy between Japanese and Korean subjects.

Assimilation policy was neither as successful as the Japanese bureaucrats wished nor as unsuccessful as postwar Zainichi intellectuals recalled, but we should not underestimate the attraction of Japanization. The search for wealth and power enticed ethnic Koreans to present themselves as loyal imperial subjects. Assimilation paved an escape route from poverty and a path toward modernity (Oguma 1998:428–34). After the passage of universal manhood suffrage in 1925, many Korean men gained the right to vote and some even became elected officials (Matsuda 1995). By the early 1940s, some ethnic Koreans proudly proclaimed Japanese affiliation and identification. The leading writer of the period, Yi Kwang-su—he had changed his name even before the 1940 law to Kayama Mitsurō (Miyata 1992:90)—predicted in 1941 that *naisen ittai* would be complete within a decade and encouraged fellow Koreans to learn both Japanese language and Japanese spirit (Kayama 1978:357, 361; cf. Kim Sokpom 1993:48). Postcolonial recollections readily condemn Yi's sedulous subservience to Japanese rule, but Japanization was very much the rule among educated ethnic Koreans (Kawamura 1999:102–6; 2000:11–12).

The term *ideology* leads some people to dismiss it as deception or delusion, but it is something much closer to the horizon of thought that shapes people's actions and beliefs. Certainly, Japanese imperial ideology, with its mixture of material benefits and moral exhortations, found many adherents among Koreans, both in *naichi* and *gaichi*. It was not purely propaganda for Noguchi Minoru (2001:1)—the Japanese name of the ethnic Korean writer Chan Hyokuchu [Chō Kakuchū]—to express the "exhilaration" of Koreans who were able to serve in the imperial military after 1938. Over 200,000 ethnic Korean soldiers fought for the Japanese empire: some died as kamikaze pilots, others were buried in Yasukini Shrine as "war heroes" (Yoon 1994:161; Kawata 2005:172–73). For some ethnic Koreans, the day of liberation was a day of defeat. In Kim Sokpom's (2005a:390) novel on the end of the war, a girl cries upon learning that Japan had lost. When her father reminds her that she should not worry because they are Korean, she responds: "Daddy, you can say that but I don't understand. We are Japanese: blood is Korean but we are Japanese nationals." Kim Hiro (1968:13), who was later to indict Japanese racism in 1968, was chagrined and cried at the announcement of Japan's defeat. The same is true for the Zainichi poet Kim Sijong, who was ignorant of the Korean language even though he grew up in Korea. As a sixteen-year-old, he was devastated by Japan's defeat and "could hardly eat for a week, ten days" (Kim Sokpom and Kim 2001:17). He vainly waited for *kamikaze* [divine wind] to save the empire (Kim Sijong 2004:5). By the early twenty-first century, however, stylized memory dominates; in Yū Miri's 2004 novel based on her grandfather's life, ethnic Koreans uniformly shout cries of joy and jubilation on 15 August 1945 (Yū 2004:613). Anyone who has encountered the incongruous situation of older Zainichi men singing Japanese military songs would be skeptical of the historical revisionism.

The identification of colonial subjects with colonial masters, after all, was not as uncommon as postcolonial reflections and recriminations would suggest. Consider Nirad C. Chaudhuri's (1989) epigraph to his 1951 autobiography: "TO THE MEMORY OF THE / BRITISH EMPIRE IN INDIA . . . / ALL THAT WAS GOOD AND LIVING / WITHIN US / WAS MADE, SHAPED, AND QUICKENED / BY THE SAME BRITISH RULE." Imperial identification and imperial nostalgia, however politically incorrect, are hardly rare sentiments among colonial subjects. In these postcolonial times, it is almost impossible to regard an ethnic Korean as Japanese patriot, or an ethnic

Indian as British loyalist, as anything but an instance of false consciousness or bad faith. The minority population that wished to believe in assimilation—as the paradigmatic instance of German Jewry suggests—cannot but be seen as fatally flawed, fooled into destructive self-delusion (e.g. Scholem 1980:26–27). Yet the seduction of colonial modernity was often irresistible. It is the anti-assimilationist position, such as that of Gershom Scholem in Weimar Germany, that is very much the minority phenomenon: Scholem himself migrated to Palestine. It is difficult to identify any ethnic Korean intellectual of note in Japan who had not converted to the Japanese cause before the war's end. The hold of the empire—however difficult it is to gauge the extent to which ethnic Korean intellectuals capitulated and assented to the Japanization process in their heart of hearts, wherever that may be—brooked very little resistance and exacted a great deal of collaboration and approbation. In spite of prevalent anti-Japanese sentiments in post-Liberation South Korea—until the mid-1990s even Japanese popular music was banned—colonial-era collaborators were never systematically prosecuted (Kim Sokpom 1993:13; Yoon 1994:232–33). How many would have been acquitted in the postcolonial judgment? To stress their "very lack of assimilation . . . essential 'Korean-ness,'" as did Edward Wagner in 1951, is anachronistic: a decidedly postwar, postcolonial misrecognition (Wagner 1951:43).

The sheer inertia of everyday life in Japan, along with the intensification of Japanization efforts, by the 1940s created an increasingly assimilated community in terms of linguistic competence, names, schools, or even food and clothing (Tonomura 2004:322–26). The first "boom" in ethnic Korean literature in Japanese occurred around 1940, anticipating by a generation the more common reference to the Zainichi literature boom around 1970 (Watanabe 2003:8, 209). Only the steady influx from the Korean peninsula kept the aggregate level of language fluency and cultural assimilation down. Over a third of Korean men married Japanese women by the 1940s, although well over 90 percent of Korean women married co-ethnics, suggesting a major sex imbalance in the ethnic community (Tonomura 2004:320–21). Kim Saryan's (2006) story, "Hikari no naka ni" [In the light, 1940], exemplifies the extent of ethnic intermingling. The ostensibly Japanese teacher turns out to be Korean, and the Korean-hating pupil turns out to have an ethnic Korean mother.

Nonetheless, there was nothing approaching Zainichi identity in the prewar period. The generational transition to a Japanese-born, Japanese-speaking, and Japanese-schooled Korean minority did not occur before 1945, as a sizable proportion of the second generation were born after the

1930s. One may very well argue that assimilation was only skin deep: language was not native; culture was an overlay on traditional Korean-Confucian schooling. Not surprisingly, ethnic Koreans in the main Japanese islands often wrote in Korean (cf. Pak Kyongsik 1983c). The cloak of Japaneseness, even when actively donned, could be tossed off at any point; an ostensibly loyal imperial subject, such as Kim Saryan, could transform into a loyal Korean nationalist after 15 August 1945. Yet, once again, we should not ignore the profound desire for the modern that animated so many ambitious Koreans to seek to write in Japanese and even to marry a Japanese person: modernity and Japaneseness were more often than not conflated. That the modern came to Korea via Japan would prove to be a repressed undercurrent of post-Liberation Korea. The very language and thought of modern Korea was deeply inflected by the brush with Japan; it would be equally blinkered, to be sure, to see modern Japan without its deep and extensive colonial entanglement. Be that as it may, the fundamental choice facing ethnic Koreans in the late colonial period was between becoming Japanese or resisting it. The logic of the colonizer and the logic of the colonized brooked no intermediary solutions. Even the very term Zainichi was not used before the end of the war.

POSTWAR JAPAN AND THE IDEA OF HOMOGENEITY

The ideology of imperial multiethnicity collapsed with Japan's defeat, only to be replaced by a counter-ideology of monoethnic Japan. Having lost its expansive empire, postwar Japanese society was considerably less ethnically heterogeneous than it had been. While expatriate Japanese returned home, many "foreigners" left the Japanese archipelago.

Ethnic minorities in general and ethnic Koreans in particular, however, did not disappear. The call for the collective repentance of a hundred million Japanese [*ichioku sōzange*] patently included the erstwhile colonial population. In the immediate postwar years, ethnic Koreans at times engaged in furious struggles and, by engaging in black-market transactions or defending ethnic schools (most notably in the 1948 Hanshin Tōsō [Struggles]), made headline news. Yasumoto Sueko's *Nianchan* [Second brother, 1958] was the best-selling title in Japan in 1959 and was made into a movie by the noted director Imamura Shōhei. Written as a ten-year-old orphaned girl's dairy, *Nianchan* is a simple but harrowing chronicle of postwar Japanese poverty and hunger. It is a curious document in the sense that the young ethnic Korean narrator describes Korean war victims as "pathetic foreigners" and Korean food as alien, while writing down the sole racist incident in the Roman alphabet [rōmaji] (Yasumoto 2003:91, 214, 200). Although everyone else is introduced using her or his real name, the glaring exceptions are the diary writer herself and her siblings, whose names are given in their *tsūmei* [Japanese alias]. Even a casual reading, however, reveals the diary writer as ethnic Korean, and *Nianchan* was read as something like the Japanese equivalent of Anne Frank's diary and generated many articles on problems plaguing ethnic Koreans in the late 1950s and early 1960s (Sugiura 2003:305). *Nianchan* is hardly alone. Ōshima Nagisa's *Kōshikei* [Death by hanging, 1968]—a searing portrait of a sensational 1958 murder case (known as the Komatsugawa Incident) involving the conviction and execution of a young Zainichi man, Ri Chin'u—appeared precisely when the discourse of Japaneseness [Nihonjinron] was popular, with one of its chief predicates being Japan's monoethnicity (Lie 2001:130–36). Paradoxical too was that some of the greatest pop stars of the 1950s and 1960s were ethnic Koreans (Lie 2001:chap. 3).

More than the demographic decline in the ethnic minority population, the collective repression of what was retrospectively understood as imperial illusions effaced ethnic diversity. In effect, most Japanese people severed their emotional ties to the prewar period: the war as the nightmare that was to be forgotten. The colonial experience was rejected as prehistory; it is as if Japan were born anew in 1945. Not coincidentally, it is almost impossible to find anything in the postwar years without the prefix "new" [shin]. This transvaluation in postwar Japanese mentality—the postwar renunciation of the prewar world of war and empire—is encapsulated in the popular 1959 TV-drama-turned-film *Watashi wa kai ni naritai* [I want to become a seashell]. Rather than honor and glory, with all its pomp and circumstance, peaceful, ordinary life was the good life: in short, better to be a seashell than a solider. It is of course not that everything changed all at once, but the defeat was cataclysmic in impact, not only in terms of utter physical destruction but also spiritual evisceration and intellectual bankruptcy. How else can one make sense of the Japanese subservience to the occupying forces—only moments ago reviled as the beast and the devil—and to the political, intellectual, and moral hegemony of the United States? Already by 30 August 1945, *Nichibei kaiwa techō* [Handbook of Japanese-English conversation] had appeared and went on to sell four million copies in three months (Handō 2006:30–31). It would take decades before even the legitimacy of having its own military force—as Max Weber among others suggested, almost the very definition of the state—would be widely discussed in Japanese politics. In the meantime, most Japanese people jettisoned tradition with abandon.

While ideologists of imperial Japan had described and defended Japanese multiethnicity, postwar intellectuals condemned not only imperialism, but also its inevitable correlate: ethnic heterogeneity. Imperial subjects *[shin-min]* became either Japanese nationals *[kokumin]* or foreigners. The 1950 Nationality Act embodied the principle of *jus sanguinis,* and restricted naturalization law (Morris-Suzuki 1998:190). The predominant postwar Japanese self-image envisioned a small, homogeneous country, without ethnic diversity. The idea of a homogeneous Japan went well with the ideals of democracy and egalitarianism. Japanese intellectuals not only contrasted monoethnic Japan with the multiethnic United States—the foil for all comparisons in the postwar era—but they also identified Japanese distinctiveness in cultural and ethnic homogeneity. Western, and especially American, commentators on Japanese society also portrayed Japan as a homogeneous society. Japanese people even looked alike to western observers, who in turn would presumably have been unable to distinguish ethnic Koreans from ethnic Japanese (cf. Riesman and Riesman 1976:6, 31).

The seemingly revolutionary transformation reveals a remarkable continuity. The prewar Japanization effort and the postwar monoethnic ideology both presumed a homogeneous society. Official discourse, prewar and postwar, rejected the ethnic other, albeit in different ways. The form, if not the ideological justification, remained the same. Similarly, the postwar rejection of the Emperor ideology and the embrace of Marxism belied the continuing adherence to ideological certitude and intellectual hierarchy. Alphonse Karr's quip that the more things change the more they remain the same has a ring of truth, especially in reputed instances of revolutionary rupture.

The ideal of Japanese homogeneity extended well beyond the ethnic dimension to encompass social inequality and regional diversity. Immediately after the war, pervasive poverty and the elimination of status hierarchy created a much more egalitarian society, both in terms of income inequality and status identification. Rapid cultural integration—facilitated by industrialization, urbanization, and militarization in the first half of the twentieth century—accelerated in the 1950s and 1960s. Tokyo aristocrats and Osaka merchants, Hokkaidō ranchers and Kyūshū farmers alike became Japanese (Oguma 2002:553–54). The new middle classes—replete with standard, though gender differentiated, uniforms—became part and parcel of a Fordist society of standardized producers and consumers. The corporation was the dominant institution in society. The expansion of the mass media—not only the media of radio and television but also the messages conveyed—relentlessly reduced dialectal diversity and promoted cultural uniformity. The convulsive churning of all of these forces within the postwar Japanese body politic spread homogeneity as the defining quality of Japaneseness. The *dankai* [baby-boomer] generation exemplified the newly imagined Japanese collectivity. Whereas the military had provided common culture among Japanese men in the prewar period, schools and workplaces, along with popular culture and the mass media, were the least common denominators of Japaneseness for the baby boomers. Uniformity—or, more accurately, uniformities—reigned. Crucially, Tokyo was the center and the standard of popular national culture. It would have been much more difficult to expunge the facts of cultural and ethnic differences in, for example, Osaka.

Ethnic elision is clear from the disappearance of Zainichi in the popular media. Ōshima Nagisa's *Wasurerareta kōgun* [The forgotten imperial military, 1963], which depicted Korean soldiers in the Japanese military, was aired on Nihon TV and garnered great critical acclaim. Yet the focus was perforce on the colonial past. Perhaps the most popular 1960s film with Zainichi characters was *Kyūpora no aru machi* [The town with a cupola, 1962], fondly remembered even today as the film that catapulted the actress Yoshinaga Sayuri as the postwar heroine *par excellence*. Two Korean siblings are portrayed empathetically in the film but they end up leaving for North Korea. (To be sure, the Zainichi intellectual Kang Sangjung remembered the film but *not* the Zainichi characters [Kang 2008:100]). Symbolically, then, the imperial, multiethnic past led to a peaceful, monoethnic present. In either scenario, Zainichi had no future: ethnic cleansing in Japan, ethnic unification in Korea. After a brief flurry of Zainichi presence in the visual media in the late 1950s and early 1960s—*Nianchan* (1959) and Kinoshita Junji's first script for television, *Kuchibue ga fuyu no sora ni* [Whistling to the winter sky, 1961] come to mind—they would reemerge on national television over a half-century later with the soap opera *Tokyo wankei* [Tokyo bayview, 2004] and the NHK drama *Kyōkai* [Strait, 2007] (cf. Takayanagi 1999–2000:48–54).

The novelist Kaikō Takeshi's *Nihon sanmon opera* [Japan threepenny opera, 1959] presents the most sustained literary depiction of the Zainichi population in the nascent era of rapid economic growth (cf. Yan 1995:127–43). Kaikō grew up in and wrote about Osaka—then as now the city with the largest concentration of ethnic Koreans in Japan. He delineates the contours of "Apache village" [Apatchi buraku], an impoverished neighborhood, and the "Casbah of Osaka" (Kaikō 1959:43) built on the ruins of prewar weapons factories. The village is replete with lumpenproletariat, petty criminals, and "most suspect people who may or may not have *koseki* [household registry], name, or even nationality *[kokuseki]*" (Kaikō 1959:45). The scenery is familiar as any industrializing city with impoverished immigrants, albeit with a Korean scent and accent where a man "whom we can know with one whiff, emitting from every pore of his body a rainbow of smells of *kimchi* and *makkari* [makkŏli, a demotic Korean liquor]" (Kaikō 1959:21). The novel offers a rare glimpse of multiethnic Japan from this period, but it ends with the destruction of the village and the dispersion of its denizens. Rapid economic growth bulldozed impoverished, multiethnic neighborhoods—including Korean *buraku* with their flophouses *[nagaya]*—such that, a mere two decades later, few would even recall their existence. As the Zainichi writer Yan Sogiru (2001:214) commented after seeing images from 1959 of his hometown, Ikuno (Osaka), over forty years later: "I remember the times very clearly, but I couldn't believe what I was seeing. Was Zainichi life that impoverished?" Recall *Nianchan*, which describes a girl's life from the early 1950s, and its descriptions of hunger. By the time the book became a best seller in the late 1950s, hunger was rare in Japan—probably a condition of possibility of its popularity. By the mid-1960s, all that remained of the state of hunger was the reminder by the school authorities not to waste food. While some left food on their plate, others were becoming targets of a new health hazard: obesity. The only flophouses visible to most people were in manga and movies. In the popular manga *Kyojin no hoshi* [The star of the Giants] from the late 1960s, there is an iconic scene that takes place in a flophouse: the inebriated father slaps the son and upends the dining table. The famous scene prompted more than one Zainichi to wonder whether it was a veiled allusion to the family's Zainichi status. But one had to look far and wide to catch glimpses of Zainichi in the 1960s popular media. In the steep upward ascent of economic growth, few had the repose necessary to register the moment or the fate of ethnic communities.

It is precisely when the *dankai* generation came of age—the height of rapid economic growth in the 1960s—that ethnic Koreans disappeared from Japanese popular consciousness. If the popularity of *Nianchan* owed to the radio broadcast of its narrative, the very world from which it sprang—the struggling coal mines—was already the stuff of nostalgia. As the political scientist Kamishima Jirō (1982:xvii) quipped: "In prewar Japan, everyone said that Japanese ethnicity is eclectic and hybrid. . . . However, after the war . . . beginning with progressive intellectuals, people began to say that Japan is monoethnic. There is absolutely no basis for saying that." What was obvious to the aging scholar was opaque to the majority who came of age after the war. The fact of ethnic heterogeneity was erased from the elementary knowledge about Japanese society. The official discourse of monoethnicity exonerated the Japanese authorities from addressing the demands of various minority groups (Pak Kyongsik 1992:81). Bullied at schools and excluded from mainstream employment, ethnic Koreans in postwar Japan lived in a society that disrecognized them.

Thus, Prime Minister Nakasone Yasuhiro could confidently declare in 1986, "Japan has one ethnicity, one state, and one language" (Terazawa 1990:64–65). In his ethnic allegory, ethnic and cultural homogeneity contributes to Japan's economic efflorescence; multiethnicity explains the decline of the United States. Regardless of the virtues or vices of multiethnic or multicultural nation-states, nary a voice was raised to question Nakasone's bedrock assumption. Indeed, it has been a truism within and without Japan that Japan is remarkable for its ethnic homogeneity. In a book devoted to the subject of multiethnicity, the historian William H. McNeill (1986:18) remarks: "More than any other civilized land . . . the Japanese islands maintained ethnic and cultural homogeneity throughout their history."

THE VISION OF INVISIBILITY, THE SOUND OF SILENCE: PASSING AS A WAY OF LIFE

The expunction of ethnic heterogeneity in the dominant discourse is only one strand of the story. If there were ethnic minorities, then why were they invisible? Why were they silent?

Invisibility was a fact of life: out of sight, out of mind. Ethnic minority populations tended to be residentially segregated prior to the 1960s, and most of them worked in distinct occupations, usually apart from ethnic Japanese people. That is, they were neither neighbors nor colleagues. Separation and isolation provided the possibility for civil ignorance. As the Zainichi poet Kim Sijong (2005:11) put it in his poem "Invisible Town" about Ikaino, a Koreatown in Osaka: "Everyone knows / But it's not on the map / Because it's not on the map / It's not Japan."

Most Japanese people, however, did not think that they lived in a mono-ethnic society in the 1950s when the ethnic minorities lived and worked separately from the ethnic majority, but rather in the 1970s when the minorities became integrated into mainstream society. The reason is that non-Japanese ethnics became indistinguishable from ethnic Japanese. This occurred precisely when regional cultures (including speech and sartorial signifiers) dissolved into the relatively homogeneous Japanese culture. For Koreans, ethnonational differences manifested themselves in everyday life, perhaps most viscerally in speech and food, in the colonial period. Yet the second-generation Zainichi by the 1970s were in no obvious ways distinguishable from ethnic Japanese people. While there was a foolproof test for identifying Koreans from Japanese in the early twentieth century—native Korean speakers could not articulate "pa pi pu pe po" in the received Japanese pronunciation—very few Koreans in Japan by the 1970s could not have passed this phonetic test. The consumption of *kimchi*—a type of pickled vegetables—and its constituents, such as garlic and chili peppers—was long regarded as the paradigmatic characteristics of Koreanness, as was the case for Yasumoto Sueko in *Nianchan*. Yet it has become a mainstream Japanese food item, readily available in supermarkets, and a person buying it today is just as likely to be Japanese as Korean. By the late twentieth century, no simple test of Koreanness besides genealogy existed.

Observable physical and behavioral differences are frequently regarded as master signifiers of ethnoracial distinction. When surface features are distinct, they become part and parcel of naturalized differences that are regarded as at once congenital and incorrigible. The stigma of otherness is readily apprehended by sight or sound. Yet appearance is highly ambiguous and subject to conflicting interpretations. When I have asked Japanese people to identify a Burakumin or a Korean person from a group of five or six people, they consistently failed to do better than statistical likelihood. Curiously, the proportion did not improve appreciably even when I included recent arrivals from East and Southeast Asia or those with one non-Japanese parent. Given the multiple geographical origins of people who have populated the Japanese archipelago over the millennia, the ethnic Japanese population incorporates distinct phenotypes. Hence, it is not surprising that someone from Southeast Asia (who may very well have a great deal of Chinese ancestry) may look more "Japanese" than a self-identified Japanese person. Once when I was walking in Tokyo with my daughter, whose mother is British, an elderly Japanese couple began a friendly conversation. When I told them that I grew up in the United States, they marveled at how long I had stayed away from Japan, all the while not suspecting that I may not be Japanese, whether by my own or any other basis of identification. After several minutes, they decided that they could detect my American accent. When they realized that my daughter could only converse in English, they looked at her very closely and the woman concluded that living in America made my daughter look more American. One may need to see it to believe it, but one must also believe it to see it.

Invisibility is not simply a matter of the majority group's inability to differentiate non-Japanese from Japanese people, but entails the minority population's ability to pass as normal Japanese people. Cultural integration should not be understood as either enforced or voluntary; there is always a mixture of constraint and choice, the proverbial carrot and the stick. We should not underestimate the minority population's desire to dissolve into the mainstream, lured by higher income, greater prestige, or the sheer avoidance of awkwardness. The reality of invisibility is thus partially a consequence of camouflage: the unwillingness to identify publicly as a minority and the willingness to play the majority. Almost all second-generation Koreans perform Japaneseness effortlessly and flawlessly. Even some first-generation Koreans, after all, took their colonial education to heart, and insistently lived as Japanese. The Zainichi writer Lee Yangji's father, for example, wanted her to be Japanese in appearance and affect (Lee Yangji 1981:157–58). In short, *passing* has been possible for ethnic Koreans and many other ethnic minority groups in contemporary Japanese society.

Passing denotes the presentation and representation of the self to attain and obtain the status that one desires in defiance of that which is denied. Generically, then, it entails the transgression of the boundary that separates the privileged from the non-privileged, the prestigious from the non-prestigious, the normal from the deviant—which in turn requires the successful performance of the achieved and desired status and the systematic occlusion of the ascribed and reviled status. In the early-twentieth-century United States, for example, passing almost inevitably meant crossing the color line, as depicted with great flair in early-twentieth-century novels, from Charles Waddell Chesnutt's *The House Behind the Cedars* (1900) and James Weldon Johnson's *The Autobiography of an Ex-Coloured Man* (1912) to Nella Larsen's *Passing* (1929) and William Faulkner's *Light in August* (1932). One of the modern masterpieces of Japanese fiction—Shimazaki Tōson's *Hakai* [Broken commandment, 1906]—delineates the trajectory of a Burakumin teacher from his effort to pass as an ordinary Japanese man to his exposure and eventual exile to Texas: an urtext of Japanese-language literature on passing (cf. Morris 2007:137–40).

Passing may very well be about other modes of identity, whether gender or generation, religion or region, sexuality or schooling, class or lifestyle, though there is something generic about its sociology (cf. Kroeger 2003:5, 216). At the individual level, it often generates anxiety from the omnipresent threat of exposure and the ethical conundrum of leading a life of deception (cf. Goffman 1974:87–91). As Gunnar Myrdal (1962:683) argued in *An American Dilemma*, passing requires more than an individual effort and includes "the deception of the white people . . . [and] a conspiracy of silence on the part of other Negroes who might know about it." The target of concealment may differ: the ethnic closet is transparent to family members in the way the sexuality closet often isn't. Furthermore, compartmental-ization of the self—permutations of the Dr. Jekyll and Mr. Hyde theme—may in fact be easier in times when the occluded identity is not under political mobilization. Thus, passing may have been easier for pre-Stone-wall gays than for their successors (Chauncey 1994:273–76). Similarly, passing was not a topic of as great psychological anguish for first-generation Zainichi as it was for their children and grandchildren. At the societal level, the norm that passing subverts—that categorical distinction is not rooted in nature but is in fact a convention, and often an arbitrary one at that—remains robust precisely because the norm remains unchallenged.

For second-generation ethnic Koreans in Japan—in fact, even for many first-generation Koreans who were being busily Japanized in the prewar period—passing is a default option. Many ethnic Koreans are willy-nilly in the closet because in everyday interaction they pass as ordinary Japanese. In other words, unlike African Americans, *not* passing for Zainichi requires a decision to be out of the ethnic closet: one must consciously assert ethnic identification by divulging one's Korean name or ancestry. The popular singer Wada Akiko claims, "I have not been trying to hide my ancestry as Zainichi. When asked, I answered. However, no one asked" (Pak I. 2005a:24–25). Thus, being out of the ethnic closet is much more about find-ing the right moment to assert one's identity rather than making a con-scious decision to pass as Japanese (cf. Fukuoka and Tsujiyama 1991b:85). The documentary foundation of ethnic distinction—expressed in everyday life as Korean name and Korean ancestry—is *koseki* [household registry]. Beyond self-disclosure, ethnic Koreans could be exposed by people with access to *koseki*, such as school officials or employers (and hence the pos-sibility of blackmail or malicious disclosure). Although many Zainichi, as well as many ethnic Japanese, are convinced that they can identify a Zainichi person, whether by their presentation of self (for example, as a loner or "lone wolf"), facial type or phrenology, the register of voice (some say high, others say low), faint aroma, or some sixth sense, the reality is that household registry and, by extension, nationality are the only reliable sources of identification. One must trumpet the documentary fact, or have it trumpeted.

Fear of exposure envelops everyday life that circulates rumors of ethnic deviance. The Zainichi writer Yū Miri's naturalized uncle became upset when she used the Korean name of a common fish and repeatedly insisted to her mother that she not use any Korean around his home (Yū 2001:168). Even today, when parents oppose a proposed marriage or someone is found to have an unregistered father in *koseki*, the suspicion of Korean ancestry surfaces. Opposition to international or interethnic marriage is garden-variety xenophobia in the world, but why the unregistered father? Given the patriarchal and patrilineal basis of the postwar nationality law that was in effect until 1985, if a Japanese man married a Korean woman, then their child could be registered under the father's Japanese registry. When a Korean man married a Japanese woman—and this was much more common—then their child must be registered as Korean or as Japanese under the mother's *koseki*, albeit at the cost of being a bastard *[shiseiji]*. There are other mechanisms for detecting Korean ancestry. Perhaps the most common, although necessarily speculative, is by considering the Japanese alias *[tsūmei]*. Many Korean surnames sound Japanese by adding another Chinese character (most Korean surnames have one character; most Japanese, two) and using the Japanese reading of the two Chinese characters. Thus, the Korean name "An" might become the Japanese "Yasumoto" or "Yasuda" (Fukuoka 1993:29–31). Someone with a common Zainichi *tsūmei*, such as Kaneda or Kaneshiro from the Korean surname Kim, is often presumed to be Zainichi, even if she or he should turn out to be "authentic" Japanese, as in Gen Getsu's (2003b:134) story "Unga," or Okinawan, as in Hwang Mingi's (1993:32) memoir.

Consider in this regard the prevalence of Zainichi sports and music stars in the postwar period (Kang H. 2001:98–115; Pak I. 2005a:14–35). That they were overrepresented in sports and entertainment is itself a product of employment discrimination, but they succeeded by occluding their ethnic ancestry. Perhaps the greatest hero in Japanese popular culture of the late 1950s was the ethnic Korean Rikidōzan, the professional wrestler, who was said to restore Japan's wounded pride by pummeling treacherous "foreign" (understood as "American") wrestlers. Rikidōzan was hardly alone in being at once popular in Japan and passing as Japanese. Whether to comply with the archaic tradition of the sumo world or to prevent the loss of popularity, the sumo wrestler Tamanoumi (who attained the august rank of *yokozuna*, or grand champion) and the *enka* [Japanese "soul"] singer Miyako Harumi, among many others, denied Korean descent. To prove their Japanese ancestry, they both claimed that their fathers—who were alive, well, and Korean—had passed away (Kim I. 1978:147, 162). In order for children to pass as Japanese, parents had to pass away. Furthermore, they adopted aliases—common enough in the world of entertainment—which were not linked in any obvious way to standard Zainichi *tsūmei*.

The greater the stigma attached to a particular identity, the greater the benefits of passing, and the greater the threat of exposure. Rikidōzan's herculean exploits in the wrestling ring were reputedly matched by his heroic efforts to hide his ancestry. The rumored room of ethnic refuge in his house—where he was said to dwell among Korean-style furniture, listening to Korean songs—existed on a much more modest scale for many ethnic Koreans (cf. Kawamura 2003:80). When the Zainichi baseball star Harimoto Isao beckoned him to "come out" of the ethnic closet, Rikidōzan replied: "When I came to Japan . . . Korea was a colony. We were treated like insects. . . . How many Japanese believe that Japanese and Koreans are equal?. . . . I became a star because people believe that I am Japanese. If they learn that I am Korean, their attitude will change" (Yamamoto 1995:269). Following this logic, Rikidōzan masqueraded as a Native American wrestler in the United States (Pak I. 1999:139).

Nagging moral concerns plague the problem of passing. If some ethnic Koreans devoted their lives to passing, what right does anyone have to expose them? Belatedly discovering her Korean ancestry and writing about it, Sagisawa Megumu (2005:142) remonstrates: "I destroyed [the secret] that my grandmother spent her whole lifetime protecting." Retrospectively, now that Korean ancestry is not quite the social curse that it once was in Japan, it would seem the most natural and authentic thing to say that truths should be out, and should have been out. Each disclosure may have contributed in whatever intangible ways to ushering in a situation—far more desirable for almost everyone concerned—where ancestral lineage across the Sea of Japan is a more or less interesting fact rather than a taint. That should not, however, necessarily translate into incursion into or condemnation of what little dignity that people who lived in a difficult situation sought to uphold, however reprehensible or self-defeating their decision may seem. Yes, lies and fakes, but don't liars and fakers deserve some privacy? The writer Tachihara Masaaki, who made his reputation as the purveyor of traditional Japanese aesthetic, literally transmogrified his Korean body into a Japanese one. As exemplified by the title of a book of conversations, *Nihon no bi o motomete* [In search of the beauty of Japan, 1983], he sought to out-Japanese Japanese writers. Recent biographies, however, remember him almost as much for his fictive self as for his fictive work, replete with retrospectively glaring examples of his effort to pass as Japanese, such as his recalcitrant refusal of things foreign, or of revelation of his "true" ethnic self, such as his support for other Zainichi writers (cf. Takai 1991:23, 189–90). Tachihara could not avoid the question of his ancestry in life or death. The melancholy silence of past passers appears to the post-Zainichi generation as nothing but another reminder of the bad old days, condemning the passer as inauthentic and insincere: callously disregarding fellow ethnics and suffering from self-hatred. The revenge of the repressed risks not only the privacy of the deceased but also confounds the very condition to which it gave rise. Some contemporary Japanese commentators see in the act of passing a treacherous trait that justifies the very discrimination to which Zainichi people were subjected. Yamano Sharin (2005), for example, upbraids Pak Chonsok's historic antidiscrimination suit against Hitachi by observing that the company had the right to rescind a job offer to someone who had used a "false" name, conveniently neglecting the reasons why so many Zainichi avoided using their "real" name in public life.

Passing was, in point of fact, something of a national phenomenon during the high-growth era from the Korean War to the 1973 oil shock. As school graduates poured into cities seeking jobs, they almost inevitably faced the reality of modern Japan that mandated cultural assimilation, such as dropping regional dialects. It is therefore not only Koreans who had to pass in mainstream society. Given the urban character of the Zainichi population, ethnic Koreans may have been more suitable for the new Japan than their rural ethnic Japanese counterparts. Befitting the theory of mass society then in vogue, ordinariness or normalness *[futsū]* was a popular ideal. A congeries of characteristics that constituted Japaneseness became the cultural capital of postwar Japanese society. In everyday interaction or in employment situations, the ability to enact one's Japaneseness was a strategic asset in getting along or getting ahead. What was the ethnic closet for Koreans in Japan was therefore merely one permutation of the more general prison-house of Japaneseness.

The protective coloration of Japaneseness afforded a mode of bearable, and potentially viable, livelihood: better to be silent and bear the blessings of invisibility to strive for normality. It is possible to see the hands of revan-chist nationalists and government bureaucrats in continuing the colonial-era policy of Japanization by another means. Certainly, they did their part to enforce ethnic conformity. It would be inadequate, however, to criticize the repressive ideology and practice of monoethnicity; minority groups actively embraced and promoted it. The 1955 formation of the Burakumin Liberation League entrenched the goal of assimilation. The League's primary political activity was to denounce people who demean and defame Burakumin, the definition of which included claims of ethnic distinction. In other words, the League attempted to deconstruct, not promote, ethnic identity. From the year of the League's formation, ethnic Korean organizations, in contrast, steadfastly refused to project the fate of the Korean population in the Japanese archipelago. If the desirable outcome of Burakumin agitation was total assimilation, the ultimate goal of Korean activism was repatriation. In spite of these distinct political desiderata, both groups supported the ideology of monoethnicity. That is, Burakumin are Japanese, Koreans are Koreans who should be in Korea, and only Japanese people in principle live in the Japanese archipelago. Passing, in this context, became a temporary expedient and ironically reproduced monoethnic ideology.

In this regard, the contrast between ethnic Koreans and ethnic Chinese is striking. Yan Sogiru (1987:39) relates how strangers presumed his "strange" surname to be Chinese when—given the ethnic demographics of Japan—it was more likely to be Korean. Whereas the Zainichi population suffered disrepute and discrimination, the Chinese in Japan by and large did not. Undoubtedly, colonial history accounts in part for the distinct valuation. Crudely put, Japan defeated and colonized Korea, but not China. Taiwanese, who had been colonized by Japan, were regarded as compliant and pro-Japanese. The widespread recognition and appreciation of the Chinese diaspora in particular and Chinese civilization in general, the small size of the population (according to a survey conducted in the mid-1980s, more than half came to Japan after 1945 [Kanagawa-kennai 1986:14]), and its political and social quiescence rendered Chinese at once foreign and forgettable, and therefore acceptable.

Invisibility and silence, then, left the discourse of monoethnicity unfettered. This was the unquestioned reality of Japanese ethnic constitution in the 1960s, which in turn would remain virtually unchallenged until the 1980s. Although individual-level interethnic interactions occurred, almost all were misrecognized (by the majority population at least) as intra-ethnic interactions. The term "foreigner" *[gaijin]* referred almost exclusively to white Euro-Americans *[hakujin]*; Koreans were clearly not *hakujin* but were not really *gaijin* either (cf. Uchiyama 1982:18). Few Japanese paid much attention to Koreans or Chinese in the postwar period; their chief concern remained the United States. The very small population of *hakujin* came to stand for the postwar Japanese perception and recognition of ethnonational otherness, and their relative rarity underscored the monoethnic worldview. The monoethnic syllogism, then, would be that there can be no interethnic relations because there are only Japanese people in Japan.

UNSCRIPTED ENCOUNTERS

Many people in Japan recognize themselves and would be recognized by others as non-Japanese. Given that they may be neighbors and colleagues or celebrities and superiors, inevitably and systematically interethnic encounters and interactions occur in everyday life. Yet they are largely understood as intra-Japanese interactions. Let me illuminate the mechanisms of misrecognition by adducing two ethnographic examples from the early 2000s, when monoethnic ideology was clearly on the wane. They suggest the ways in which the contradictions between monoethnic ideology and multiethnic reality almost always leave the ideology unscathed, and so much worse for the facts.

After a typically overextended academic seminar, several scholars retired to a nearby bar for a recap and nightcap. Besides me, there was a man who passed himself off as Japanese but was in fact of Korean ancestry and another man who was married to a Japanese citizen of Korean ancestry (who explicitly identified herself as "Korean"). After a round of drinks, a Japanese scholar pilloried a presenter for his academic shortcomings and used the derogatory term for Koreans *Chon*. Curiously, perhaps out of deference to his seniority, no one intervened to "correct" his racist language. Even more curiously, the "racist" took some pride in his progressive politics, especially on matters of ethnic inclusion in Japan. Afterwards, I asked the Zainichi scholar about the incident but he shrugged it off by saying that it didn't mean much, being at worst a reminder and a legacy of the colonial era (though the "racist" scholar was not even enrolled in elementary school at the end of the war). The man with a "Korean" wife merely observed that the "racist" was a decent person. The enforced politeness of public interaction mandated the utterance of improper language a logical impossibility. Rather, it was taken as informal talk—even as evidence of camaraderie, of exposing the backstage *[honne]* instead of the formality of the front stage *[tatemae]*—and was translated as being devoid of any racist intent or content. To underscore this point, the Zainichi man pointed out that the "racist" scholar was very friendly to me during the bar-time conversation and engaged in neither explicit nor subtle effort to disparage me. Divorced from any substance, then, the racist terminology had merely a phatic function—or so it was taken by two people who should be sensitive to manifestations of racism against Koreans in Japan. The matter never came up again. The irruption of the racial epithet became a nonevent, smoothed over by the polite patina of everyday academic interaction.

At the loudest event I experienced, Burakumin Liberation League members used megaphones to denounce a writer whom they deemed to be denigrating Burakumin. They were adamant that they are in no ways different from ordinary Japanese people and categorically denied that they are members of an ethnic minority group. When I suggested that external discrimination and internal identification made Burakumin fit the sociological definition of an ethnic group, they interpreted my argument as a casuistry that revealed my ignorance of Japanese reality. When I conveyed my conversation to several Japanese sociologists, they generally agreed with the Burakumin activists. An eminent social scientist added that classifying Burakumin as an ethnic minority would incur their wrath. Burakumin activism squelched all discussions of Burakumin, thereby making them invisible to a public that persists in believing in essential Japanese homogeneity. The loud, mechanically amplified speeches of the Burakumin activists not only silenced dissident voices but also added to the nationwide chorus that, unthinking, insisted on the fact of Japanese monoethnicity.

These encounters occurred outside of the contemporary Japanese cultural repertoire. To put a bit differently the syllogism that there can be no interethnic relations because there are only Japanese people in Japan, instances of interethnic tension or conflict lack relevant interpretive frameworks or conceptual schemes. A racial epithet or interethnic tension evaporates into the hurly-burly of metropolitan life and in no way threatens the presumption of homogeneity. They are therefore invisible to the vast majority of the population, and the few who speak out are ignored or silenced. I once observed a Southeast Asian man yelling at a politician who was campaigning. The angry foreigner was saying in English that the politician was a racist and a fascist. The politician smiled, politely bowed, and thanked the Southeast Asian man for his support: "I am very pleased that even our foreigner friend is supporting my candidacy!" The screaming man was not only misrecognized as a supporter but also classified as a temporary migrant worker, soon to return to his homeland. That is, when the population of foreign workers became nonnegligible, a new category was created that retained the myth of monoethnicity. In short, the fact of multiethnicity can be neither seen nor heard.

Interethnic conflicts do occur. In Tsukiji Fish Market, where many foreigners work, Theodore Bestor (2004:233–35) discusses a brawl between a Chinese and a Japanese worker and describes a Japanese account of why interethnic misunderstanding and conflict arises. The account is no different from many interviews I conducted and focuses on foreigners' failure to understand the Japanese cultural repertoire. A well-known South Korean "newcomer" in Japan, O Sonfa (1999:66–68), insists that most instances of Japanese racism merely reveal the outsiders' ignorance of Japanese behavior and culture. It is perhaps not surprising that she exemplifies the oft-voiced tension between the relatively recent South Korean immigrants and the Zainichi population, which is less interested in the nuances of Japanese culture and more eager to lambaste its injustices. In Bestor's account, the brawl was quickly forgotten and is his book's only reminder of the large presence of foreign workers in Tsukiji.

The dissipation and dissolution of interethnic tensions and conflicts are not simply due to cognitive or cultural lacunae. The general tilt toward homogeneity and harmony—assiduously reproduced in interpersonal interactions as well as by the major organizations and institutions ranging from school to work—provides the master cultural backdrop against which these specific instances of ethnic tensions and conflicts are smoothed over. Informal social controls that animate social life continued to stifle conflict in face-to-face settings (cf. Bestor 1989:208–14), but with the additional overlay of harmonious civil indifference. That is, the dominant mode of urban interaction operated under the mantra of "not bothering others" [*meiwaku o kakenai*]. In postwar Tokyo, civil indifference and informal social control both work to suppress interpersonal conflicts and emotional outbursts to sustain a veneer of civility and harmony. In the classroom and workplace, historical facts of contention are expunged and present instances of disharmony are disavowed. The culture of consensus is a highly stylized interpretation that fits neither the past nor the present of Japanese society. Yet there are psychological, interpersonal, and organizational mechanisms that mask the generic expressions of diversity and dissonance in popular discourse and everyday interactions.

THE ABSENCE OF ESCALATION, THE ABSENCE
OF ORGANIZATION

Why don't these individual instances of altercation, bickering, and conflict spiral into newsworthy interethnic tensions and recognitions? After all, Japanese people are far from being brainwashed into submission or living under totalitarian surveillance. Even when monoethnic ideology was at its most powerful in the 1970s and 1980s, there were self-identified Koreans and other nonethnic Japanese people living in Japan. Everyone I talked to at any length could recall an ethnic Korean person as a firsthand acquaintance. Consider Harimoto Isao, one of the greatest hitters in Japanese baseball history. His girlfriend's mother told him: "Because Japan lost the war it came to this but if Japan had won someone like you would not be able to come near my daughter" (Yamamoto 1995:130). He speculates that he might have ended up as a yakuza member had he not pursued a career in baseball. The ferocity of ethnic prejudice haunted him throughout high school; spectators hurled racially derogatory remarks throughout his professional career

(Yamamoto 1995:218–20, 282). Yet Harimoto remained openly and proudly Korean, as was his friend, the home-run king Oh Sadaharu, of his Chinese ancestry. Why didn't these and many other famous sports stars and performers remind Japanese people of the multiethnic constitution of Japanese society? Beyond rapid economic growth and harmony norms, the sublimation of ethnic diversity was ensured by the absence of institutions that propagate evanescent facts to constitute a recorded reality. In other words, very few organizations promoted the voices of discontent to generate sustained discourse and popular recognition.

V. I. Lenin (1988) argued that without a revolutionary party, workers would only promote a reformist agenda. By projecting a particular vision of current reality and future possibilities, intellectuals lead the masses to regard themselves as members of the working class. The theory then may become so robust that reality cannot be understood apart from that particular framework. The Stalin-era Soviet Union, for example, used class categories as the master scheme of political identification and social classification (Fitzpatrick 1999). Conversely, the absence of a class-analytic frame may misrecognize class-based expressions of social reality. In the post-civil rights United States, for example, ethnicity and race became critical categories of social analysis. Hence, many instances of individual altercations or class-based conflicts came to be seen indisputably as instances of interethnic conflict (Lie 2004a). Put differently, the diffusion of ethnic categories and identities in Japanese society may challenge Japanese people in the near future to reinterpret my first anecdotal case as a manifestation of well-entrenched Japanese racism.

Another way to think about the phenomenon is in a choice-theoretic framework. Albert O. Hirschman (1970) argued that there were three fundamental individual responses to organized life: exit, voice, or loyalty. Living in a society that denies the existence of ethnic minority, the discriminated and invisible minority may very well choose to exit. Certainly, that was a common solution among ethnic Koreans in Japan. Alternatively, they may learn to live with monoethnic ideology and society. As I have suggested, both Burakumin and Korean activists complemented and strengthened the dominant ideology of monoethnic Japan. Yet there is the third possibility: voice. Only when individual voices are articulated as collective expression does social transformation become possible. In the absence of organized opposition to the prevailing interpretation of social reality, individual voices become marginalized and ignored, as we saw in the ethnographic examples I adduced. Social movements shift the interpretive framework and acknowledge hitherto neglected reality, such as the prevalence of poverty in the Cold War United States or the existence of ethnic minorities in Japan.

Following the lead of Lenin or Hirschman, we can say that discourses and ideas that are embodied in political organizations or social movements are crucial for framing and making sense of social reality. In postwar Japan, there were no major organizations or movements to dispute the dominant ideology of monoethnicity until the 1980s. In the inauspicious climate of opinion, individuals and instances remained marginalized. Even the actually existing organizations of ethnic minority groups assiduously sustained the social myth and channeled individual energies away from voice and recognition, engendering resigned frustration or heroic expression. The virtual absence of ethnic-based activism and of public protest reproduced the belief in monoethnicity.

THE SUBSUMPTION OF SUBPOLITICS

Ethnic nonrecognition and misrecognition reveal not only the strength of monoethnic ideology, the relative paucity and diffusion of minority groups, the prevalence of passing, and the absence of organizations that advocated ethnic identification, but also the overarching character of postwar Japanese politics. The broad structural forces that shaped postwar Japan—the Golden Age of economic growth and the entrenchment of Cold War politics—crystallized in the mid-1950s. The postwar period produced a classic division between right and left that refracted the supranational politics of the Cold War. Squeezed between national politics and the superpower conflict, subpolitics—defined broadly to include concerns about subnational groups—was sublimated in the Cold War's rather more epic struggles.

Who speaks of postwar Japanese politics speaks of the Liberal Democratic Party: neither liberal nor democratic or even a party in the conventional sense. It was as subservient to the United States as it was dominant in domestic politics. Its sheer presence eclipsed subnational political concerns, whether the rights of women or the demands of minority groups. The fundamental fact of rapid economic growth tamed systematic expressions of discontent and entrenched the power of the ruling party and the national government. Subpolitics rarely played in the proscenium in the drama of national and international politics.

The left, which was most sympathetic to the claims of ethnic minority groups, was radically circumscribed by the nationalist mind-set and geopolitics. The outpouring of progressive political sentiments in Japan in the

1960s—the decade that began with the massive mobilization against the renewal of the U.S.-Japan Security Treaty and ended with the escalating student and anti–Vietnam War movements and protest against another renewal of the Security Treaty—decisively tilted the *bien-pensant* opinion to back North Korea and bash South Korea. One would be hard-pressed to find an article critical of North Korea in progressive Japanese journals such as *Sekai* in the 1960s and 1970s, whereas searing indictments of the military dictatorship in South Korea were ubiquitous. That the bedrock of Japanese support for South Korea was the Liberal Democratic Party, which was mired in corrupt money politics and unreflexive obeisance to U.S. policy, merely confirmed the progressive distaste for the South Korean regime. All this was not merely a matter of ideology. We should not forget that, at least according to CIA estimates, the North Korean economy outperformed that of the South until the early 1970s (Lie 1998:74). There were also well-intentioned efforts to consider North Korea and North Koreans as an "ordinary" country and people (Oda 1978:245), precisely to avoid beatification or demonization. Meanwhile, South Korea was ruled by the aging, corrupt autocrat Rhee Syngman in the 1950s, only to be replaced by the authoritarian military officer Park Chung Hee in the 1960s and 1970s. The South Korean polity was the antipode of the idealized image of the new Japanese polity: autocratic, not democratic; militaristic, not pacific.

The problem of the Zainichi, very much an afterthought to the few Japanese who thought about Korea or Koreans at all, was an appendage to the problem of the Korean peninsula. The Zainichi population became pawns in the struggle between North and South Korea in particular and the communist and capitalist worlds in general. As pawns, they were easy to sacrifice or ignore. The Liberal Democratic Party that ignored the colonial past and its legacies considered the Zainichi problem as a matter of foreign policy. The Japan Communist Party supported North Korea but neglected the Zainichi population (Yoon 1990:100–101; Jon 2005:213–15).

The subsumption of ethnic politics turned all eyes away from the actually existing situation of ethnic Koreans in Japan. Although the immediate postwar years had generated a great deal of Zainichi engagement in domestic Japanese politics, the Korean War turned the gaze of many Zainichi to homeland politics. From the mid-1950s to the mid-1970s when educated Zainichi were almost uniformly, deeply politicized, Zainichi politics spelled geopolitics: the struggles between communist North and capitalist South. And the vast majority favored North Korea. In the early twenty-first century, the attractions of communism seem opaque. Outside of North Korea, Kim Jong Il is an object of derision when he is not one of terror, but his father elicited a great deal of respect not only from the North Korea–oriented Zainichi population but also from the educated Japanese public. At least until the mid-1970s the primacy and legitimacy of North Korea were largely unquestioned by the majority of the Zainichi population. Even after the 1965 Normalization Treaty between Japan and South Korea, many Zainichi persisted in declaring themselves North Korean nationals. This is remarkable because the treaty provided profound incentives, such as the possibility of overseas travel and welfare benefits from Japan, to be South Korean citizens. Yet only in the early 1970s did the proportion of South Korean nationals among the Zainichi population exceed that of the North. And, as I elaborate in the following chapter, the founding principle of the North Korea–affiliated Koreans was the ideology of return. To think of Zainichi as anything but temporary residents in Japan was heresy. Given that the leadership, as well as the majority, of the Korean population in Japan in the 1950s and 1960s had been born in Korea and spoke Korean, the pull of the homeland was at once visceral and natural. It should not be surprising, then, that there was hardly any book on the Zainichi experience until the 1970s. As late as 1985, the Zainichi scholar Yoon Keun Cha (1990:95) could remark that "studies on Zainichi are almost absent" except for some collections of documentary materials. The pioneering works of Zainichi historiography, for example by Pak Kyongsik (1973, 1979), can be read as an extension of the Cold War by other means in their indictment of Japanese colonialism and its contemporary extension in U.S. imperialism. The involuntary character of enforced migration [kyōsei renkō] justified repatriation.

The prevailing opinion in Japan—right or left, ethnic Japanese or ethnic Korean—presumed the imminent disappearance of the Zainichi population or ignored it altogether. What the right and the left also shared was the nationalist understanding of the Zainichi population, which legitimated the repatriation movement. It is to this topic that I now turn.

2. Exile

The Korean population in Japan already included many Japanese-born, Japanese-speaking children by the end of the war. Because the influx of migrants declined precipitously after 1945, the proportion of second-generation Zainichi increased throughout the postwar period. Although no longer considered the Emperor's children, they were undoubtedly children of the empire. By the early 1970s, over three-fourths of Zainichi were Japanese-born, and more than half of Zainichi marriages were to Japanese citizens. Most ethnic Koreans could pass easily as Japanese, and they did so using Japanese aliases and speaking Japanese fluently. Very few aspects of their lives betrayed their Korean ancestry: clothing or schooling, the kind of television shows they watched or the leisure activities they pursued. Simultaneously, there were indisputable improvements in their livelihood. Rapid economic growth from the Korean War to the early 1970s ensured that benefits more than trickled down to ethnic Koreans.

Nonetheless, ethnic Korean life in postwar Japan remained precarious. Most critically, they were foreign nationals of countries with which Japan had no official diplomatic relations until the 1965 Normalization Treaty with South Korea, which excluded the majority who were North Korean nationals. Educational attainment lagged well behind their Japanese counterparts. Public-sector jobs were closed to foreign nationals and most large companies did not hire ethnic Koreans. Housing discrimination was rife. Many Japanese presumed Koreans to be truculent, even criminal, and certainly Other. Surveys from the 1950s consistently showed Koreans to be the most disliked national group in Japan. Hence, most postwar observers exuded pessimism: for the Zainichi scholar Pak Cheil (1957:137), the future of Zainichi spelled, "to answer in a word, impoverishment"; the U.S. historian Richard Mitchell (1967:158) concluded that "the traditional Japanese dislike for Koreans remains strong, and may even have increased." The 1950s and 1960s were the decades of darkness and desperation for ethnic Koreans in Japan.

The xenophobic refrain—"Koreans, go back to Korea"—is the stuff of Zainichi infantile memory. Its kinder, gentler permutations—"why do you speak Japanese so well if you are Korean?" or "why are so many Koreans living in Japan?"—disclose historical ignorance but also underscore the pervasive nationalist mind-set—one nation, one people—that gripped both Japanese and Koreans in the postwar period. One conclusion that the ethnic Korean leaders, and indeed almost everyone, in Japan agreed upon until the 1970s was the destiny of the Zainichi: their inevitable repatriation. Ethnic Koreans were temporary residents in Japan. In the dominant line of thinking, they should have returned to their homeland after the end of colonial rule. In fact, the majority—up to three-fourths—repatriated, but some 600,000 remained on the Japanese archipelago.

The salient point is not the reality of no-return but the ideology of return. The idea that Japan might be a permanent home for ethnic Koreans—a place to be buried or a country in which descendants will live long and presumably prosper—was alien and abominable. Whereas many Japanese excluded Koreans from the ambit of Japan, Koreans too rejected Japan in theory. Powerful anti-Japanese sentiments manifested themselves in rejecting rapprochement with Japan and Japanese; for example, in opposing intermarriage or naturalization. In this mind-set, articulated most forcefully by what I call Sōren ideology, Zainichi are exiles in Japan. "An exile is someone who inhabits one place and remembers or projects the reality of another" (Seidel 1986:lx).

In this chapter, I explore distinct resolutions of the problematic of exile by three well-known writers of Korean descent in Japan: Kim Sokpom, Lee Yangji, and Lee Hoesung. In particular, I focus on their depictions of actual return to Korea. Before I explore disparate modes of exilic and diasporic identity, let me delineate the postwar trajectory of the Korean population in Japan.

THE POSTWAR PERSISTENCE OF THE KOREAN POPULATION IN JAPAN

The immediate postwar period generated mass confusion and mass mobilization (cf. Hirabayashi 1978:3–5). Some ethnic Koreans reveled in their newly independent status. As the novelist Tanabe Seiko (2004:130, 153) recollects, the situation changed from the prewar period, when any ethnic

Japanese could declaim, "Shut up, Chōsen!" to the postwar years, when any ethnic Korean could retort, "Japan lost; don't be so arrogant."

If the received Zainichi historiography were true—the colonial period as unremittingly oppressive and exploitive—then almost all Koreans should have hastened back to the Korean peninsula. The majority (1–1.4 million) did leave the Japanese archipelago (given the absence of an official census, these numbers are rough estimates), but notwithstanding the U.S. and Japanese authorities' effort at ethnic cleansing, some 600,000 remained (Kim Yondal 2003b:188). Thus arose the problem of *Zairyū* [remaining] Koreans or *Zainichi nanmin* [refugees] (cf. Kim T'ae-gi 1997:162–63). Edward Wagner's (1951:1–2) description is symptomatic of the mind-set of the U.S. authorities: "the Koreans have remained a highly vocal, emotional and cohesive group." He goes on to charge them with producing "considerable civil turmoil," creating "an obstacle to reconstruction," and interfering with various reform efforts by the Japanese government and the U.S. occupation forces. It is as though they stayed in order to wreak havoc on Japanese reconstruction efforts. Yet, as Wagner goes on to relate, several factors contributed to their continuing residence in Japan.

In spite of suffering racial discrimination and economic exploitation, some ethnic Koreans had achieved successful careers in business, the imperial bureaucracy, and even the military during the colonial period, while others seized economic opportunities that opened up immediately after the end of the war (Wagner 1951:41–42, 62–63). Hence, the U.S. occupational authorities' enforced limits on repatriation—1,000 yen and 250 pounds of luggage—provided a profound disincentive to return (Hōmu Kenshūjo 1975:70–72). Although we have no exact records of the demographic differences between those who left and those who stayed, there is no question that some who stayed in Japan enjoyed a relatively privileged status. There were, to be sure, impoverished Koreans who could not afford the train fare to one of the departure ports (Jon 1984:131).

The vast majority of Koreans in Japan may have supported what eventually became the North Korean regime, but most did not regard northern Korea as home and southern Korea was convulsed by constant uprisings and upheavals. It is a characteristically nationalistic trope to depict the nation as a home, but a tangible home is not located in some homogeneous national space but in an actual place: a building, a village, a neighborhood. The generally impoverished, unhealthy, and unmodern conditions in post-Liberation Korea also repulsed some returnees, who made a U-turn back to Japan. Che Sogi (2004:42) returned to Japan after six months in Korea: "There was no place to live, there was no place to work. . . . Furthermore, I couldn't speak Korean well." As the Zainichi writer Kim Sokpom reminisced: "I suppose it was better here [in Japan], after all. By 1946 one couldn't live in Seoul: inflation was staggering, and it was a town of unemployment, beggars, and hunger. . . . I would probably have died [had I stayed]" (Kim Sokpom and Kim 2001:40). Nearly 16,000 ethnic Koreans were, however, evicted to Korea in 1946, and over 7,600 in 1949 (Pak Cheil 1957:127–29). The threat of deportation would serve as the proverbial sword of Damocles for many ethnic Koreans in the postwar years.

Risks of financial loss and political instability were far from the only reasons people stayed. Pak Kyongsik, the eminent Zainichi historian, hoped to marry his Japanese lover and therefore remained in Japan even as the rest of his family left. Although he did not marry her, he was unable to see his siblings for over thirty years (Pak Kyongsik 1981:11, 79–81). The anti-colonial activist Kim Hyonpyo (1978:184–86) was in Seoul but—wary of the disorderly country and longing to be with his German wife, whom he met in Dalian—he entered Japan illegally. The prewar government had, after all, encouraged intermarriage as a matter of national policy. In some rural prefectures in the 1950s, the ratio of Korean-Japanese "mixed" households exceeded two-thirds of all local "Korean" households (though in Osaka the ratio was below 5 percent) (Pak Cheil 1957:132–33).

As the web of personal relationships that crossed ethnonational boundaries shows, we should not merely stress the economic and political. The vast majority of ethnic Koreans, and indeed most ethnic Japanese, suffered all manner of hardships during the war and immediate postwar years. In a 1951 survey of a Tokyo ward, only 41 percent of ethnic Korean adults were employed, mostly in the informal sector, such as scrap recycling and casual day labor (Zainichi Chōsen 1978:285). Scrap recycling was a euphemism for garbage collection, and the first postwar decade was an unenviable time for many Koreans in Japan (Yang 1994:178–80). Rather than merely stressing the economic advantages, often a decisive factor was that Japan was, for all intents and purposes, and in spite of poverty and discrimination, a home. Perhaps half of those who stayed after 1948 had moved to Japan before 1930 (Mitchell 1967:104). In the aforementioned 1951 study, 63 percent of ethnic Koreans were born in Japan, and 43 percent of them could not speak Korean (as opposed to 18 percent who could not speak Japanese) (Zainichi Chōsen 1978:289–90). Pak Kyongsik (1992:612) recalls that in 1949, a third of the faculty members at his ethnic Korean school were not fluent in Korean. An elderly Japanese policeman asks the ethnic Korean character in Chon Sunpak's story "Tonsha no bannin" [Guard of a pig house]: "Korea has become independent and is now an impressive country; why don't you return?" Thinking to himself that he knows that his homeland is independent, he ponders: "I cannot return. I grew up in Japan from my infancy. I have forgotten Korean and the village to which I should return" (Chon 1994:80). Although one survey shows that roughly 80 percent of the Korean population in Japan wished to return in the immediate postwar years (Pak Cheil 1957:35), over 60 percent had expressed their intention to reside permanently in some 1930s surveys. Clearly, to remain or to return is not a question to be resolved solely by intention but also by personal attachments, perceived opportunities, and concrete contingencies.

Repatriation was difficult because the traffic between the Korean peninsula and the Japanese archipelago was severely restricted in the postwar period. While millions of people had been ferried between Shimonoseki and Pusan from 1905 to 1945, the line was not resumed until 1970 (Kim Chanjung 1988:iv). As late as the 1960s, there were no Japanese books on immigration law because immigration was so rare (Iinuma 1983:24–25). Although illegal entries from both North and South Korea continued, the stringent surveillance of Japanese national borders limited them (cf. Han 2002:103). The return journey was therefore likely to be a one-way trip, especially for those who went to North Korea (Zainichi Chōsenjin 1964:40). By the outbreak of the Korean War, the prospect of immediate repatriation had vanished for the remnant population. Until the 1965 Normalization Treaty, the fundamental freedom of travel was severely curtailed for the Zainichi population.

In the year following the end of the war the population of ethnic Koreans in Japan settled at roughly the same figure it had been during the mid-1930s (some 600,000). The population—except for one major episode around 1960—would by and large remain in Japan. It is in the immediate postwar years that the term *Zainichi* begins to appear. It would not be misleading to call the period between August 1945 and August 1946 as the year zero of Zainichi history.

THE POLITICS OF EXCLUSION

The recalcitrance of the Japanese government and the persistence of colonial racism in the postwar period made life difficult for ethnic Koreans. They had been Japanese nationals under colonial rule, but they gradually lost their rights after the war. In so doing, the government belied its prewar claim that they had achieved theoretical equality with ethnic Japanese. Quite frequently, the Japanese authorities had it both ways. Ethnic Koreans were stripped of their suffrage in 1945 presumably because they were not

Japanese, but their effort to create ethnic schools was denied in 1948 because they were Japanese nationals. Although Koreans were arrested as *Japanese* war criminals—twenty-three were executed (Utsumi 1982:ii)— their co-ethnics were fired from government jobs because they were no longer Japanese nationals (Hōmu Kenshūjo 1975:116–23, 147). The United States—the official governing body until Japanese sovereignty was restored in 1952—classified the Korean population in Japan alternately as "liberated peoples" and "enemy nationals" (*Zainichi Chōsenjin* 1978:10–12). Lacking knowledge, understanding, or vision, the U.S. policy generally sought to repatriate them (Wagner 1951:41–42), and otherwise followed the decisions of the Japanese authorities (Kim T'ae-gi 1997:743–52). Underlying their predilection was the prejudice that ethnic Koreans were unable to shed their "essential 'Korean-ness'" (Wagner 1951:43). They served as a convenient scapegoat for the problems afflicting Japanese society, ranging from the defeat itself to economic hardship. The Japanese authorities attempted at various points to deport all ethnic Koreans—true to their status as scapegoats—though they ultimately were rebuffed by the U.S. occupation forces (Kim T'ae-gi 1997:576–80).

The alienation of resident Koreans from the Japanese body politic occurred steadily during the decade after 1945: their rights and recognition as Japanese nationals were exfoliated (Ōnuma 1993:chap.3). Already by December 1945, Korean voting rights were revoked (Kashiwazaki 2000:21). Anti-Korean hysteria in response to black marketeering led to the 1947 Alien Registration Law, which relegated ethnic Koreans to foreigner status (Mitchell 1967:112–13). The 1950 nationality law decreed patrilineality as the basis of Japanese citizenship, thereby stripping "Korean" children of Japanese mothers of their Japanese nationality. A 1952 law mandated governmental registration and surveillance of foreigners, though it also provided a temporary measure for the continuing residence of ethnic Koreans (Kim T'ae-gi 1997:739–40). In 1955 all registered aliens were forced to be fingerprinted [*shimon ōnatsu*], the beginning of a dreaded practice that was the focus of an oppositional movement in the 1980s (Zainichi Chōsenjin 1964:83–84). Ethnic Koreans were even excluded from the rights enshrined for non-nationals in Japan's postwar constitution; it would take legal challenges and political struggles beginning in the 1970s to restore those rights.

By the 1952 San Francisco Peace Treaty, ethnic Koreans in Japan, the Japanese authorities, and the larger Japanese public regarded the Zainichi population as irredeemably Korean. The government defined ethnic Koreans as foreigners who should be encouraged to return to Korea.

Japanese people readily accepted the ethnonational distinction that belied the colonial Japanization project. The term "Zainichi" captured the temporary nature of Koreans' residence.

For ethnic Koreans, postwar Japanese society was an inhospitable environment even beyond their separate and unequal treatment as resident foreigners. Korean entanglement in the black market and other illegal activities accentuated the association of Koreans with criminality and violence. Between the Rhee Line—the 1952 decree by the South Korean president to extend South Korean territorial waters—and the Komatsugawa Incident—the 1958 murder case involving the eighteen-year-old Ri Chin'u—the surname Lee (Rhee, Ri) reigned as "the pronoun of evil" in the late 1950s (Hwang 1993:80). Worse, Koreans' identification with communism rendered them vulnerable in the 1947 "red purge" and in subsequent anticommunist measures. In short, Korean identity in Japan was at once polluted and taboo; Koreans were to be excluded and quarantined. Colonial racism transmuted into outright racial discrimination.

The exclusionary principle structured all public-sector jobs as well as prestigious private-sector employment. The majority of ethnic Koreans had worked in mining, construction, and factory jobs before 1945, but they were expelled from "Japanese" jobs after 1945. Ethnic Koreans therefore pursued informal-sector employment and, in so doing, created a new ethnic economy. In the immediate postwar years, many engaged in illegal or marginal economic activities, ranging from illegal alcohol production to scrap recycling. Some became racketeers and yakuza members. Lacking official protection, Koreans created mercantile organizations to promote their interests (O 1992:43–50).

The remaining population congregated in Korean ghettoes, especially in Osaka, but they were also dispersed throughout the archipelago. Many were isolated. As a first-generation woman recalls, "I had no other relatives or family around me. If there had been someone, a relative or someone, then I don't think that I would have had to endure such *kosaeng* [suffering]" (J. Kim 2005:12). Lacking ties to other ethnic Koreans, the rural Zainichi population—many were mixed households, as we saw—sought to blend into the local community.

Thus, Zainichi existence was at once parallel to and occluded from mainstream Japanese society: parallel because they often lived and worked apart from their Japanese counterparts, and occluded because to the extent that they participated in Japanese life they were invisible as they passed as Japanese. Their invisibility and silence were predicated in part on the expectation of return.

THE RISE OF SŌREN

The politics of exclusion inevitably raises potentially racist questions: Why didn't Koreans return to their homeland? And if concrete possibilities of repatriation were minimal, then why didn't ethnic Koreans seek assimilation and naturalization in Japan? The answer, in brief, was that most did intend to return. As something of a destiny, it was merely a matter of timing, with the modal time being when Korea was unified. Ethnic organizations played a powerful role in shaping the ideology of return.

Postwar ethnic Korean organizations arose to combat discrimination, aid fellow ethnics, and engage in politics. After the end of the war, Zainichi Chōsenjin Renmei [League of Resident Koreans in Japan; usually abbreviated as Chōren] announced in its Manifesto, "Our historical mission is to eliminate the remnants of Japanese imperialism and feudal forces, and to realize the fundamental political, economic, social, and cultural demands of our people and to construct a complete independent state on the basis of true democracy" (*Zainichi Chōsenjin dantai* 1975:37). Chōren functioned as a de facto government for Koreans in Japan: collecting "taxes," dispensing welfare, and trying criminals (Mitchell 1967:104–6). It provided critical bulwarks against Japanese media criticisms of Korean black-market activities and the Japanese government crackdown on Korean-language schools (Mitchell 1967:108–15). It also worked closely with—and often followed—the Communist Party, purging from the leadership pro-Japanese, nationalists, and other non-communists (Ri 1971:4–5).

Reflecting the Cold War in general and the division of the Koreas in particular, Chōren failed to sustain a united front among ethnic Koreans in Japan. Its communist orientation generated a splinter group to the right: the South Korea-affiliated Zainichi Daikanminkoku Kyoryū Mindan [Community of Resident [South] Koreans in Japan; usually called Mindan] in 1948. The term *kyoryū*—used, for example, for Japanese residents in colonial Korea—highlights the organization's homeland orientation. Mindan's expectation was that Koreans would soon repatriate and, unlike Chōren, it assiduously avoided intervention in Japanese politics, aligned itself squarely behind South Korea, and was broadly pro-Japanese because of South Korea's pro-U.S. stance (Ri 1971:102–3). With its unity largely based on ideological anticommunism, Mindan suffered from factionalism (Tei 1982:62–63, 74–75). It was also widely seen as a front for middle-class people with ties to South Korea (Mitchell 1967:125–26). Furthermore, Mindan's pro–South Korea sentiments were not exactly reciprocated. Unlike North Korea, the South Korean government willfully neglected the

Korean diaspora in Japan until the 1970s (Kim Chanjung 2004a:145). Rhee Syngman's ferocious anti-Japanese sentiments extended to the Zainichi population (Kim Chanjung 2007:20–22), who were suspected of communist sympathies (Kim T'ae-gi 1997:762–65).

Beside Mindan, numerous ethnic groups rose and fell in the immediate postwar decade (Ri 1971:5–29), but Chōren and its allied groups dominated ethnic politics. Although Chōren leaders expressed passionate interest in homeland politics, their activities often focused on Japanese matters, such as the 1948 struggles to protect ethnic education of Koreans [Hanshin Tōsō]. As one Zainichi man recalled: "We couldn't send Korean children to Japanese schools. We were finally liberated" (Kim Teyon 1999:73). In effect, they fought for Koreans' place in Japanese society (Yan 1995:61–68). At its first meeting in 1946, the Chōren leader Kin Tenkai (Kim Chone) demanded political rights and economic betterment for Koreans in Japan "to make our Japan a wonderful place to live" (Pak Kyongsik 1979:56). Chōren also fought to restitute Korean suffrage (Yang 1994:66). Led by the Communist Party, it engaged at times in highly publicized demonstrations (Ri 1971:29–36). In 1949, in the context of escalating anticommunism, the U.S. authorities dissolved Chōren.

The Korean War destroyed much of the homeland but its primary impact on the Zainichi population was to deepen the conflict between ethnic factions. Whereas the majority backed the North, some supporters of the South volunteered as soldiers. Anticipating the experience of later returnees, the volunteers—many of whom could not speak Korean—were targets of considerable suspicion. Worse, many of them were unable to return to Japan (Kim Chanjung 2007:209–10). In contrast, the communist-inspired activists, including both ethnic Koreans and ethnic Japanese, sought to end the dispatch of weapons in particular and the war in general, most famously in the Suita Incident and the Hirakata Incident (Nishimura 2004:122; Wakita 2004:271–72). Waged in the context of rearming Japan, the two incidents, along with other major demonstrations, signaled the continuing influence of the Communist Party and its ethnic Korean affiliate, Zainichi Chōsen Tōitsu Minshu Sensen [Koreans' United Democratic Front in Japan; usually called Minsen]. Established in 1951, Minsen succeeded Chōren and continued its support for North Korea and international communism as well as protecting ethnic Korean rights in Japan (Mitchell 1967:120–21).

Beyond deepening the divided allegiances, the Korean War also oriented ethnic Koreans to homeland politics. Minsen was superseded by Zainichi Chōsenjin Sōrengōkai [General Federation of Resident Koreans in Japan;

usually called Sōren, Chōsōren, or Chongryun] in 1955. The establishment of Sōren is linked to a major turn in ethnic Korean politics: henceforth, the dominant organization among ethnic Koreans subordinated itself to the North Korean regime. In 1954, North Korean Foreign Minister Nam Il had declaimed the Zainichi population as North Korean citizens *[kōmin]*. Han Doksu—Sōren's founding secretary, who would remain in the leadership position until his death in 2001 at 94—delivered an influential speech in 1955 that affirmed the new North Korean line. In the speech, he was explicit about the political and ontological status of ethnic Koreans in Japan: "In a word, the movement of Koreans in Japan takes the standpoint of North Korea" (Han 1993:610). That is, Koreans should no longer follow the Japan Communist Party but follow and fight for the North Korean government (Han 1993:525). A "major mistake" of the Communist Party in the imme- diate postwar years was to define Koreans as an "ethnic minority" *[shosū minzoku]* rather than as Korean nationals (Ko 1985:306). Sōren members resigned en masse from the Communist Party and affirmed their Korean- ness. Many Sōren documents were written in Korean (see, e.g., Pak Kyongsik 1983a, 1983b), despite the spread of Japanese as the native lan- guage for ethnic Koreans in Japan. There were even efforts to suppress the use of Japanese in the 1950s (Kim Sokpom and Kim 2001:151–52).

Han's 1955 speech made clear that the Zainichi population was in Japan temporarily as North Koreans. They are "part of the homeland people *[honkoku minzoku]* and their constituents" (Han 1986:13). As Pak Cheil (1957:166) suggested: "The solution to the problem of Zainichi cannot be achieved unless we assume the solution to be the problem of Korea," includ- ing land reform in South Korea and unification. As a population waiting to return, they were to prepare for the eventuality, not to meddle in Japanese affairs. As a Sōren official explained, they had made a "mistake" earlier: "We were disliked by Japanese people because we interfered in Japanese domestic politics"; henceforth, Koreans will engage in educating the "chil- dren of the Republic [North Korea]" (Ri 1956:123). The support for the homeland and the expectation of return mandated Sōren's insistent anti- assimilationist stance (Zainichi Chōsenjin 1996:15–18). Sōren thereby redirected the energy of the left-leaning activists who struggled for ethnic rights and recognitions in the immediate postwar years to the political exigency of the North Korean regime.

Homeland orientation was the foundation of Sōren ideology, but the organization provided indispensable infrastructural support for ethnic Koreans living and working in Japan. Sōren was less a cult of personality and more of a culture of mutual uplift. Its two critical pillars were finance and education. At a time when Japanese banks were loath to lend to ethnic Koreans, Chōgin Bank, as Sōren's financial arm, filled a critical need. Even more significant was ethnic education. Sōren schools sought to prepare for eventual return and therefore stressed the teaching of Korean language and history. Needless to say, ethnic education was also communist education, highlighting the flaws of capitalism and the perfidies of U.S. and Japanese imperialism (*Zainichi Hokusenkei* 1967:1–5). Sōren curriculum did not offer Zainichi history qua Zainichi history but only as part of the "revolutionary activities of General Kim Il Sung" (Kim Chanjung 2004a:5; cf. Ko 1985:401–2). Whatever the parents' expectations of return or commitment to communism, Sōren schools not only provided a respite from potentially racist Japanese schools but inculcated ethnonational pride. Curiously for a self-consciously communist organization, Sōren betrayed what might be called a petit-bourgeois orientation: while Chōgin loans promoted small (and later larger) businesses, ethnic schools educated relatively well-off pupils, as poor Zainichi parents were unable to afford the tuition and sent their children to fee-free Japanese public schools. Paradoxical, too, was the efflorescence of Zainichi capitalists who were ideologically and organizationally communist (cf. Yan 1987:59). Yet Sōren was at once the local and national government of the Zainichi population.

In the late 1950s, Sōren's hold over ethnic Koreans in Japan was nearly total. Although the vast majority (more than 90 percent) of ethnic Koreans in Japan hailed from southern Korea, an equivalent majority identified ideologically with North Korea after the 1948 North-South split. To speak of Zainichi in the 1950s almost always meant North Koreans in Japan [Zainichi Chōsenjin] (e.g. Rōdōsha 1959). Kim Il Sung's regime basked in the glow of heroic anti-Japanese colonial struggles and promised a communist utopia. Sōren derived its legitimacy from North Korea, and the North Korean regime sought in turn to control Sōren. Criticizing the organization was tantamount to insulting both Kim Il Sung and the Zainichi community as a whole (cf. Yan 2006:25). Expulsion was excommunication, the experience of social death (cf. Kim Sokpom 2005b:35).

Even today, there remain die-hard Sōren members who support the North Korean regime financially and ideologically. But the legitimacy of and even passion for North Korea was most robust in the 1950s and 1960s, a trend that owed in no small part to the Communist Party's support for Koreans before and after World War II; the Korean communists' impeccable credentials in resisting Japanese colonialism; the appeal of freedom, equality, and solidarity; and the ostensible economic successes of North Korea. More generally, the postwar world of Zainichi was profoundly shaped by international communism. Chan Myonsu (1991:3–4) writes that Sōren "was my everything." As an elderly Zainichi said: "Communism was the youth *[seishun]* of our generation" (cf. Kim Chanjung 2004b:4). The intellectual culture of Zainichi was dominated by the collected works of Marx, Engels, Lenin, Stalin, and Kim Il Sung. The editor of the pioneering Zainichi journal *Madan* recalls that reading Stalin's *Dialectical and Historical Materialism* was the "most moving experience" of his life (Honda 1992:108–9). The Zainichi writer Yan Sogiru (1995:67, 74) spent much of his high-school years studying Marxist-Leninism, and spent some twenty-three years reading *Das Kapital*. Kim Il Sung was revered and glorified: One Sōren official recalls being told to read Kim Il Sung's revolutionary memoir a hundred times, and apparently some did so (Han 2002:76–80). North Korea was paradise on earth, which was not so much a statement of fact as one of promise. As Czeslaw Milosz's (1981:30–35) social psychology of the communist mind-set suggests, not only did Kim Il Sung's *juche* [self-reliance] philosophy and dialectical materialism provide a more or less coherent history and sociology, as well as liturgy and rites, they also provided *meaning:* freedom *for* an ideal future, rather than the prevailing capitalist refrain on freedom *from* constraints. Japanese imperialism had also promised meaning, but it was a cataclysmic failure. The United States brought liberation but it could neither bring about a unified Korea nor defend the Zainichi population. For many disappointed and disillusioned Zainichi in the 1950s and 1960s, North Korea, with its active propaganda, became the beacon of hope.

Just as significant as the historical legacy of struggling against Japanese imperialism and the future destination of the paradise on the earth in sustaining Sōren was its status as a bulwark against Japanese racism and the embodiment of ethnic pride. Sōren supplied not only history and teleology but also community and welfare, as should be clear from its cardinal role in finance and education. Around the cadres at the core revolved satellites of followers and fellow travelers, many of whom believed passionately in the cause that guided their lives and community. Sōren activists and followers expressed, not unlike the U.S. communists described by Vivian Gornick (1977:13), "inner radiance: some interiority of illumination that tore at the soul." We should not forget the flame that burned brightly for a while and not merely shake our head at the bitter ash that remained after the dream had turned out to be a nightmare. For every crime committed by the North Korean regime or the Sōren leadership, there are countless instances of mutual aid and ethnic uplift by Sōren members. As one of them said, "How many ethnic minority groups in the world can boast that they teach their children the language of their ancestors? Can third-generation Japanese Americans stage a play in Japanese? The third-generation Koreans in Japan can." Whereas Mindan members had long ceased any serious commitment to language reproduction or ethnic education, Sōren schools continued to teach the Korean language and the North Korean–Sōren brand of nationalist communism. Sōren was also the main conduit of information and support, especially for rural Zainichi. Sōren, in short, was born and thrived as an organization of "overseas nationals" *[kaigai kōmin]* of North Korea (Zainichi Chōsenjin 1996:19). Sōren ideology was predicated on and promised repatriation.

THE IDEOLOGY OF RETURN, THE DREAM OF UNIFICATION

Sōren ideology followed the North Korean brand of communist nationalism and promised Zainichi repatriation, but not to southern Korea whence most ethnic Koreans in Japan came. Sōren portrayed South Korea as an impoverished dictatorship: a puppet of the U.S. imperialist government. If the United States was giving massive aid to South Korea, it was paradoxically in order to "enslave 'South Korea' militarily, politically, and economically" (Kim Chonghoe 1957:44). In a rare study of the Zainichi population published in the 1950s, Pak Cheil (1957:154) argued that South Korea was not the ancestral land for the Zainichi population but merely a "site of graves." Because they would in effect be immigrants, they would need the South Korean government's support, for which they would wait in vain: "what will await them are confusion, unemployment, and hunger" (Pak Cheil 1957:154). Curiously, the ire did not extend to Japanese society but only to the Japanese government, which was considered a lackey of the United States (Ri 1956:23–24).

If the return to South Korea was discouraged, then why didn't the Sōren leadership encourage repatriation to North Korea? Some blamed the interference of the United States, Japan, and South Korea (e.g. Ko 1985:106); the U.S. imperialists were seen as the inevitable source of North Korean problems and are the target of insults to this day. Others insisted on the importance of preparing for imminent return (Pak Cheil 1957:155). The struggle for North Korea was in fact the struggle for unification; ethnic Koreans were to contribute toward the reconstruction and strengthening of the Korean nation. As a popular Zainichi saying at the time went, "love the future" (Han 2002:43). Sōren cadres thereby conflated the hope for repatriation and the desire for unification. Nearly every Zainichi favored unification then as now, but it would be misleading to attribute the same level of consensus and enthusiasm to the idea of return. After all, many of them stayed in Japan for a reason or two.

In the late 1950s, however, there was a major repatriation project when Kim Il Sung promised "a new life after their return to the homeland" to celebrate the tenth anniversary of North Korea's founding (Mitchell 1967:138). The North Korean government sought to relieve labor shortage and to strengthen its claim as the sole legitimate nation of Koreans; the Japanese government hoped to achieve ethnic cleansing (cf. Takasaki 2005:26–28; Morris-Suzuki 2007:178–79). Backed by Japanese politicians on the right and the left, as well as the International Red Cross, the repatriation project accorded with the prevailing nationalist mind-set: population transfer to achieve ethnonational isomorphism. It faced only sporadic opposition, primarily by Mindan and the South Korean government—which even sponsored terrorist acts to halt the project (Kim Chanjung 2007:234–36)—and achieved a remarkable show of unanimity (Lee Chang-soo 1981:101–2).

The repatriation project responded to the problematic of discrimination and diminished Zainichi prospects in Japan by presenting North Korea as the counterpoint to their miserable existence in Japan (cf. Shin 2003:15; Satō 2005:93–94). The propaganda campaign exploited the trope of a paradise on earth where every refrigerator was full of beef and pork and youths could study at Kim Il Sung University and possibly Moscow State University (Hagiwara 1998:361). As a primary school pupil, Hwang Mingi's (1993:61) friend longed to return because "I can eat ham free every day and live in a large house." The poet Fujishima Udai (1960:8) claimed that some ethnic Japanese people masqueraded as part of Zainichi families to escape the poverty of Japanese life. The reality is that economic growth in Japan stirred the social psychology of frustration for ethnic Koreans, who by the late 1950s were only beginning to take part in the prosperity that ethnic Japanese had been enjoying. For ethnic Koreans, the sheer difficulties of livelihood made the promise of a new life—any life—alluring: as one Zainichi man wrote in the early 1960s: "My meager, humble life is no longer sustainable today. Therefore, I have decided to repatriate" (Iwata 2001:143). Terao Gorō's 1959 travelogue of North Korea was widely read (Jon 2005:216–17; cf. Fujishima 1960:356–57). Terao (1961:15) reported a Zainichi returnee gushing: "From the standpoint of my Japanese period, I must almost apologize for my [affluent] life [in North Korea]." As he wrote in another book, North Korea was a country where 80,000 Zainichi could "live without any inconvenience," or as a "star of hope" (Terao 1965:71).

The parliamentary member Iwamoto Nobuyuki (1960:19) observed that "for Koreans leading tough, pathetic lives in Japan, [returning to North Korea] is literally returning to heaven from hell."

The repatriation project also reaffirmed the Sōren leadership's new alliance with North Korea and rejection of the Communist Party in particular and Japan in general (Hagiwara 1998:309–12). Sōren activists organized Zainichi to join the repatriation project; one activist hoped to prove his mettle by sending as many Zainichi as possible to North Korea (Han 2002:59–60). In any case, repatriation appealed especially to idealistic Zainichi youths. Yan Sogiru (1995:148) comments, "I think every Zainichi youth at the time thought of repatriation. When friends would randomly meet one another on the street, the conversation would somehow turn to repatriation, and we parted in some excitement by shaking hands and saying we would next meet in the Republic [North Korea]."

In the two-year period from 1960 through 1961, some 70,000 Zainichi journeyed to North Korea but the number dropped to about 3,500 in 1962 and steadily declined thereafter (Kim Chanjung 2004a:160). The repatriation project officially ended in 1984, having dispatched 93,340 people to North Korea, including 6,731 Japanese and 4 Chinese spouses and dependents (Morris-Suzuki 2007:12), but it had effectively ended by the early 1960s.

Why did the repatriation effort dry up so quickly? Some Sōren supporters pointed to interference by the Japanese government (e.g. Un 1978:197; Han 1986:213–17), but both Sōren leaders and followers had clearly lost their enthusiasm by the early 1960s. Sōren retained Zainichi activists in Japan in order to protest the impending Japan–South Korea Normalization Treaty (Sasaki 2004:156–57). Undoubtedly, many Koreans had simply chosen to stay in Japan (see, e.g., Chan 1989:220). As I have repeatedly stressed, cultural assimilation had been manifest as early as the late 1930s, and many Koreans were entrenched in Japan by 1960.

More important, as the former Sōren official Kim Sangwon (2004:64–67) argues, the suffering of Zainichi in North Korea blatantly contradicted the promise of paradise and thereby stemmed the flow (cf. Ri 1971:58–60). North Korean poverty and autocracy were manifest almost instantly (Han 2007:18–22). As early as 1962, the Zainichi variant of "the god that failed" had appeared, describing Zainichi returnees to North Korea as political prisoners in an impoverished dictatorship, and going so far as to compare the North Korean regime to that of Hitler's Germany (Seki 1962:85–87, 134). In the North Korean class system, Zainichi literally were second-class citizens (though not as ill treated as the third class that constituted enemies of the state, such as former landlords and Christians). The North Korean regime regarded them with suspicion, and they were liable to be indicted as spies for the South or Japan (Hagiwara 1998:159–61; Lee Y. 1999:106–7). Even loyal communists experienced difficulties because of the economic, cultural, and linguistic differences between North Korea and Japan.

By the time Zainichi were able to visit their returnee relatives in the late 1970s, the claim of North Korean paradise tested ordinary credulity. Its failure anticipated the open disavowal of North Korea in the 1980s by erstwhile Sōren supporters (see, e.g., Kim W. 1984, Chan 1991). More immediately, the repatriation project spelled the declining prospect of return for Sōren Koreans. After the 1965 Normalization Treaty, South Korea—which, after all, was the actual land of ancestry for nearly all ethnic Koreans in Japan—became the destination for repatriation. Just as Mindan members who visited South Korea after the 1965 treaty found the homeland alien—as we will see in the narratives of exile below—the brush with the reality of difference confirmed the implicit decision to stay in Japan. Rapid economic growth that was manifest at the time and would continue unabated for another decade would merely seal the fate of Zainichi in Japan. The iron cage of Japanese life had transmogrified into the golden cage by then: a cage, to be sure, but a glittering one.

In spite of the unrealistic prospect, the ideology of return would long survive beyond the early 1960s. The false promise of colonial-era assimilation and the brute reality of contemporary discrimination left future repatriation as the best hope for ethnic Koreans in Japan. The extent of actual assimilation was, at least ideologically, immaterial. Shin Sugok's grandfather, though born in Korea, spoke only Japanese, decorated his house with a Japanese flag and Japanese sword, and insisted that his wife and children wear kimonos, but he decided to repatriate (Shin 2003:28).

Zainichi identification—and the prospect of a viable future for ethnic Koreans in Japan—was precluded because there were really only two options: assimilation or repatriation. As Pak Kyongsik (1981:5) explained: "Before [the end of the war], I was unable to experience pride because I was unable to have ethnic subjectivity [minzokuteki na shutaisei] as I was incorporated in the process of Japanization [kōminka] and Imperial Japan's ethnic discrimination." That is, one could aspire to be and thereby be accepted as Japanese, or to remain and be despised as Korean. The idea of Zainichi was something of an excluded middle. Even when over 600,000 Koreans more or less opted to stay in Japan, the idea of a hybrid identity was elusive, if not oxymoronic. The justification for tarrying was the prospect of unification. As late as the mid-1980s, the eminent Zainichi intellectual Yoon Keun Cha (1987:250) equated Zainichi with unified Korea, and Yamada Terumi (1986:14, 19) declared that "the problem of Zainichi cannot be told without the perspective of Korean unification. . . . The major key to the solution to the problem of Zainichi is Korean unification" (cf. Pak Chonmyon 1995:319). Even today, Sōren has not embraced the idea of conviviality *[kyōsei]:* of ethnic Koreans settling down in Japanese society (Kim Chanjung 2004b:191). The idea of temporary residence—enshrined in the *zai* in *Zainichi*—and the expectation of ultimate return remained resonant. A book from the late 1990s defines the Korean population in Japan in terms of its history of colonization, the present reality of discrimination, and the consciousness of ancestral land *[sokoku]* (Ko 1998:58). The *après-garde* of homeland consciousness—like the nationalist-communist regime in North Korea—survived the short twentieth century. To the question— why are there Koreans in Japan?—the modal answer until the 1970s would have been that they had nowhere else to go until unification. They were, in a sense, waiting for the message to arrive that recalls the contemporaneous work of Samuel Beckett: Zainichi were permanent exiles.

DIASPORIC DISCOURSE OF EXILE

Let me now focus on three narratives of exile. They are taken from the 1980s and 1990s, but the dream of return survived the collapse of Sōren ideology. Having achieved the long-standing desire, the reality of return transforms the nature of homeland and exile.

Kim Sokpom's Utopia

Kokoku kō [To the ancestral land, 1990] recounts Kim Sokpom's travel to Chejudo, an island off the southwestern coast of South Korea that is the locale of his *magnum opus, Kazantō* [The volcano island, 1983–97]. The seven-volume novel depicts the April 1948 uprising in which many insurgents and citizens sympathetic to communism were killed. Although Kim was born in Osaka, Chejudo is not only an important locus of his fiction but a place he calls his ancestral land *[kokoku]*.

Kim had repeatedly attempted, but failed, to visit South Korea for forty years. His original intention was foiled by the political turbulence that culminated in the Korean War (though confusion and poverty also contributed to his decision to stay in Japan). Several planned trips were stymied either by the South Korean government's refusal to grant a visa or by other unfortunate occurrences. He had also spurned an opportunity to travel to South Korea: "The reason I could not return to my country for over forty years is, in a word, the political one of the division between North and South Korea" (1990:6). In 1981, his fellow editors of the journal *Kikan sanzenri* traveled to South Korea. The journal was founded by former members-turned-critics of Sōren; Kim himself had left the organization in 1968 because of his opposition to its stultifying hierarchy. He refused to join his co-editors because of his opposition to the South Korean military dictatorship that had just massacred civilians in the 1980 Kwangju Incident. He also resigned from the journal's editorial board. In other words, he opposed the North Korean and South Korean regimes, their respective organizations in Japan, and even his closest allies who had left Sōren with him in the late 1960s (see also Kim Sokpom 1981, 2004).

Thus, Kim's independent position precludes his loyalty to ready-made identities: North Korea, South Korea, Sōren, or Mindan. Furthermore, his chosen language of writing—Japanese—and his break with *Kikan sanzenri* implied writing largely for the Japanese reading public and Japanese periodicals. *Kazantō* was published by Bungei Shunjū, one of the leading Japanese publishers usually associated with the political right.

Because of his long absence from his ancestral land—he was born in Osaka, after all—Kim's relationship to Korea exists almost solely in memory and imagination. There are only two tangible connections to Korea that he mentions. First, he has a stone that he received from a Japanese friend who had visited Chejudo. He would "occasionally smell the faint aroma of the ocean." Secondly, *Asahi shinbun*—a leading, and left-leaning, Japanese daily—chartered a small plane to fly him near Chejudo in 1984 in order to see the "Volcano Island" that he had been writing about. Like exiles around the world, he sought assiduously to recuperate a memory of home. If his concrete experiences with homeland seem rather thin materials to generate fully formed memory—he had been born and reared in Japan—we should remember that the realm of imagination frequently reigns majestically over the impoverished land of reality. In this spirit, André Aciman (2000:51) writes of himself as "a Jewish boy landlocked in Nasser's anti-Semitic Egypt, yearning to be back in France I had never seen and did not belong to." Or, somewhat conversely to Kim's narrative and more mundanely, the literary critic Nan Bujin reports the first visit of his friend's South Korean father to Japan. In response to the question how he finds Japan, the father repeats: "I feel nostalgic, I feel nostalgic." Asked what he is so nostalgic about, he says: "The landscape is absolutely the same as in my childhood. I feel like I have somehow returned to my home *[kokyō]*" (Nan 2006:i). Nostography and nostomania are frequent outcomes of not only exile but also of old age.

Kim describes his 1988 trip as an effort "to bury forty years of time in two hours [the flight time from Tokyo to Seoul]" (Kim Sokpom 1990:21). The much-anticipated trip is anticlimactic. He recognizes very little of Seoul or Chejudo. "As I walked I looked for the shape of the past. . . . Chejudo was utterly transformed. . . . The shape of the past was virtually absent" (90). The site of a massacre, for example, has become a tourist site. Memory serves him poorly; in fact, the photographs he had seen prior to his trip afford him the few glimpses of recognition that he experiences. South Koreans he encounters outside of his admirers confound—in fact, shock—him: the daredevil taxi drivers, the rude waitresses, the arrogant subway station attendants, and so on (50). He refuses to recognize that the rhythm and resonance of his everyday life are fundamentally Japanese. The dissonance he senses in South Korean life is an accurate measure of his forty-year-long residence in Japan and the forty-year transformation of South Korea. Given that his life experiences have been inescapably Japanese, it should not be surprising that he should recognize so little of South Korea. What would feel the same after nearly half a century, especially since his most extended period of stay on the island was for half a year when he was thirteen (37)?

Kim concludes: "Unified Korea . . . is my ancestral country [*sokoku*]" (138). This remembered past is problematic, because Korea was colonized by Japan; hence, the desire to return cannot be to the past but to a future ideal. Recognizing that Korea is not the place of his birth, he acknowledges that his ancestral land is a place of conscious construction shaped at once by his ethnic consciousness and by his anti-Japanese philosophy (113). Kim's ancestral land is a projection of his desire for a unified Korea and a rejection of his de facto home.

By posing a utopia, Kim rejects all actually existing Korean nation-states or Zainichi organizations. Confident in his identification as an ethnic Korean (albeit exiled in Japan), he lives in fact as a Japanese and writes for the Japanese public. Although completely dependent on the Japanese intellectual establishment (his Japanese publisher defrayed his travel expenses and even sent bodyguards for him), he castigates Japan. Symptomatically, he had abandoned the Korean-language version of his magnum opus in the mid-1960s, after publishing nine installments in a Korean-language journal published by a Zainichi organization (Nakamura 2001:29–30). His main justification is the ethical injunction that he must write "in a language that has an element of the enemy" (Kim Sokpom 2004:202).

Kim's exile is sustained by his denial about his diasporic status. His fictional focus is the Korean past that he barely remembers, and his imagined community of unified Korea exists in the undefined future; meanwhile his concrete community is the Japanese reading public. Longing for an imaginary homeland, the exile remains beholden to an actually existing host country that he castigates. It is a private and comfortable exile, devoid of danger or desperation. "Counseling despair is the traveler's prerogative, a luxury available to all for whom withdrawal by boat or air provides a personal solution, relieving them of the pressure to act" (Nixon 1992:174). Worst of all, by averting his gaze from his diasporic status, he elides all the concrete problems of Zainichi life (see Takeda 1983:118–19). By the turn of the century, however, Kim begins to employ the term diaspora and defines diasporic literature as oppressed people's literature, in contradistinction to "Japanese literature that is on the side of the rulers" (Kim Sokpom 2004:196). Quite obviously, he does not regard his oeuvre as part of Japanese literature.

Lee Yangji and the Irreconcilable Gulf

Toward the end of *Kokoku kō*, Kim mentions a meeting with another Zainichi writer, Lee Yangji [Yi Yang-ji]. Over a drink at an open-air stall, he is surprised to learn that Lee, who had been studying traditional Korean dance in Seoul, is relieved to be speaking in Japanese with him (Kim Sokpom 1990:133). Although she considers Yamanashi Prefecture (where she can see Mt. Fuji) as her home [furusato], Kim reflects that Chejudo is his home even though he was born in Osaka. He conjectures that their difference is generational. After her death, he extends his willful speculations and wishful projections in *Chi no kage* [The shadow of the land] (Kim Sokpom 1996:184–86). In fact, Lee was born in Japan, her father sought to Japanize her, became naturalized when she was nine, and had earlier written that Yamanashi is *not* her *furusato* (Lee Yangji 1981:151–52).

The relief that Lee expresses is a central tension in her novel *Yuhi*, which takes place on the day when Yuhi [Yu-hŭi], a Zainichi woman studying at S University, leaves South Korea for Japan. The story first appeared in the literary journal *Gunzō* in 1988, and was published by Kōdansha the following year. Its phenomenal popularity generated a backlash. Norma Field (1996), for example, offers an insightful but withering reading: "reactionary," "distasteful" (cf. Ryu 2007:328).

The anonymous narrator, who works at a small publishing company, has misgivings about not seeing Yuhi off at the airport. The story intertwines the narrator's recollections of Yuhi and the narrator's conversations with her aunt, with whom she lives in a house in an older, quieter neighborhood of Seoul. Yuhi's return to her homeland—the constant refrain of *uri nara* ("our country" in Korean) punctuates the narrative—was motivated, we learn toward the end of the story, by her desire "to defend her own country against her father" (Lee Yangji 1993:440). Because of unsavory business dealings with deceitful fellow Koreans in Japan, her father had repeatedly expressed his distaste for Korea and Koreans during her childhood. In an early essay, Lee (1981:157) writes that her father "hoped that I would become more Japanese." Growing up among Japanese, she learned little about Korea except for her father's lamentation, while she did not experience discrimination. "Yes, I was surprised to hear about [discrimination against Koreans in Japan] in the past, but I have never been directly discriminated against or bullied" (Lee Yangji 1993:410). The narrator is puzzled by Yuhi's literary taste, which encompasses the work of both Yi Kwang-su and Yi Sang. Although dissimilar in many ways, a striking unity between the two is the profound influence of and interest in Japan. She decided to study abroad in South Korea because she was attracted to the music of Korean flute.

The narrator depicts Yuhi linguistically; the narrative reveals Yuhi's problems with Korean and her continuing attachment to Japanese. Despite majoring in linguistics at a prestigious university, Yuhi commits simple solecisms and, like native Japanese speakers, cannot properly pronounce Korean words (Lee Yangji 1993:413). The narrator is surprised and exasperated by Yuhi's inability to make Korean her own. Yuhi's mode of language acquisition is to memorize and to regurgitate: a characteristic Japanese mode of language learning. She reads her large Korean-language dictionary cover to cover (she underlines the word for "torture"). (This reliance on rote regurgitation also prevents the protagonist of Lee Hoesung's 1975 novel, *Tsuihō to jiyū* [Exile and freedom], from mastering Korean [Lee H. 1975:21].) Her writing skills, not surprisingly, far surpass her oral abilities. At the same time, Yuhi refuses to watch TV and rarely goes out. The narrator's first outing with Yuhi was disastrous, as Yuhi turns nauseous from mingling with the crowd in the bustling city.

The flip side of Yuhi's inability to learn Korean is her attachment to the Japanese language. The narrator is troubled to find over ten boxes of Japanese books in Yuhi's room, and relates how she heard Yuhi speak in Japanese—when she enters the house for the first time, or late at night when Yuhi is alone in her room. Most strikingly, the narrator finds that what turns out to be Yuhi's keepsake for her—a brown envelope containing over 448 pages of writings—is in Japanese, which the narrator cannot decipher. The linguistic wall would often prove to be an insurmountable obstacle for Zainichi who sought to become Korean in Korea (see, e.g., Kan 1998:190).

Language is not the only thing that separates the narrator from Yuhi. The narrator finds Yuhi inscrutable and feels ambivalent about her diasporic, pseudo-Korean status. The story expresses two common stereotypes that South Koreans held in the 1970s and 1980s about Zainichi: their possible entanglement with North Korea, and their propensity to frivolity. It is possible to detect the narrator's envy of diasporic Koreans in the affection her aunt shows for Yuhi (Zainichi) as a substitute for the aunt's daughter (now Korean American). The narrator's aunt, for instance, calls her daughter in the United States after she reminisces about Yuhi with the narrator.

The narrator is angry that Yuhi was able to enter S University, the most prestigious school in South Korea, because of special provisions for overseas Koreans. She is troubled that Yuhi finds faults with *her* country. Yuhi accuses South Koreans of taking advantage of foreigners, of not apologizing when they step on others' feet, and of other rude behavior, such as students who spit in restaurants. The violence and aggression that Yuhi experiences in Seoul is exemplified by her discovery that there is a dearth of passive-voice expressions in the Korean language. The narrator retorts: "Zainichi are Japanese. No, they look down on Koreans more than Japanese do, and resent Koreans" (Lee Yangji 1993:426). Zainichi visitors and residents in South Korea generally experience the converse situation: being looked down upon and resented by ordinary South Koreans. Zainichi baseball players who played in the fledgling South Korean professional league in the mid-1980s were frequently and pejoratively called *Panchoppari* [half-Japanese; *Choppari* is a pejorative South Korean term for Japanese] (Sekikawa 1984a:230, 267). Convinced of Yuhi's supercilious attitude toward South Korea, however, the narrator responds: "You just don't know South Korea" (Lee Yangji 1993:436).

The narrator is correct: Yuhi's experience of South Korea is textual and passive. Although she loves the view of the rocky mountain, she refuses to hike there. She idolizes the sounds of Korean flute but declines to take lessons. Yuhi's quest for *uri nara* [our country] is, like Kim's search for "ancestral land," idealistic. The narrator's aunt, who remains empathetic throughout, observes that Yuhi "probably came just with ideals, without knowing anything about South Korea" (Lee Yangji 1993:436). In part because of the school tie—her husband also graduated from the prestigious S University—the aunt sees a parallel with her deceased husband and Yuhi. Because he hated Japan as a colonizer, he could never master Japanese or even watch Japanese television even as his business trips repeatedly took him to Japan. The protagonist of Lee Yangji's *Koku* [Time, 1985] feels similarly: "the words I use are always repeatedly quoting someone else's words" (Lee Yangji 1985:192). And the inevitably Japanese accent and the concomitant failure to master Korean are constant refrains in Lee's fiction (e.g. Lee Yangji 1985:57, 178).

For Yuhi, the distance and difference between the Korea of her ideals and the reality of Seoul are irreconcilable. Recounting the moment when she froze during an examination, Yuhi says that she just could not write the four letters of the Korean alphabet *[han'gŭl]* for *uri nara* (Lee Yangji 1993:437). Although she "believes in King Sejong [the fifteenth-century monarch who oversaw the creation of the Korean alphabet], [she doesn't] like the *han'gŭl* of today" (437). She finds it hypocritical to see other students writing *uri nara*. The Korean she hears in contemporary Seoul she finds intolerably ugly, like "tear gas" (437). Likewise, in *Koku*, the protagonist complains: "The Korean language that people are going back and forth is several hundred phons of noise. I am nostalgic for that soft, moist, gentle atmosphere of Japan" (Lee Yangji 1985:12). Seoul is unhygienic and polluted (57, 155). The protagonist of *Koku* is constantly washing herself—presumably cleansing herself from the "dirty" environment of Seoul—and putting her makeup on (3, 198). Just as the dirt of Seoul must be washed away, she cannot face Seoul without a protective mask.

Yuhi loves the neighborhood of the narrator and her aunt because it is peaceful; the Korean they speak is, moreover, not ugly. Yuhi's ties to contemporary South Korea, which she otherwise finds so repugnant, are to the tape of Korean flute music and the written texts. The two people she likes—the narrator and her aunt—are themselves alienated. The narrator is on the verge of depression when Yuhi arrives, and deals with texts at her work (not unlike Yuhi). The widowed aunt refuses to move to an apartment in Kangnam, which represents Seoul's modern face. The gulf between the ideal and the reality of homeland that Yuhi expresses in Korean that she has not mastered is but an instance of her profound ambivalence about South Korea. After all, Yuhi's father, not her Japanese friends and neighbors, despised Korea; it was her intention to redeem Korea against her father's ire. Finding Yuhi drunk one night, the narrator notes that Yuhi writes in Korean that "I am a fraud. I am a liar" (Lee Yangji 1993:429). Soon thereafter Yuhi writes that "I cannot love"—in effect, Yuhi cannot love the actual *uri nara* she finds—but goes on to note that she loves the sound of Korean flute, the sound of the ideal *uri nara* (430). The distinction she detects between the reality of contemporary South Korea and the serene ideal of *uri nara* is redolent of Hannah Arendt's (1978:66) distinction between "pariah" and "parvenu" Jews: "It is the tradition of a minority of Jews who have not wanted to become upstarts, who preferred the status of 'conscious pariah.' All vaunted Jewish qualities—the 'Jewish heart,' humanity, humor, disinterested intelligence—are pariah qualities. All Jewish shortcomings—tactlessness, political stupidity, inferiority complexes and money-grubbing—are characteristic of upstarts."

The story ends with the narrator saying "ah," a common letter in both Japanese and Korean alphabet, but unable to follow it with another sound. The ambiguity of the sound—it is impossible to decipher whether it is Japanese or Korean—signifies the incompatible worlds of Japan and Korea.

It would be simple to depict Lee's Yuhi as a Korea-hater, just as it would be easy to celebrate Kim as a Korea-lover. But the similarities are telling. Both—as we will see also for Lee Hoesung's narrator—are troubled by the rude public behavior of South Koreans. The labyrinthine roads and the congested public spaces, although to superficial observers no different in Tokyo from those in Seoul, baffle them. The Korea they imagine is rooted in the past: the imaginary reconstruction of Chejudo for Kim, and the mythical past of King Sejong for Yuhi. Most important, both return to Japan. In spite of his discussions of ancestral land and homeland, Kim treats the return to Japan as unproblematic, as something obvious. Ironically, it is Yuhi, who belongs more unquestionably in Japan, who sees return (and who spent much more time in South Korea) as problematic, a sign of defeat. But Yuhi herself experiences none of the problems that confront her co-ethnics in Japan.

Thus Japan for all intents and purposes is a home for both Kim and Yuhi. It is the country in which their lives are embedded, from the ability to navigate urban crowds, the familiarity with landscapes and the built environment, to language. Life in South Korea [*kokoku* for Kim, *uri nara* for Yuhi] is implausible, if not impossible. Hence, both idealize—the future utopia of a unified Korea for Kim, the distant past of King Sejong and Korean flute for Yuhi. Trapped between the idealized homeland and its alien reality, both find themselves snugly, if inescapably and troublingly, at home in Japan.

Between the Living and the Dead

Lee Hoesung's *Shisha to seisha no ichi* [The market of the living and the dead, 1996] is another narrative of return. The thinly veiled fiction recounts the Zainichi writer Munsok's trip to South Korea. What differentiates his narrative from the other two is that, rather than seeking a return to an idealized past or an imagined future, he resolves to ground himself in the worldwide Korean diaspora that transcends existing national divisions. This book marks a profound transformation in Lee's outlook, which was no different from Kim Sokpom and other Zainichi intellectuals with strong sympathy for Marxism and nationalism. His five-volume epic novel, *Mihatenu yume* [The unrealized dream, 1975–79], chronicled the struggle for unification and underscored the isomorphism of Zainichi destiny and Korean unification.

The novel recounts a Zainichi author in his 60s who returns to South Korea for the first time in twenty-three years. Like Kim, Munsok—who is based closely on Lee Hoesung himself—has left Sōren, regards South Korea as the southern land of his ancestral land [*sokoku*], and has been denied visas to enter South Korea. Furthermore, he feels elated to be in South Korea (his impulse is to kiss the floor after he passes through the customs at Kimpo Airport in Seoul), but everyday life in South Korea confounds him. He fears the "unknown world" (Lee H. 1996:6) and repeatedly remarks on the rudeness of people who bump into him on the streets. Like Kim and Yuhi, then, Munsok realizes that the tempo and texture of life in Seoul are far from that in Japan. His discomfort in South Korea is due in part, like Yuhi's, to his inadequate command of Korean.

Munsok's narrative is interspersed with his accounts of visiting and re-visiting people and sites significant to him, and musings on his past that focus on Korean and diasporic Korean politics. As he drives down to Kwangju with a famous dissident poet and several others to pay homage to those who died during the Kwangju Incident, he thinks back on his encounters with Korean expatriates in Germany, particularly those sympathetic to the North Korean regime. On another occasion, he meets a friend from his college days with whom he had worked together on the repatriation project. "It was almost sad that the dream of returning to 'North' had become a nightmare" (Lee H. 1996:186). He ponders the powerful rhetoric of Sōren and how its followers reproduce it (cf. Ryang 1997:chap.2). He cannot quite fathom why an owner of a "soap land" [a bathhouse that often doubles as brothel] remains loyal to Sōren and donates his earnings to the North Korean regime.

Munsok also feels distant from South Korea and South Koreans. Although he is glad to be in South Korea, he is constantly irritated. He is angry with a publisher who has not properly paid his royalty; he feels that the publisher had treated him like a "foreigner," not a brother. Although

Munsok favors unification—"What's bad is the division between North and South" (Lee H. 1996:208)—his identification with his homeland, unified or not, is far from total.

Munsok is, rather, concerned about the fate of the Korean diaspora: "What Korean people expect is . . . not the rapprochement based on the benefits and costs of the divided nation-state, but pan-ethnic solidarity" (Lee H. 1996:210). He insists on his diasporic identity as Zainichi. He claims an "appreciation"—even "ecstasy"—of being and continuing to be Zainichi (210). His diasporic and pan-ethnic vision is, moreover, nonracial. As he states early on: "In our clan, Japanese blood, Ainu blood, and Russian blood are all mixed and melted together" (59). He came to this realization after visiting ethnic Koreans in Sakhalin, Central America, and elsewhere; in each of these places, Koreans have intermarried with different ethnic groups (see Lee H. 1983). Hence, for Munsok, there is no simple return to the imagined homeland that is Korea, unified or not. What has come asunder as a global diaspora cannot be reassembled on the Korean peninsula.

What motivates Munsok is, rather, that "the living should pay homage to the dead" (Lee H. 1996:213). In this spirit he seeks to honor the memory of Kim San, the Korean revolutionary who fascinated Helen Foster Snow and led her to write (or co-author) a book on his life, *Song of Ariran* (Wales and Kim 1941). "In my youth, I read *Song of Ariran* as my Bible" (Lee H. 1996:114). He encourages South Koreans to lobby the South Korean government to honor Snow, who was at the time living in a home for the elderly in Connecticut (cf. Lee and Mizuno 1991).

In praising the dead, Munsok hopes not only to carry on their spirit, as it were, but also to live as a diasporic Korean. He quotes a Korean expatriate in Germany who says that Koreans who live in Germany act like Germans, while those who live in France act like French. His resolution to reside in Japan as Zainichi, who is affiliated with neither Korea, is grounded in his belief that it will be a reminder, "a cause of conscience," for both Japan and Korea (Lee H. 1996:210). In grounding himself in the Korean diaspora, Munsok avoids glorifying the mythical past or the utopian future.

FROM EXILE TO DIASPORA

Exiles yearn for a simple remedy: a return to a home or a situation *ex ante.* Whether Adam and Eve's expulsion from the Garden of Eden or Ovid's banishment from Rome, Western literature is replete with the theme of exile and the concomitant longing to return. Expulsion and ostracism were cruel and unusual punishments—at times reckoned as worse than physical death, and equated with spiritual or social death—that upended the lives of the expelled. The pathos of exile resonates across disparate cultures and periods, from Odysseus to Aeneas, Dante to Pushkin and Brodsky, from the elegiac poetry of the Tang Dynasty to the contemporary lamentations of African intellectuals. One must wonder what world literature would be like without the phenomenon of exile, without the impulse of romantic lamentation. Is the rapture of literature possible without the experience of rupture? Especially baffling is that the condition of exile is fundamentally subjective; for Proust's Marcel, for example, banishment was simply nocturnal separation from his mother.

The resonance of the exilic condition reverberates most forcefully in the political allegory of exodus and deliverance. From Moses to Cromwell to Martin Luther King Jr., the commingling of individual exile and collective exodus nourishes on apocalyptic hope and points toward a promised land (cf. Walzer 1985:3–7). Next year in Jerusalem or Zion, *Heimat* or utopia. Paradise lost, oppression and liberation, paradise regained: the archaic narrative structure of exile, whether for Jews in Egypt or Koreans in Japan, begins with expulsion, expatiates on the wandering in the wilderness replete with tales of woe, and ends—or promises to end—on the collective return to homeland: deliverance and redemption.

In post-traditional societies, the rapid tempo of change engenders a pervasive sense of displacement that potentially renders everyone an exile, even those who experience no spatial movement. The past, as we hear endlessly, is a foreign country. Nostalgia and melancholy become symptoms of transformative modernity. Martin Heidegger (2006:175–80) suggested that we are thrown into the world, evoking at once our fallen nature and our exilic condition. Being homeless and *unheimlich* is the essential human condition and the source of modern restlessness. Rather than embracing our newfound nature as *Homo viatores*—in perpetual peregrination—we accept the received, negative connotations and strive for roots. The desire to recapture, or at least to connect to, the past—to remedy cherished infantile memories or plain old homesickness—emerges as a powerful motivation in the human sciences. From Hegel to Proust, the remembrance of things past is the secular search for meaning. We moderns are, in this sense, all exiles; exile is an endemic condition of modernity.

In temporal displacement, the search for home (the remembered, reified past) is inextricable from the condition of exile (the lived, and ever changing, present). Paradise lost—what other kind of paradise is there?—unleashes a desire to regain it. Symptomatically, arguably the first modern novel is *Robinson Crusoe:* exiled on an island, he struggles to return home. Never mind that what is taken as a temporary, transient abode is a stationary, stable abode. For the exile the stay is necessarily "temporary" even "though it lasts a lifetime" (Tabori 1972:27). Kim Sokpom (2001:29) writes: "I could not imagine that I would continue the life of 'Zainichi' to this day." The very passage of time, however, makes a return impossible. This is true for time travelers or historians, exiles or migrants. John Berger (1984:67) writes: "Every migrant knows in his heart of hearts that it is impossible to return. Even if he is physically able to return, he does not truly return, because he himself has been so deeply changed by his emigration. It is equally impossible to return to that historical state in which every village was the center of the world." The impossibility of return to the remembered past precludes, to be sure, neither the incessant search for the past nor a searing critique of the present. Indeed, the very impossibility or the very loss may make all the more urgent the desire to recover and preserve the pristine past.

My concern is, however, with the social and the spatial—the more common—meaning of exile. A ubiquitous ideology of modernity in this regard is modern peoplehood, the idea that everyone belongs to a particular nation, ethnicity, race, and that identity is primary and primordial (Lie 2004b). In its modern articulation, home is no longer a concrete place but an imagined space. While few people in Chosŏn Korea had any inkling of being Korean, the rather abstract idea of Korea had become well nigh universal by the twentieth century. In the age of nationalism and the nation-state, every instance of banishment or displacement outside of one's own national borders stands as an example of exile. Every migrant, under the reign of nationalist ideology, is an alien, an exile. Hence, a constant yearning for a return to homeland—the only place where one can truly belong, truly *be*—is constitutive of modern peoplehood.

Not surprisingly, modernist writings pullulate with melancholy and nostalgia. Intellectuals are—by their very ability to articulate their grievances—perforce the loudest voices to call for, and even demand, a return to their homeland. The space of exile is the exilic condition itself: the discursive space of thinking and writing about exile. Their presumed privilege as intellectuals, however, often enmeshes them in their condition of exile. An exile often lives in a state of mutual incomprehension with the host society, and suffers the indignities of patronizing comments, if not outright racist remarks. The situation is, however, not infernal. As Rob Nixon (1992:43) writes of V. S. Naipaul: "The irony here ought not to be missed: Naipaul, secure, esteemed, and integrated into the high culture of metropolitan England, asserting his homelessness, while considerable numbers of genuinely disowned people battle to be acknowledged as legitimate members of the society he is at liberty to reject rhetorically, although he depends on it in every way." Irony inflects the exile literature, to be sure. Although an exiled writer may bemoan the loss of artistic powers, the work of art may in fact belie the deleterious impact of exile. Gareth D. Williams (1994:99) argues that: "Ovid remains firmly in control of the abilities which are misleadingly portrayed as all but destroyed by exile." In fact, new people and places may engender fresh insights and inspiration. But my concern is not with irony but with bad faith.

The agony of an intellectual exile may be but an expression of bad faith: a cosmopolitan writer laments his displacement, and impugns his host country, all the while benefiting from his exiled but exalted status. Whether for Ovid or Dante, Rome or Florence was literally life itself. That they produced great works of literature in exile should not lead us to conflate their pathos with more or less voluntary modern exiles, who should properly be called expatriates. The two ostensibly contradictory positions—exiles' incessant longing for return and their entrapment in their host country—are in fact part and parcel of the very condition of an exile who longs for a mythical past or a utopian future. Because a return to the original condition or time travel is impossible, there is a temptation to idealize the remembered homeland or a fanciful future and to denigrate the here and now. This is all the more striking when one is basically a denizen of the host country, who may be luxuriating in the inescapable desire to escape: that inevitable modern type, the tourist.

All these concerns manifest themselves in especially acute ways for postcolonial intellectuals. Colonialism is remembered as a simple, hierarchical binary: the Manichean world that structures not only social understanding but also moral judgment. The suspicion and condemnation of collaboration—who could in fact have escaped the forces of colonialism?—color all colonial subjects, albeit in various ways, but in the postcolonial era, the colonizers and the colonial culture and history are things to be denied and denigrated. "Postcolonial poets often figure the desire to recuperate the precolonial past as the troubled search for an ancestral home, irreparably damaged by colonialism" (Ramazani 2001:10).

Living as a Zainichi intellectual and dependent on Japan in nearly every way, whether sponsorship or readership, Kim Sokpom can nonetheless state that anti-Japanese thought is a major pillar of his philosophy. Yuhi's homeland is similarly mythical, albeit projected into a distant past. Like Kim, she cannot abide by the reality of everyday life in contemporary

South Korea. Unable to denigrate Japan as Kim, she takes refuge in Korean texts and Korean flute on the one hand and Japanese books on the other. Neither can ground their lives in any existing group or place. In their line of reasoning, exile, the desire for return, and its impossibility are one and the same. By drawing a sharp line between homeland and host country, national boundaries and categories are in turn reified. But there is more: intellectual exile (or expatriation) stands above the hoi-polloi world of (voluntary) migrants and (involuntary) refugees who metaphorically wash ashore in a foreign land to toil or rot. The world of Zainichi intellectuals is far from that of their compatriots who were enforced migrants in the 1940s, the few refugees that the recalcitrant Japanese government accepted in the 1970s, or the foreign workers from Southeast Asia who sought manual and menial labor in Japan in the 1980s. The deracinated, cosmopolitan nomad exults in the pathos of exile, eliding thereby the lives of local yokels, migrants, and refugees. As Joseph Brodsky (1988) warned, the situations of menial laborers and refugees "make it difficult to talk about the plight of the writer in exile with a straight face." It is emblematic of the contrasting fates that the exile is almost always depicted in the singular whereas the refugees are almost always characterized *en masse*. More concretely, the twentieth century witnessed a phenomenal level of interregional migration and a "radically new form of homelessness" in millions of refugees (Marrus 1985:4). To the less privileged masses experiencing exile, the vatic pronouncements of return and home are vapid palaver.

For Zainichi returnees, whether to North Korea in the late 1950s and early 1960s (the repatriation project) or to South Korea in the late 1960s (after the 1965 Normalization Treaty), a common realization was the profound distance between their idealized homeland and their diasporic existence. It is a shibboleth that many Zainichi harbor an inferiority complex against homeland Koreans. In part this is an accurate indication of the unrequited love of diasporic Koreans toward their supposed homeland. As a Zainichi baseball player in South Korea said, "In Japan I am discriminated against as *Chōsen* [Korea], but I am derided in South Korea as *Panchoppari*. Both sides say 'go home'! Where am I going to go? Is our country under the ocean?" (Yamamoto 1995:287; cf. Sekikawa 1984a:206). As suggested by the bitter words on Kim Dae Jung's failure to mention the importance of Zainichi supporters (Chong 2006:167–68), the peripheral status of Zainichi among the principals of homeland politics was not lost. In part it points to the imperfect ways in which Zainichi were Koreans, such as in the mastery of the Korean language.

The rejection by the homeland—usually as *Panchoppari*—may enhance the desire to be "perfectly Korean," but the task would be nearly impossible and thereby facilitate distinct Zainichi identification (cf. Kim Teyon 1999:100–103). In terms of language or livelihood, the world of Zainichi was far from the world of homeland. Already by the early 1950s, most of the more than 600 Zainichi volunteers in the Korean War could not speak Korean well and South Koreans believed them to be Japanese soldiers (Kim Chanjung 2007:54–55). When the U.S. military rebuffed their demands, they threatened to perform the quintessentially Japanese ritual of *seppuku* [hara-kiri] (Kim Chanjung 2007:71). They may have been patriotic Koreans in spirit but were linguistically and culturally Japanese. The nineteenth-century definition of language as the soul of the people seems romanticized but its converse seems all-too-real: it's hard to call a place home without a common language.

This rift merely widened for both North and South a half-generation after the war's end. Kim Hyandoja (1988:64) was one of the early Zainichi travelers to South Korea in 1967: "For me, who was born in Japan, grew up in Japan, received education in Japanese school, and could express myself only in Japanese, South Korea was a foreign land." The baseball star Kanemura Yoshiaki realized that he had no "homeland" after he went to South Korea for the first time in 1981. He could not communicate with fellow Koreans, and "positively became conscious of being 'Zainichi'" (Kanemura 2004:129). The Korean language was at best an aspiration—for native Japanese speakers a relatively easy language to master grammatically but a very difficult one phonetically—and at worst a reminder of bad infantile moments. The protagonist in Yū Miri's first novel, *Ishi ni oyogu sakana* [The fish that swim in stone, 2002], remembers Korean as the language that her parents fought in and in which her father forced her to memorize the song of Arirang "while beating her with a broom" (Yū 2002:43). Yū claims that she covers her ears whenever she hears Korean because of baleful memories (Yū 2001:171). The Zainichi protagonist of Gen Getsu's novel *Oshaberina inu* [Talkative dog, 2003] visits Seoul at his Japanese girlfriend's behest but finds it so painful that he only lasts five days there (Gen 2003a:98).

The inescapable fact is that the passage of time widens the rift between homeland and diaspora, however it may also deepen the longing. Unification certainly did not come to Zainichi; as Kim Suson's poem "Ariran Tōge" [Arirang Hill] put it: "Half century / Children became adults / Older people died / Students became elderly / I still cannot see Arirang Hill" (Morita and Sagawa 2005:176). Most of those who returned found an alien land and people. Second-generation Zainichi travelers to South Korea in the 1960s and 1970s frequently failed the immigration authorities' stentorian demand to speak "our language" and, failing to do so, invited vituperative condemnation. If home implies a warm and fuzzy place, neither North Korea nor South Korea provided the imaginary hearth. It is an enduring theme of Zainichi writings from the 1960s that South Koreans callously treat—and at times defraud—their diasporic compatriots. In Yi Kisun's novel *Zerohan* [Zero half/Korean, 1985], the protagonist's visit is marred by the usual annoyance and befuddlement: the unavoidable otherness of the ostensible co-nationals. Fleeing Japan, he cannot eat in South Korea and seeks to flee again, to Japan. The one man—not coincidentally someone who grew up in Japan—with whom he gains a measure of intimacy turns out to have been a habitual liar. Yū Miri's aforementioned novel features a South Korean who translates the protagonist's play but wants her to pretend that she wrote it in Korean herself. The translator's marketing ploy—the predicted appeal of a Zainichi playwright writing in Korean—incenses the protagonist, leading her to make an abrupt exit.

The infeasibility of repatriation underscored the thorough immersion of Zainichi in Japanese life. Most critically, there was the Japanese language. The representative postwar Zainichi writer Kim Dalsu chose to write *Genkainada* [Genkai Strait, 1952] in Japanese for a Japanese readership (Isogai 1979:55–56). If he admired the Japanese novelist Shiga Naoya, then much the same can be said of literary Japan at the time that regarded Shiga as the "god of the novel" (Kim D. 1998:47; cf. Kawamura 1999:115–16). No postwar Zainichi writer of note wrote in Korean. The broad literary background—what they read, what they discussed—was not so much Korean as Japanese. Because the cosmopolitan strain in Japanese intellectual life ensured a fair dose of non-Japanese writers on any self-respecting person's reading list, Zainichi writers dutifully perused them. Yan Sogiru (2001:64) recalls his youthful enchantment with the poetry of Ishikawa Takuboku and Nishiwaki Junzaburō, Baudelaire and Rimbaud—which would not differentiate him from any aspiring postwar Japanese poet. Kin Kakuei's "Kogoeru kuchi" [The frozen mouth, 1966], for example, invokes Raskolnikov without mentioning Dostoevsky because *Crime and Punishment* was an inescapable literary touchstone for Zainichi and Japanese writers alike. Although it would be easy to identify major Japanese literary influences on Kin's exemplary Zainichi fiction—whether Shiga Naoya or Natsume Sōseki—one would be hard-pressed to find a Korean literary trace. Ri Chin'u's youthful criminal spree—before he achieved notoriety in the 1958 Komatsugawa Incident, which I discuss in the following chapter—was to have stolen fifty-three volumes of world literature, including Dostoevsky. Lee Hoesung (2002:240), in turn, had his complete works of Dostoevsky stolen. The pursuit of Dostoevsky's work, wrote the naturalized Zainichi Yamamura Masaaki (1975:19), was his "only goal in life." Both Ri and Yamamura, perhaps not surprisingly, would turn to Christianity for salvation. Even the appeal of abstract, universal humanism revealed the preponderant impact of Japanese culture on Zainichi life.

As many Zainichi would come to recognize, another resolution to the dialectic of idealization and disappointment was to create solidarity among diasporic people. This is, as we have seen, the path that Lee Hoesung stakes, though he later would revoke his neutrality and assume South Korean citizenship (Lee H. 1998). In an era when nation-states are hegemonic, one must in fact belong to one nation-state or another; when nation-states are increasingly in eclipse, an alternative to exile, or diasporic identity, emerges. Instead of belonging to a nation-state, there is a new, dispersed sense of a peoplehood. As Kim Chonmi (1998:56) observes: "state [kokka] is not *Heimat* [kokyō], *Heimat* is not state." Kyō Nobuko (2000:5–8) would go so far as to jettison the very idea of *Heimat*. By grounding oneself in the transnational diaspora, it may be possible to avoid the contradictory position between an impossible return and an idealized homeland.

Diasporic recognition proffers a postnational source of identity. In the transition from the national to the postnational, or from exile to diaspora, the dialectic of exile and complicity is transcended, as well as the idealization of the homeland and the denigration of the host country. Simultaneously, the diasporic standpoint challenges and destabilizes the fixed national boundaries and categories. No longer divided into "us" and "them" within national borders, the transition from the exile to the diaspora locates homeland in its very dispersion. Exile may exult and achieve that moral state "not to be at home in one's home" (Adorno 1997:43). Hugh of St. Victor (1961:101) said much the same thing in the early twelfth century: "The man who finds his homeland sweet is still a tender beginner; he to whom every soil is as his native one is already strong; but he is perfect to whom the entire world is as a foreign land. The tender soul has fixed his love on one spot in the world; the strong man has extended his love to all places; the perfect man has extinguished his."

In the early twenty-first century, we continue to experience rumblings of nationalist sentiments that result in human tragedies. The desire for return among diasporic peoples is, in many ways, part and parcel of the ideology of modern peoplehood that offers little room for ethnic heterogeneity within a nation-state. As class politics wane among rich nation-states, another politics—that waged between those inside and those outside, or between those who belong and those who do not—has come to the fore: the battle over migration, the reassertion of national identity, and other conflicts over belonging are some of the manifestations of the politics of inside and outside, the politics of belonging and exclusion. In this context, the identity of diasporic peoples, especially postcolonial people in their former colonizer country, faces a crossroads: the return to a country of their origin or to de-exile themselves and to carve out a place as a diasporic people. Zainichi narratives of exile are, in this regard, concrete instances of a wider phenomenon, and their distinct resolutions of the problematic of exile and identity will, for Zainichi, as well as all other diasporic peoples, have profound significance on the shape of the twenty-first century.

3. Cunning

Oka Yuriko grew up in an affluent family and fully imbibed an imperial, military education. Fifteen at the end of the war, she attended the prestigious Ochanomizu University and became a communist, not an uncommon reaction to the destruction of wartime illusions. As she participated in revolutionary politics, she met Ko Samyon: "When I learned that he was Korean, I was not particularly surprised. There were many Korean comrades in the Communist Party then. Some of my cellmates were in romantic relationship with Korean comrades. They probably faced problems but we were not particularly concerned" (Oka 1993:84). She attributes her lack of prejudice to the international orientation of the Party. Ko initially hesitated, arguing that they "live in different worlds" (93): not only were their nationalities different but he was a factory worker and she, a bourgeois girl [ojōsan]. The Communist Party, which attempted to regulate every aspect of Party members' lives, eventually approved the relationship but her parents ferociously opposed it. Ko, however, enlisted his acquaintance, the eminent novelist Noma Hiroshi, to convince her parents. After a two-hour meeting, her parents relented; the couple married in spring 1955. At the wedding ceremony, no one mentioned Ko's ethnicity. This was in part because the Communist Party did not discuss people's past, but Oka (138) also believes that there was "nothing particularly important" about Ko's ethnicity, which was "not Korean, of course not Japanese, 'not anything.'" Ko did not wish to naturalize, but (unlike many other Koreans in the 1950s) he also had no intention of returning to Korea. Confronted with the choice between naturalization and resignation (an ethnic Korean had to choose between Sōren and the Communist Party after 1955), he found a deeper commitment to the liberation of Korea and therefore quit the Party and his job, and nearly ended his life itself. Because Oka's teaching job depended on having Japanese nationality, she could not give up her citizenship. Going to Shimonoseki, where Ko grew up, Oka (152) was struck by the warm reception she received from his family and neighbors: "they had the goodness of human being, the sensitivity of equality, which transcended the fact that basically they didn't like Japanese." Ko eventually turned to reading—Tolstoy, Turgenev, Chekhov, Maupassant—and writing. The couple reared their child as Japanese, but the boy killed himself in part because of the confusion over his "mixed" status. Oka's memoir is necessarily shaped by the impasse between her and Ko, Japan and Korea, and the tragedy of their offspring: "I continued to suffer from the fact that we couldn't go over the gulf no matter how hard we tried, but we ourselves had created that gulf" (200).

Though published in 1993, Oka's book focuses on the dark decades of Zainichi disrecognition in the 1950s and 1960s. In spite of its pessimistic assessment—ethnonational origins as destiny, the impossibility of bridging the gulf—her memoir is in fact replete with positive moments: the triumph of romantic love, the warmth of Ko's relatives, the success of his writing career. The lives of Oka and Ko anticipate the reciprocal recognition and reconciliation between Zainichi and Japanese.

In this chapter, I explore the prehistory, or proleptic articulations, of Zainichi identity: the cunning of ethnic recognition. Homeland orientation and identification persisted well into the 1970s. The postwar erasure of the prewar reality and its consequences, including the postcolonial minority, was most effective then, but had evidently reached its limits. Precursors of Zainichi identification, nascent and inchoate though they may have been, seeped through the pentimento of postwar uniformity and homogeneity.

THE 1965 NORMALIZATION TREATY AND ITS REPERCUSSIONS

The 1965 Normalization Treaty between South Korea and Japan, concluded in the context of escalating U.S. intervention in Vietnam, was an awkward resolution to the legacy of Japanese colonialism. The peace that excluded North Korea seemed illegitimate and thereby elicited political mobilization, among not just the pro-North Zainichi population but also the progressive Japanese public (Nihon Shakaitō 1970:3–5; Un 1978:39–40).

Whatever the eventual consequences of the 1965 treaty, it underscored the primacy of geopolitics. The Zainichi population was a convenient object of North-South struggles for influence, legitimacy, and primacy. Not surprisingly, the homeland orientation of the two major ethnic organizations intensified; their conflict continued the Korean and Cold wars by other means (Chong 2006:57–58). The treaty would mark a major turning point for the Zainichi population in the longer run. For ethnic Koreans in Japan, it provided profound incentives to seek South Korean citizenship, which would offer relatively secure footings in Japan, the relative freedom to travel abroad (and return to Japan), and access to Japanese medical and welfare benefits. The treaty also signaled to the Zainichi population that unification was far from being imminent and therefore the likelihood of prolonged, perhaps permanent, residence in Japan. This realization would in turn vitiate Zainichi organizations.

Sōren faced an irreversible decline in membership. A functioning passport from South Korea and social benefits from the Japanese government ultimately superseded any emotional or ideological commitment to Sōren and North Korea. Other factors contributed to the decoupling of Sōren and Zainichi, as well. The anticipated paradise, as we saw, turned out on inspection to be an impoverished autocracy. The North Korean regime, along with the international communist movement, was bureaucratically calcified and viscerally authoritarian. Sōren, true to its satellite status, followed the North Korean regime in its autocratic turn from the mid-1960s on. The 1972 speech by Han Doksu (1980:24–25) is emblematic of Sōren's revolutionary rhetoric: "The Great Leader Chairman Kim Il Sung is the sun of the people [minzoku] and the father of overseas Koreans. He led the Korean revolution to victory based on the immortal self-reliance [juche] philosophy that he himself created and contributed not only toward the development of world revolution but also developed a unique philosophy and theory of overseas Korean movement." Revolutionary jargon and jeremiads were disseminated and reproduced throughout the organization. The suspension of disbelief gradually gave away to the suspicion of charlatanism. Han's nationalist communism veiled ham-fisted devotion to power and hierarchy; he ruthlessly purged rivals and dissenters. Whereas silence enveloped purges, the revolutionary rhetoric was everywhere amplified and exaggerated, undoubtedly fueled by the inhospitable environment of postwar Japan. The Ōmura Camp that imprisoned potential deportees, for example, was called "Auschwitz" (Choe 1978:228). However unjust the deportation decisions or unpleasant the camp conditions, the inflated comparison did not incite the reader to revolutionary activities but rather to jettison the book in favor of the television set. Sōren's stultifying hierarchy seemed all the more archaic in the relatively egalitarian, democratic, and dynamic society that was postwar Japan. Over time, Sōren members would find the catechism of juche philosophy or the discipline of bureaucratic centralism unpalatable. It is one thing to sustain irrepressible interest in *juche* philosophy when there isn't competition; it is another thing to do so against the seductions of popular amusement, material plenty, and intellectual freedom.

The secular decline in the fortunes of North Korea—and international communism in general—dictated Sōren's descent. For every ex-Sōren member there is an experience of rupture, the new gestalt that revealed North Korean poverty, corruption, and autocracy. A former Sōren official ran into his former classmate in North Korea, doubly disturbed by how weathered his friend looked and by what he took to be the food for his friend's pet being in fact for his friend's family. Others expressed disgust with the Sōren leadership: an ex-Sōren member expectorated bitterly as he lambasted Han Doksu's penchant for luxuries (cf. Ri 1995; Han 2002). Just as the misgiving about the Russian Revolution may have begun with Kronstadt for some and Stalin's Great Purge or Khrushchev's exposé for others, Sōren had generated heretics and excommunicated them from its very inception: those who disagreed with Han's 1955 speech, Sōren's elevation of politics over literature in the late 1950s, or the inevitable disappointments with the repatriation project. Even as late as 2003, the North Korean regime's acknowledgment that it had kidnapped twelve Japanese women prompted horrified Sōren members to resign, sometimes after a long lifetime's commitment to the organization and its ideals. That the god had failed does not negate the individual experience of tragic exit, as an explosion or a whimper, that recalls the words of Ignazio Silone (1949:113): "The truth is this: the day I left the Communist Party was a very sad one for me, it was like a day of deep mourning, the mourning for my lost youth."

Sōren Koreans retained their faith much longer than their communist counterparts elsewhere. While North Korea initially bankrolled Sōren—the Japanese Foreign Ministry reported the total North Korean contribution at 8.3 billion yen between 1957 and 1969 (Gaimushō 1969:52)—by the 1970s Sōren's financial and technological contribution was helping to prop up North Korea. Beginning in the mid-1970s, Sōren members invested millions of yen in joint ventures with and donated gifts in cash and kind to the North Korean regime (Miyatsuka 1993:112–13). Some speculate that the annual Zainichi contribution to North Korea was as high as 60 billion yen per annum in the 1990s, though the figure was likely to be much, much lower (Chan 1995:118–19). Whatever the actual amount, what is indisputable is the North Korean regime's reliance on Zainichi contributions (Lee Y. 1999:90). Ironically, the very capitalists and merchants that the regime denounced constituted the pillars of North Korean national communism by the mid-1970s (cf. Tamaki 1995:42–43). Yan Sogiru's fictionalized portrait of his demonic father in *Chi to hone* [Blood and bone, 1998] has the dying patriarch donating his entire wealth—the money that he had spared no means to accumulate—to North Korea.

Nonetheless, the communist bubble within Japan was ultimately unsustainable. As I argued in the previous chapter, the brush with actually existing North Korea revealed the gaps between the idealized paradise and the infernal reality. The language instruction that so many Sōren members are proud of produced a Korean dialect in its own right: Sōren language [*Sōrengo*] or Chongryun Korean (Ryang 1997:43–49). Chongryun Koreans and—owing to linguistic drift occasioned by over a half-century of division—North and South Koreans became divided by a common language. More generally, the enthusiasm for North Korea waned precipitously after the 1980s (Sekikawa 1992:3). Sōren's extensive national network and its two principal institutional pillars—the ethnic banks and schools—long remained robust, but by the mid-1990s, with the collapse of Chōgin branches, and certainly by the 2003 exposure of the North Korean kidnapping of Japanese citizens in the 1970s, Sōren's downward trajectory seemed irreversible (cf. Ri 2003:150; Kim Chanjung 2004b:21). As recriminations mounted, the brilliantly obfuscatory revolutionary rhetoric seemed irritatingly irrelevant and irresponsible.

If the 1965 Normalization Treaty augured the decline of North Korea in Zainichi life, why didn't Mindan benefit from it? The growth in Mindan membership resulted not from ideological conversion but rather from practical exigencies. Mindan never captured the moral imagination of the Zainichi population but functioned as a glorified passport agency. The baseball player Harimoto, for example, refused to join Mindan because he opposed its practice of collecting membership fees from Zainichi wishing to obtain a visa to South Korea (Yamamoto 1995:251). It is difficult to generate loyalty and love for a government agency.

More significantly, the unsavory character of not only Japanese society but also South Korea deflected the Zainichi embrace of Mindan and delayed the departure from Sōren. One would have had to be a dyed-in-the-wool anticommunist to love the South Korean regime in the late 1960s and 1970s, a time of reckless disregard for democratic niceties. In April 1971, the Suh brothers, who had been studying in Seoul, were arrested as North Korean spies, and spent much of the 1970s and 1980s in prison. They came to exemplify not only courageous resistance to South Korean dictatorship (Suh 1988:236), but also fierce commitment to nationalism and unification (Suh 1981:12). They were part of second-generation Zainichi who sought to live as "Korean" (Suh 1988:110). Even as the Suh brothers were part of a new South Korean government program to attract overseas Koreans, Zainichi faced official and popular suspicion (Suh 1981:19). The National Security Law under Park Chung Hee's Yusin regime created a proto-total-itarian society in which the failure to answer a commonsense query—such as the price of a pack of cigarettes—brought one suspicion of being a North Korean spy. Autocrats are of course not always wrong; a Zainichi man attempted to assassinate Park in 1974.

The political and ideological rift between South Korea and the Zainichi population was deep and wide in the 1970s. Living in democratic Japan, even Mindan members found the South Korean government's human rights abuses unsavory. In 1973 the Korean CIA abducted Kim Dae Jung, who had lost the 1971 South Korean presidential election, in a Tokyo hotel room. The egregious crime generated a great deal of protest and fury in Japan. As some Mindan members sought to rescue Kim, the surveillance and intimidation of the Korean CIA reached their South Korean relatives (Chong 2006:49). The Park regime disciplined Mindan by rescinding the organization's con-trol over the right to issue visas. Bereft of its main funding source, Mindan came to depend on the South Korean government and thereby became a puppet of Park's dictatorship (Chong 2006:72–74). The military dictatorship thereby distended diasporic discontent. Many Zainichi, as well as the edu-cated Japanese public, came to revile South Korea and Mindan.

The Suh brothers' trial and the Kim Dae Jung abduction pointed to the primacy of homeland politics among ethnic Koreans in Japan in the 1960s and 1970s. No major protests or mobilizations dealt with essentially Zainichi issues. Chong Jaejung (2006:192), who was a leading figure in the effort to rescue Kim Dae Jung, concludes his memoir by affirming his devotion to "the democratization of South Korea and the unification of homeland." Although his memoir was published in the twenty-first cen-tury, Chong was born in 1917 and much of his activities took place in the postwar era. Long residence in Japan, including a series of successful busi-ness ventures, did nothing to avert his political gaze away from the Korean peninsula.

More profoundly, the geopolitical struggles of the 1960s convinced the majority of the Zainichi population that unification was by no means imminent, signaling the permanence of their fate in Japan (Kim Sokpom 2001:16–25). The receding dream of unification was accompanied by the bitter reality of actually existing homelands. As I have stressed, returnees to both the North and the South were frequently regarded suspiciously. Meanwhile, their counterparts in Japan were obedient and loyal to the divided homeland regimes, both of which were politically suspect. By the 1980s, several former Mindan and Sōren activists would acknowledge the ineffectiveness and irrelevance of the two major ethnic Korean organizations in Japan. One former Mindan member exclaimed: "What have Mindan and Sōren done? They only express the egoism of the leadership, and do nothing for Zainichi." Losing the prospect of an immediate return, the temporary shelter that was Sōren and Mindan seemed sorry and shabby.

The Normalization Treaty augured the end of Sōren ideology and the ideology of return and thereby facilitated the Zainichi recognition that their fate would transcend the divided homeland and be intimately intertwined with that of Japan. The condition of possibility of Zainichi identity was to go beyond the North-South divide and to forgo the ideology of imminent return. An elderly woman in Ikaino said, "We must unify Korea from Ikaino!" (Kim Chansen 1982:84). For Suh Kyungsik (1988:112), who had stayed in Japan unlike his imprisoned two elder brothers, Zainichi are "people who have not been divided." Or as his brother Suh Sung (1994:149) concluded, "For us, clearly, ethnicity is above the state. One ethnicity is more important than the two states." Rather than being peripheral, the focus was now on Zainichi themselves. The prospect of Zainichi identity loomed: to cultivate, as it were, ethnic Korean gardens in Japan.

EXCLUSION AND INCLUSION

The period between the end of the Korean War and the oil shock (1953–73) were not only the high years of the Cold War but also the era of rapid economic growth in Japan. Symbolized by the 1964 Tokyo Olympics, Japan achieved phenomenal development and popular democracy. However tentatively and precariously at first, ethnic Koreans were enmeshed in the dominant trends of Japanese society: trickled-down economic benefits and diffuse beliefs in human rights.

Few mood-enhancing drugs work better than rapid economic growth and its almost inevitable correlate of expanding opportunities. This was especially true for those who had endured scarcity during the war and immediate postwar years. Riding on the Korean War–generated economic boom, ethnic Koreans succeeded in several industries, especially the service sector. According to one police report from the early 1950s, 70 percent of Koreans worked in the service and sex industries [fūzoku eigyō], such as cabarets, dance halls, pachinko [Japanese-style pinball] parlors, and restaurants (Pak Cheil 1957:142). Although the significance of sex-related industries declined, the ethnic Korean occupations concentrated in the service sector and small, family-owned enterprises. In a mid-1980s survey of Shimane Prefecture, restaurants, pachinko, and recycling constituted half of all Zainichi employment (Naitō 1989:288). Roughly the same picture emerges from a contemporaneous survey in Kanagawa Prefecture. Often facing obstacles in gaining loans from mainstream banks, ethnic Koreans relied on family savings, mutual aid, and ethnic banks (Kanagawa-kennai 1986:50–53). In the Kanagawa survey, nearly 70 percent of the jobs were in family-owned businesses or obtained through co-ethnic networks (Kanagawa-kennai 1986:75–77).

In the postwar period, the Zainichi population created a new ethnic economy. Whereas prewar Korean establishments primarily catered to fellow Koreans, the postwar Korean services principally targeted Japanese customers. Zainichi came to be associated above all with *yakiniku* [barbecued meat] restaurants and pachinko parlors. Yakiniku is a Zainichi adaptation that arose in the postwar years and attained popularity in the 1960s. The neologism "yakiniku restaurant" was a political compromise between existing North Korean [*Chōsen*] and South Korean [*Kankoku*] restaurants (Miyatsuka 1999:164–65). Zainichi owned 90 percent of the roughly 20,000 yakiniku restaurants in Japan in the 1990s (Nomura 1996:44). Its centrality in the Japanese palate can be seen in the movie *Purukogi* (2006) (Gu 2007). In the 1990s ethnic Koreans owned an estimated 70 to 80 percent of the 18,000 pachinko parlors, which generated turnover twice that of the Japanese automobile industry and even exceeded the South Korean GNP in 1994 (Nomura 1996:93). Han Chan'u graduated from the prestigious Hōsei University but, unable to land a suitable job, pursued entrepreneurship and reigned as the pachinko "king" (Nomura 1996:99). First-generation owners hoped that their children would not inherit the business, but college-educated, second-generation Zainichi did so in part because of continuing discrimination in mainstream employment (Sung 1990:193). Although ownership of yakiniku restaurants and pachinko parlors is an ethnic marker, identification is inconclusive, as in the case of the pachinko millionaire family in Yū Miri's 1998 novel *Gōrudorasshu* [Gold rush].

Ethnic Korean successes in self-employed, service, and entertainment sectors were the unintended consequences of their systematic exclusion from prestigious professions and occupations. Job discrimination was an unquestioned fact of life in the postwar period. All public-sector jobs were reserved for Japanese nationals until 1972. (In that year, when a private child-care facility became a public entity, a Chinese child-care worker appealed the dismissal and was ultimately retained by the facility [Nakahara

1993:15].) In a 1971 survey, 42 percent of large employers responded categorically that they would not hire ethnic Koreans, and a further 38 percent
said that they would find it "problematic" to do so—a euphemism for
employment discrimination (Nakahara 1993:16–17). As late as 1976, Sakura
Bank (then Kōbe Bank) stated, "We have no intention of hiring . . . Korean
men," and Asahi Garasu [Glass] observed that "if we employ Koreans the
workplace harmony would be destroyed" (Nakao 1997:59). The 1969 law
against Burakumin discrimination and Pak Chonsok's successful 1970–74
discrimination lawsuit against Hitachi (discussed below) ended the era of
outright employment discrimination against minorities and foreigners.
Pak's successful suit upended the Zainichi conviction that they could not
work for a prestigious firm or emerge victorious in a Japanese court of law
(Nakahara 1993:33). The predominant preconception was that, outside of
baseball for boys and singing for girls, self-employment in the ethnic
economy, whether scrap recycling or yakiniku restaurants, was the fate of
Koreans in Japan. The exclusionary practice of mainstream industries and
companies continued well into the 1980s and 1990s (Kanagawa-ken
1984:101–2; Pak I. 2005a:176–81). Hence, ambitious Zainichi youths sought
professional and technical self-employment in fields such as medicine (Kim
Chanjung 1983:54–56). Employment discrimination also spurred ethnic
Koreans toward entrepreneurial pursuits, and though most of the establishments were modest, some became remarkable successes, such as Lotte
and Softbank.

Beyond employment discrimination, ethnic Koreans faced the exclusionary practices of national and local governments. Although the postwar
Japanese Constitution guaranteed basic human rights, the Japanese welfare
state systematically neglected foreigners. In spite of equal treatment as tax-
payers, non-naturalized Koreans categorically lacked access to social welfare
provisions, ranging from child support to old-age pensions (Yoshioka
1980a:93–95, 1980b:226–29). Ethnic organizations and networks were crucial in the 1950s and 1960s in part because of the almost complete absence
of safety nets and public services for the Zainichi population. The 1965
treaty mandated access to national medical insurance for South Korean citizens (Yoshioka 1978:38, 45). Until the 1980s, however, Zainichi faced barriers to receiving medical, welfare, pension, and other benefits of the welfare
state that they supported through their labor and taxes. The situation
improved after the Japanese government compliance with the 1948 Universal
Declaration of Human Rights in 1979 and the UN International Refugee
Convention (1951) and Protocol (1967), which extended government services
to non-nationals, in 1982 (Yoshioka 1981:139–40).

Government bureaucracy purveyed the idea of ethnic heterogeneity as illegitimate. Fingerprinting for the Certificate of Alien Registration proved a particularly vexing emotional experience for most Zainichi youths. During the anti-fingerprinting movement in the mid-1980s, many Zainichi born in the 1950s and 1960s mentioned fingerprinting as a degrading and dispiriting experience. Being fingerprinted was tantamount to being treated like a criminal. A second-generation Zainichi youth, who felt Japanese in almost every way, realized that he was "a foreigner, after all" when he registered for the Certificate (Miyata 1977:12–13).

Schooling, too, provided a powerful lesson in otherness. In the mid-1970s many Zainichi children experienced "the immovable wall of discrimination for the first time when they sought to enter high school" (Miyata 1977:59). Ethnic Korean school graduates were frequently ineligible to transfer to Japanese public high schools or to apply to Japanese colleges and universities. It was only in the mid-1990s that lawsuits challenged the discrimination against ethnic Korean schools (Nakao 1997:88). Most Zainichi children used Japanese aliases *[tsūmei]* and passed as Japanese. The very effort to pass, however, inevitably highlighted their difference and discriminated condition. In any case, attending a Japanese school reminded them that they were *not* Japanese and that they had to hide their Koreanness. School lunch is an enduring theme in Zainichi school memories of shame, teasing, and self-loathing (Ozawa 1973:112–16). Similarly, some Zainichi children hesitated to invite their friends home because of the fear of exposing the existence of elderly, non-Japanese speaking relatives or of other signs of Koreanness or non-Japaneseness. In 1969, the middle-school pupil Pak Kyonja wrote: "How much I hated being Korean . . . Sometimes I wondered why I was born Korean. . . . I was afraid of being found out that I was Korean. . . . I did not want to be known as Korean" (Iinuma 1983:91). In some cases, one's Koreanness was literally pounded in by bullying classmates. Physical violence against Zainichi students was common throughout the postwar period (Zainichi Chōsenjin 1963:6–16; Miyata 1977:75–77).

Housing was frequently denied on the basis of foreignness or Koreanness (Miyata 1977:72–74). Until 1979, foreigners were not permitted to live in public housing (Nakao 1997:74–75), and it was not until 1989 that a court upheld a housing discrimination case, providing a powerful precedent against discrimination based on national origins (Nakao 1997:73). Opposition to intermarriage and discrimination against its offspring were omnipresent, as I elaborate below. Curiously but perhaps predictably, most country clubs excluded ethnic Koreans, though some of the most eminent professional golfers were Zainichi (cf. Ueda 1995:69).

In summary, there was systematic exclusion of ethnic Koreans from Japanese life in the first quarter-century after the end of the war. Discrimination manifested itself at critical junctures in the life course—education, employment, housing, and marriage. Government policy came close to apartheid or Jim Crow—"apartheid by default," according to Hicks (1998:4)—but the Japanese stress was on excluding Koreans as outsiders rather than dominating them or establishing separate institutions. More critically, exclusion turned to tentative inclusion in the era of rapid economic growth. It was difficult to sustain the myth in the irremediable otherness of the Zainichi population. A 1950 survey of ethnic Koreans from Chejudo living in Tokyo demonstrated residential concentration but also significant signs of assimilation (Izumi 1966:242, 258–60). In the postwar period, even as governments and employers engaged in outright exclusion, countervailing forces integrated ethnic Koreans into Japanese society. Already by the mid-1950s Pak Cheil (1957:131–37) had identified assimilation as a major fact and master trend of Zainichi life. The mass media, ranging from the ubiquity of manga to the explosive popularity of television, did not exclude ethnic Koreans. The pervasiveness of Japanese popular culture in turn vitiated Korean tradition and culture. A 1974 study of ethnic Koreans in Osaka showed that only a fifth used Korean as their primary language at home, whereas a fourth never used it (Hong and Han 1979:97). As Kaikō's 1959 novel Nihon sanmon opera [Japan threepenny opera] anticipated, Korean neighborhoods disappeared in the course of the 1960s (Kim Chanjung 2004a:173–76). Yan Sogiru (1995:23) found the Korean neighborhood in the immediate postwar years "noisy," in contradistinction to the "quiet" Japanese areas, but by the 1970s the distinction disappeared. There was also a steady increase in intermarriage: already by the late 1950s, roughly 25 percent of Korean men married Japanese women, and 11–14 percent of Korean women betrothed Japanese men (Tonomura 2004:410).

The critical institution that differentiated but also assimilated the Zainichi population was education. Enforced assimilation characterized late-colonial-period policy. The extension of this mind-set was the government effort to suppress ethnic education in the immediate postwar years. However, Zainichi struggles for ethnic schools in Osaka and Kobe in April 1948 [Hanshin Tōsō] led the Ministry of Education to approve ethnic Korean education in Japan, which in turn was compatible with the Zainichi ideology of return. As the second-generation Zainichi Kim Kyonghae (1982:7) wrote: "Unless we weren't taught even in an 'instant' way, we would be useless as a 'Panchoppari' when we returned." Ethnic pride sought to overcome the shortage of qualified teachers and the paucity of textbooks

(Yang 1982:42–43). Sōren schools instilled North Korean ideology, such as the primacy of unification (Pak Sangdok 1982:257–60). Whatever their shortcomings, Sōren schools cultivated ethnonational pride and inculcated Korean language, history, and culture. To the larger Japanese society, however, ethnic Korean schools often signified juvenile delinquency. For Kim Hanil (2005:5), fighting was a "requirement" when he attended an ethnic Korean school in the 1970s.

The disjuncture between North Korea's socialist ideal and authoritarian, stagnant reality only widened in Sōren consciousness throughout the 1970s and 1980s; in spite of continuing loyalty, Sōren schools' homeland orientation was in tension with the likely prospect of permanent residency in Japan. As much as liking and becoming Japanese was tantamount to betrayal, the creeping influence of Japanese society was impossible to resist (Kim Hanil 2005:29–30, 111–14). Sōren graduates sought enrollment and employment in Japanese institutions. In response Sōren schools underwent a major revision in 1993 to incorporate more pragmatic and more Japanese-oriented curriculum. The ideology of return succumbed to the culture of Japanese orientation.

By the 1970s, the existence of ethnic Korean schools notwithstanding, the majority of Zainichi children attended Japanese public schools. In spite of racist incidents and racialized treatments, Korean children learned to act and be Japanese. The Ministry of Education promoted a standardized curriculum that was insistently monocultural and monoethnic. The absence of multicultural education—and, more importantly, multicultural sensibility—was glaring in the 1960s and 1970s. As a 1989 survey shows, the two most important topics that Zainichi parents hoped that their children would learn, but were neglected in the Japanese curriculum—and to a large extent in Sōren schools as well—were Zainichi history and ethnic discrimination (Kyoto Daigaku 1990:28). In spite of the curricular and social problems that confronted Zainichi pupils, the majority of parents acquiesced to the reality of Japanese life. A 1979 survey conducted in the Osaka area shows that only 30 percent of parents valorized learning Korean and just over 1 percent expressed desire for their children to return to Korea (Hong 1982:69). Nearly four-fifths agreed that Japanese schools were better for their children because they live in Japan (Hong 1982:71; cf. Kyoto Daigaku 1990:35).

Frequently denied the opportunity to pursue advanced schooling themselves, many Zainichi parents—following the prevailing cultural priorities in both Korea and Japan—stressed schooling as the privileged route to upward mobility. In a 1980s survey, whereas over 40 percent of ethnic

Koreans older than 60 did not attend school (as opposed to less than 1 percent for their Japanese counterparts), the ratios for those in their 20s and
30s were roughly the same (Kanagawa-kennai 1986:124–25). Zainichi passion for literacy and education was not so much a quintessentially Korean
trait, but it was just as much, if not more, a Japanese cultural practice and
belief (cf. Suh 1998:14–15). The campaign for literacy as a form of antidiscrimination (Iwai 1989) or the diploma disease that afflicted almost everyone, or the simple pleasure in reading and attaining *Bildung [kyōyō]*,
expressed the desire for democratic education that was hegemonic in Japan
(traditional Korean education was thoroughly elitist). Both in intention and
in consequence, then, Japanese schools contributed to the cultural integration of Zainichi children into Japanese society.

Cultural integration occurred without any serious attempt to redress
prevailing prejudice against ethnic Koreans. As a form of protective coloration to navigate monoethnic Japanese society, passing (as I discussed in
chapter 1) was the normative presentation of the Zainichi self. In a survey
from the late 1970s, only 14 percent of students used ethnic Korean names
(Hong and Nakajima 1980:109). In another survey from the 1980s in
Kanagawa Prefecture, the figure was even lower, at 12 percent (Kanagawa-
kennai 1986:188). Japanese aliases were used in order to protect Zainichi
youths from prejudice and discrimination, but the virtual universality of
Japanese names contributed to the public perception of Japanese monoethnicity (and therefore the deviant ring of Korean names). Curiously, Japanese
authorities frequently urged Korean children and employees to use *tsūmei*,
but not Chinese students and workers (Kanagawa-kennai 1986:176–77).
The practice was socially functional but psychologically dysfunctional, as
it had a profoundly shameful repercussion, tantamount to abdication of
authenticity and betrayal of culture, for Zainichi youths. For some the
adoption of a Japanese name resuscitated and reminded them of the 1940
Japanese imperial edict that stripped all Koreans of their ethnic names
[sōshi kaimei]. Hence, what might strike outsiders as a mere inconvenience
or a reasonable accommodation struck ethnically conscious Zainichi as an
ethnic betrayal (Kim I. 1978:9–11).

Ironically, this sense of shame or guilt was often much more pronounced
among those who had employed *tsūmei* from birth. For the first generation, an alias was a mask that they could don or cast off; the distinction
between the "true" and the "false" was clear. For the second generation,
however, the experiential basis of distinguishing the real and the fake was
absent; they had grown up with their Japanese name, frequently using it
much more often than their Korean name. That is, the "false" name was

more "real" than the "real" name, which sounded "foreign" to boot. A third-generation Zainichi woman decided to naturalize because she could not abide her Korean name, which was used on official occasions. Having used her Japanese alias at home and at school and work, she claimed that she hardly recognized her "real" name: "It is so unnatural." Devoid of these confounding identity issues, most parents mandated the use of *tsūmei* for their children (Hester 2000:194).

Even for those who use their Korean names, however, there are ambiguities about whether to use the Japanese or Korean reading of their Chinese character–based names. Recall the Zainichi writer Kin Kakuei, who consciously used the Japanese reading of his Korean name. An individual may very well shift one's position over time. For example, Lee Hoesung has only belatedly urged the Korean reading of his name; he had earlier used the Japanese rendition, Ri Kaisei. The problem, to be sure, does not end so easily. Lee is a common Chinese—and Japanese—reading of the surname that Koreans pronounce as Yi. However, following the traditional Chinese practice, North Koreans tend to transliterate it as "Ri," whereas South Koreans modally employ "Lee." The author Yū Miri insists on the Korean reading of her name, but the more accurate rendition of "Yū" is in fact "Yu" (cf. Kure 2007:46).

Name was one of the most salient issues in the making of Zainichi identity. As Denise Riley (2005:117) proposes: "the name hovers at some midpoint between the tattoo and the state register." For Zainichi youth, neither is it fixed nor is it singular, but the question weighs constantly and heavily nonetheless. No wonder that the reigning temptation, as articulated in Lee Chong Hwa's (1998:n.p.) discourse on muttering [*tsubuyaki*], is to "resist everything that names." In Sagisawa Megumu's story "Meganegoshi no sora" [The sky through the spectacles, 2001], the character Naran bemoans her "strange" Korean name yet later regrets using a Japanese name as she hears ethnically insensitive comments by her best friend. When a fellow student asks a senior who goes by her "real name" why she has such a "strange name," she matter-of-factly answers that she is Korean. "The simple fact told as fact momentarily pierced Naran's spirit" (Sagisawa 2004:62). It is this very simplicity—that ethnic Koreans might have ethnic Korean names—that long eluded the Zainichi population in monoethnic Japan.

DISRECOGNITION

Zainichi served as a repository of Japanese people's suspicion and xenophobia, but ethnic Japanese and ethnic Koreans by the 1970s were indistinguishable in terms of appearance, behavior, and culture. As the specter of impoverished Zainichi receded from the reality of affluent society, any test of distinction besides genealogy was likely to fail. Few ethnic Koreans harbored any realistic plan to return to either Korea; one late 1970s survey of Korean parents showed that less than 2 percent hoped that their children would reside in Korea, whereas 35 percent wished that they would "live just like other Japanese" (Hong and Nakajima 1980:122). It should not be surprising that even Zainichi observers believed that unless ethnic Koreans would return to Korea soon, the Zainichi population would become integrated into Japanese society (see, e.g., Zainichi Kankoku 1970:377–80).

Passing, as I argued in chapter 1, was a default condition. Not to pass as Japanese required a conscious effort to use one's Korean name or to proclaim one's Korean ancestry. Yet "coming out" was difficult not only because of Japanese xenophobia but also because of the generalized Japanese dislike for difference that was especially pronounced in the era of rapid economic growth. Passing was, then, natural and comfortable, but also unenviable and unviable. It was tantamount to living a lie; ethnic pride and individual dignity militated against the inauthentic life of passing. The disclosure of Korean ancestry, moreover, could jeopardize a personal or employment relationship. The omnipresent threat of outing invalidated the ostensibly sensible solution.

Beyond the statistics and the structures of discrimination, what seared Zainichi consciousness was their illegitimacy—*disrecognition*, or lack of recognition—in postwar Japanese society. Here I use *recognition* not to mean re-identification but a complex of attributes—love, right, and esteem—that endow people with a sense of acceptance and acknowledgment. In the prewar period, ethnic Koreans may have been deemed inferior, but they were a familiar group with their rightful, albeit lesser, place in Japanese society. In the postwar period, though the legacy of colonial hierarchy slowly dissipated, ethnic Koreans lost their legitimate place in monoethnic Japan. That is, when acknowledged, they were deemed inferior, but more commonly they were not even acknowledged. In spite of the existence of "good" Japanese and the invariable variability of individual experience, colonial hierarchy and its postcolonial legacy made Zainichi objects of dislike, disenfranchisement, and degradation that were simultaneously unrecognized: in short, objects of disrespect and disrecognition. They lacked what the sociologist T. H. Marshall (1992:8) calls "social citizenship": "the right to share to the full in the social heritage and to live the life of a civilized being according to the standards prevailing in the society." Ethnic Koreans were not welcome in Japan; they shouldn't have been there; they weren't there in official discourse. In short, their lives were congenitally tragic; no wonder that *sinse t'aryong* [traditional Korean narrative of lamentation]—hardly heard in contemporary South Korea—proved such a popular Zainichi genre.

The most emblematic expression of disrecognition is that the name of the group doubled, unaltered, as the racial epithet. For both Kim Dalsu, born in 1919, and Lee Chongja, born in 1947, the earliest memory of discrimination is being teased for being "Korean" [*Chōsenjin*] (Kim D. 1981:20–21. As early as 1930, Kim (1977:44–45) encountered a chorus of "Chōsenjin" on his first day out in Japan. There was no welcome, only disrecognition. The baffling situation is expressed by Fujiwara Tei, whose best-selling 1949 memoir depicted her family's arduous return to Japan after the end of the war: "We were called Japanese. No one got angry about it since it was obvious. Yet, when we called Koreans 'Koreans,' they got very angry" (Fujiwara 2002:60). What was puzzling to the colonizer was plainly obvious to the colonized: *Chōsen* signified undesirable attributes and traits: the usual racist litany of dirty, smelly, lazy, and stupid (cf. Kim Chanjung 1983:31). The Korean word, after all, is *Chosŏn*, not *Chōsen*; only a Japanese person would employ what for native Korean speakers is an odd-sounding word, a signifier of colonial conquest. Furthermore, the utterance was an illocutionary act that embodied the will to dominate and discriminate. The seemingly innocuous nomenclature embodied and disclosed the history and sociology of Japanese domination.

The sense of Japanese superiority and Korean inferiority that developed during the colonial period persisted in the postwar period. Not only were ethnic Koreans deemed poor (with its associated attributes, such as dirty and smelly), they were also associated with criminality and treachery. In short, they needed to be contained and excluded. Whereas the adult world prevented ethnic Koreans from joining their games for power and wealth, the childhood world frequently unleashed physical and symbolic violence. As we have seen, teasing and bullying were staples of recess activities at school. School authorities often averted their gaze from naked displays of exclusion and intolerance. A twelve-year-old Zainichi student committed suicide after his classmates called him "dirty" and "stupid" and admonished him to "die." The school authorities, however, denied the existence of bullying or discrimination (Kim Chanjung 1983:16–20). Although such callous disregard was at times an expression of ethnic discrimination, it was just as often a commitment to Fordist education, in which every pupil was supposedly equal and alike.

Self-hatred, hatred of things Korean, and guilt for hating the self and the group stirred many Zainichi psyches, damned to ponder endlessly on the irresolvable question of identity. Not surprisingly, like the twelve-year-old schoolboy, a popular solution was self-mortification. Rare indeed is it to encounter a Zainichi memoir from the dark decades of disrecognition that does not mention the contemplation of suicide. It is disheartening to note the striking series of Zainichi suicides: Ko Samyon's father attempted suicide; his son, as we saw, killed himself (Ko 1986:85–87, 2004:1, 12). Kin Kakuei and Sagisawa Megumu committed suicide. Yū Miri repeatedly sought to kill herself, arguing that suicide can "activate life" (Yū 1999:65).

The third-generation Zainichi Son Puja was born in a Burakumin village in Nara in 1941. Growing up, she was mercilessly teased for being Korean, so much so that she "came to hate [my] mother" and told her: "Kill me. Why did you give birth to me as Korean? . . . I want to die" (Son 2007:47). She continuously contemplated suicide as a schoolgirl. By the time she was married at twenty, she had changed her job twenty-two times, often having to leave her job when her Korean ancestry was divulged (Son 2007:65). Yet the tragedy was that Korean ancestry or ethnicity meant little, if anything, to Zainichi children. As Arai Toyokichi described his Zainichi life course in "Taegu e" [To Taegu]: "I started writing short stories when I was a high-school student / But I still cannot read *han'gŭl* / The first time I held the Certificate of Alien Registration / It was like a spy movie and I didn't think I could show it to others . . . / I wanted to vote / But I did not have suffrage / I couldn't get used to the name Pak that I only used at the local authorities. . . . " (Morita and Sagawa 2005:316). Rejection and dejection, ethnic discrimination but cultural assimilation tormented Zainichi youths who came of age in the postwar period.

A sentimental commonplace states that it is corrosive to the soul to dominate or discriminate; if true, many a Japanese came to personify social evil in the postwar period. What is certain, however, is that the structure of disrecognition had corrosive effects on Zainichi psyche. One of the enduring motifs of Zanichi literature is the violent father (Takeda 1983:14–16). Yan's aforementioned novel *Chi to hone*—later made into an award-winning 2003 film by Sai Yōichi—is a wrenching rendition of a son's memory of his alcoholic and violent, wife-beating and mistress-keeping father (cf. Gen 2000b:16–18; Kin 2006a:256–57). As Yan Sogiru (1995:10) remarks: "Whenever I recall my father, I cannot understand what he was thinking of as he led his life. He never once loved his family. In particular he looked down on women and sought to express his existence by wreaking violence." Whatever the place of colonialism-induced poverty and ethnic discrimination in making sense of the traumatized and traumatizing father figure, there is little doubt that ethnic Koreans who lived in prewar Japan were marred by intra-ethnic problems of conflict and crime, patriarchy and violence. As the first-generation Zainichi woman Pak Sun-Hui explains, "most of our fathers were involved in manual labor. I think because they had to experience prejudice from the Japanese society, and felt frustrated and angry about their lives and poor standard of living, they came home and took it out on their families. That is why many Korean men would come home drunk and beat their wives and kids. This was the sole image embedded in my mind" (J. Kim 2005:164). The violent father faded with the dominant trace of ethnic trauma only in the 1990s.

The involution of disrecognition did not merely affect the emasculated, inebriated patriarch. Inferiority complex was pervasive, leading to a denial of Korean ancestry—and even hatred toward parents as in the case of Son Puja—and to the unwelcome embrace of Japanese identity. In the volatile mixture of widespread poverty, ethnic isolation, and traditional patriarchy, postwar memories of prewar Korean ghetto life are rampant with incidences of alcoholism, domestic violence, and other social dysfunctions (Kim Saryan 1973:18; Chan 1966:10–12). They would also find contemporary counterparts in Zainichi literature, which is replete with sexual violence, family dissolution, gambling addiction, substance abuse, alienation and anomie, murder and mayhem, to parricide, pederasty, and incest (cf. Yū 1998; Gu 2002; Gen 2007). Instances of mental illness, from depression to suicide, afflicted Zainichi lives. Paranoia gripped some Zainichi; one man was convinced that he was under constant police surveillance and that "Prime Minister Nakasone [and others] are discussing taking a photograph of my anus . . . and plan on making me confess by injecting poison in my anus" (Kurokawa 2006:55). It also may not be coincidental that the representative Zainichi writer Kin Kakuei and the representative Zainichi intellectual Kang Sangjung both suffered from stuttering. The stutter, with considerable sexual overtone, weighs as a burden that must be urgently overcome, even more so than the division of the homeland, in Kin's "Kogoeru kuchi." Suicidal narratives—and deeds as I noted—are ubiquitous in Zainichi fiction and autobiography. It would be hopelessly reductive to blame disrecognition for Zainichi mental illness or self-mortification— one would be foolhardy to dismiss the physiological and intrapsychic sources of psychological problems—but the ferocity of disrecognition made the reduction at once plausible and meaningful to Zainichi themselves.

The internalization of disrecognition is implicit in the phenomenon of passing. The protagonist in Sagisawa Megumu's story "Hontō no natsu" [Real summer] notes: "I didn't have any intention of hiding my being

Korean. At least, I didn't consciously seek to hide it" (Sagisawa 1997:31). Yet his initial reaction after getting into a car accident is to ask his girl-friend to leave the car; the police interrogation would inevitably uncover his use of a Japanese alias and his nationality. For Sugihara, the protagonist of Kaneshiro's Go (2000), occluding his ancestry is far from his intention, yet not only does he hesitate to disclose his ethnic identity to his girlfriend but the disclosure is greeted with his girlfriend's confession that her father regards Koreans as having "dirty blood" (Kaneshiro 2000:179). As a char-acter in another Kaneshiro novel remarks: "In the darkness of [the] movie theater, we can become different human beings, not Zainichi North Koreans, Zainichi South Koreans, Japanese, or Americans" (Kaneshiro 2007:28). Yet what happens outside in the glare of daylight? In spite of his bravado, Sugihara cannot will national boundaries or disrecognition to disappear (cf. Wender 2005:200–201). Having become almost perfectly Japanese, many Zainichi people unwittingly incorporated the Japanese dis-recognition of Koreans.

WHICH SIDE ARE YOU ON?

The Zainichi population faced the infeasibility of returning to Korea, the implausibility of being Japanese, and the impossibility of being otherwise. Zainichi were condemned—according to the "second-generation" Zainichi writer O Rimjun (1971:195), born in 1926—to struggle to "escape from being half-Japanese [Panchoppari] [and] to become Korean." Lee Hoesung similarly posits the quintessential Zainichi cycle of superficial assimila-tion, the realization of being half-Japanese or half-Korean, and the attempt to achieve Koreanness (cf. Takeda 1983:69). For O and Lee, the possibility of a hybrid status—both Korean and Japanese—is not seriously mooted as they urge Koreanness, albeit in Japan and not in Korea. Rather than assim-ilation or repatriation, the Zainichi choice was between Japanization and Koreanization. The decision was either/or but not both, or in-between, or beyond.

A minority pursued the path of naturalization. Only 233 Koreans were naturalized in 1952, and throughout the 1960s there were several thousand cases per year. It would be tempting to blame the xenophobic policies of the Japanese government. Between 1952 and 1985, the Japanese government projected an ethnoracially homogeneous vision of Japanese society: one race, one ethnicity, one nation. In general, citizenship, race, ethnicity, and nationality were all conflated: the obviousness of Japaneseness underscored monoethnic ideology (Lie 2001:144–48). Only people who can claim blood descent—and preferably pure at that—deserved citizenship (Kashiwazaki 2000:27). Furthermore, the Immigration and Naturalization Bureau was often culturally insensitive and bureaucratically recalcitrant, and therefore appeared arbitrary and authoritarian, though the same charges of being tedious and odious could be cast on most government bureaucracies (Kim Yondal 1990:29–34; Asakawa 2003:58). Yet we should not dwell exclusively on rebarbative Japanese policies and practices. Having assimilated culturally, most ethnic Koreans hesitated to take the next step. Three-fourths of ethnic Koreans in Osaka in 1974 were categorically against naturalization (Hong and Han 1979:125).

Zainichi resistance expressed not only instinctive anti-Japanese sentiments but also the nationalist mind-set that precluded the possibility of in-between identity. The category of Korean American or Korean Canadian is possible and plausible when the question of citizenship is decoupled from that of ethnic identification. Given the essentialist mind-set that asserted a homogeneous Japan and Korea, hybridity was dismissed. The world of either/or manifested itself in one of Aesop's tales—which were immensely popular in postwar Japan—that sticks deepest in my memory from my schooldays in Japan in the 1960s. The bat, which was neither of land nor of air, was banished from both sides. The dreadful destiny of the lonely bat was a moral allegory for everyone, Zainichi included. As the "mixed-blooded" writer Iio Kenshi (1993:11) remarks, the eyes of the bat "seek hope in darkness. The harsh and cold glare of its eyes is lonely and enveloped in pathos." Darkness visible was an otiose poetic fantasy to those who experienced disrecognition. The possibility of recognition mandated being Japanese or Korean. Kim Kyongdok (2005:86) spent his four years in college pondering, Hamlet-like, "to be Korean or to be Japanese." The question was: Are you Japanese or are you Korean? Which side are you on?

Colonial and historical memory made naturalization a gesture of national betrayal, an act of treason. As late as the mid-1980s, Yoon Keun Cha (1987:195) declared: "In essence 'naturalization' is on the same line as the past Japanization policy that ignored the historical existence and subjectivity of 'Zainichi' and their dignity as human beings" (cf. Kim Sokpom 2001:32, 156). Because naturalization required the adoption of Japanese-sounding names (based on approved Chinese characters) until the 1990s, it reprised the 1940 edict that outlawed non-Japanese names [*sōshi kaimei*]. It also stipulated compliance with the Japanese practice of household registration [*koseki*], which was overlaid upon the traditional Korean landlord practice of lineage registry [*chokbo*]. From the perspective of the Confucian—and Korean—value of venerating ancestors, naturalization implied a brutal uprooting of the family tree. Never mind that lineage registry was a province of the landed elite, the group, at least according to the received Zainichi historiography, that was underrepresented in the Zainichi population.

More prosaically, Japan remained the ideological enemy that had never atoned for its colonial-era brutalities—or continuing maltreatment and injustices—and therefore had not been exonerated. Colonialism is apparently never having to say you're sorry: for a society in which "sorry" is ubiquitous, the Japanese government has been remarkably intransigent in its refusal to proffer formal apology for historical wrongs or contemporary mistakes (cf. Lie 1991). Thus, naturalization signified rejection of Zainichi experience and ethnicity. As Bei Happō recounts his life, it begins with his "slave-like condition" during the prewar period and sixty years of struggling against discrimination; naturalization would be a denial of his life (Tsubouchi 1998:161). The protagonist of Lee Hoesung's 1997 story "Ikitsumodoritsu" likens changing nationality to *fumie:* the humiliating ritual imposed on Japanese Christians during the sixteenth century of stepping on a portrait of Jesus to prove one's indifference to the banned religion (Lee H. 2005a:36). As the mother cries in Chon In's poem "Kika" [Naturalization]: "We lost our name / We sold our country" (Morita and Sagawa 2005:131).

The expected costs of ethnic betrayal frequently outweighed the anticipated benefits of switching sides. Naturalization did not ensure the end of disrecognition. Like Burakumin, who were indisputably Japanese citizens but continued to suffer discrimination, Japanese citizenship did not promise an impregnable defense against prevailing anti-Korean discrimination. Naturalization merely offered another form of passing, albeit with a government imprimatur. Yet could the blemish be repaired by cosmetic, bureaucratic overlay? Far from becoming truly Japanese, a naturalized Zainichi might still fear the exposure of one's rejected ancestry. Simultaneously, the "convert" might lose Zainichi community support (cf. Pak I. 1999:85).

Naturalization thus threatened the very definition of Zainichi. Retaining Korean nationality was the only legitimate way to be Zainichi. This was literally true in the sense that the population figure for Zainichi depends on the census, which in turn only has categories for foreigners. Because neither the Japanese government nor social scientists systematically collect data on ethnic diversity—according to monoethnic ideology, what would be the point?—there are only Japanese nationals and Korean nationals. To be a Japanese citizen means to assume Japanese ethnicity as well. The logic of Japanese government officials and demographers was shared by most ethnic

Koreans. As a second-generation Zainichi journalist put it in the mid-1980s, his refusal to naturalize "is connected to losing the last thing that should be defended as Zainichi" (Won 1986:17). As late as 1998, Kim Kyonbu (1998:178) dryly observes: "Zainichi are, needless to say, foreigners who do not hold Japanese nationality within Japan." Nationality was a sticking point [kodawari], the last redoubt of Koreanness. Naturalization implied exchanging the soul of Koreanness for that of the ideological enemy.

If the Zainichi ambit precluded naturalization, it also cast into doubt intermarriage. Ethnic Koreans were just as likely to resist ethnic exogamy as ethnic Japanese. In the major Zainichi novel of the first postwar decade, *Genkainada* [Genkai Strait, 1954], Kim Dalsu (2006:259) recounts the romance between the ideologically "half" Japanese So Gyente and the Japanese woman Ōi Kimiko. When So confesses his ethnic ancestry, Ōi merely responds, "aren't Koreans now Japanese?" His simmering national loyalty leads him to quit at once his "Japanese" job and girlfriend. Ideologically, at least, this becomes a symptomatic characterization of interethnic relationship. The first-generation Zainichi who experienced the strident racism of the colonial period and the immediate postwar decade found it difficult to trust Japanese or to dilute the blood and the culture of Koreans in Japan. Kim's novel is based on his real-life romance and break-up with his Japanese girlfriend. After the war, Kim returns to Japan, runs into his old girlfriend, and decides to marry her: "Korea is independent. I am no longer a member of the people invaded by the Japanese but a member of the liberated Koreans" (Maekawa 1981:270). Yet when he finds out that she had an American soldier as her boyfriend during their separation, he cannot forgive her for having harbored love for someone who took part in the suppression of the Korean people's struggles (Maekawa 1981:270). Whatever the accuracy of this narrative, it captures the political and ideological overlays that bedeviled personal relationships across ethnonational lines. Yoon Keun Cha (1992:89) glosses the topic by commenting that ethnic conflict only deepens with age and generates "unbearable sadness." The essence, so to speak, cannot be changed and merely shows its true color over time. The opposition to intermarriage persisted long after it was ubiquitous. As late as 1982, the marriage between the Japanese novelist Oda Makoto and the Zainichi artist Hyon Sunhye was a media sensation and something of a "scandal" (Hyon 2007:81).

Intermarriage is of course a matter of definition. Ko Yon-i (1998:61) asks rhetorically if his North Korean nationality and his wife's South Korean nationality make them an instance of an international marriage and their daughter a *hāfu* [half]. Lee Seijaku (1997:36) describes her parents' union as an instance of "international marriage": a first-generation South Korean father (Sōren) and a second-generation Zainichi mother (Mindan). Some ethnic Koreans balked at Zainichi marriage to naturalized ethnic Koreans (Kim Masumi 2004:115).

In spite of ideological opposition, the postwar period continued the prewar trend. Although a 1974 survey showed that 61 percent of responding ethnic Koreans in Osaka were against intermarriage (Hong and Han 1979:125), by then over half of Zainichi marriages were to Japanese nationals (Kang and Kim 1989:156–57). To be sure, Japanese nationals included not only naturalized ethnic Koreans but also other non-ethnic Japanese. It is worth remarking that intermarriage was by definition a contravention of the traditional Japanese and Korean patriarchal practice of family-arranged marriage. It is only in the early 1970s that the ratio of romance-based marriage exceeded that of family-arranged marriage in Japan. The decline of prewar patriarchy and the rise of individualism occurred in tandem with the increasing incidence of intermarriage, which in turn would generate a social basis for Zainichi identification beyond the Japan-Korea binary. As the Zainichi poet Chon Jan wrote in "Nihonjin to koi o shite" [Falling in love with Japanese]: "Falling in love with Japanese / I realize how I am not Japanese / And not Korean / I realize that I am Zainichi [in katakana, the script to denote things foreign]" (Morita and Sagawa 2005:357). The rapidly rising rate of intermarriage, perhaps more than any other metric, portended the permanent residency of ethnic Koreans and their integration in Japanese society.

The offspring of intermarriage—"mixed" children [konketsuji], often called hāfu—fared poorly in the imaginaries of both ethnic Koreans and ethnic Japanese. Given that Japan's patrilineal law held force until 1985, children of a Japanese mother and Korean father were often registered with just the mother. Their bastard [shiseiji] status was a legal encapsulation of the conceptual anomaly of ethnic hybridity. The only recourse was therefore to choose one side or another. In the repatriation project, about 1,800 Japanese women followed their ethnic Korean husbands partly in order to avoid a problematic existence as "mixed" couples and the dim prospects for their "mixed" children (Aoki 2005:122). In the 1960 film Umi o wataru yūjō [The friendship that crossed the sea]—the best-known Japanese film on the repatriation project—the "mixed" child decides to give up trying to be "pure Japanese" in order to be "pure Korean" in North Korea (Takayanagi 1999–2000:144). In Fukazawa Kai's 1992 novel, Yoru no kodomo [The child of the night], one of the characters divides Zainichi into four classes; and the lowest are those who were naturalized, but "the mixed-blood [kon-

ketsu] don't belong anywhere. . . . The mixed-blood are invisible men" (Fukazawa 2006:56). Sagisawa Megumu belatedly discovered and discussed her Korean ancestry, going so far as to study Korean in South Korea. To herself, she is a quarter Korean: "I am a quarter. I came to [South Korea] bringing the naturally felt interest and love for my quarter ancestral land" (Sagisawa 1994:44). When she says that her background is "very difficult to explain," the cabdriver responds, "It's not very difficult. You're a *kyoppo* [diasporic Korean]" (Sagisawa 1994:45). When she is with other *kyoppo*, however, she feels that she is neither Zainichi nor *kyoppo*.

Naturalized or mixed Zainichi often suffered double exclusion, and the excluded middle at times was a space of auto-extinction. In 1970, Yamamura Masaaki, a Waseda University student, burned himself to death. He wrote (1975:121–23): "I didn't want to be born in this country. I wanted to live in ancestral Korea, however poor. . . . I would have refused naturalization if I weren't nine years old. . . . Rather than living as an incomplete half-Japanese, I had a strong desire to live as a Korean. . . . [My fellow Korean students] regard me as a betrayer who abandoned his ancestral land. I am not Japanese. I am no longer Korean. . . . Where is my land of repose?" In 1974 the aforementioned writer Ko Samyon—married to Oka Yuriko—published *Ikirukoto no imi* [The meaning of living], which was "a message he sent to his son" (Oka 1993:193). The twelve-year-old had committed suicide, in part because of the confusion of ethnic identity. A viscid gloom enveloped non-Zainichi Zainichi during the dark decades of disrecognition.

The ideology of monoethnicity affected both ethnic Japanese and ethnic Koreans. The vocabulary of blood purity was frequently invoked by Zainichi to shun intermarriage and to resist naturalization. In effect, the belief in ethnic essence—presumably carried by "blood"—accompanied the pursuit of purity. Yet the boundary line that separates the two groups inevitably leaves impurities, not least from colonial-era intermarriages. In the immediate postwar years, Pak Cheil (1957:136–37) estimated the existence of 70,000 to 80,000 "semi-Koreans" [*jun Chōsenjin*] in Japan, well over 10 percent of the total Zainichi population. The corrosive consequence of the search for purity manifests itself most dramatically in the narrowing circle of people with true ethnic essences. This is the context in which intra-ethnic marriage between members of Sōren and Mindan was problematic.

Lee Hoesung's 1975 novel *Tsuihō to jiyū* [Exile and freedom] exemplifies the trap of essentialism. A naturalized protagonist is married to an ethnic Japanese woman. Tokio constantly regrets his naturalization and remains ambivalent about miscegenation: his "mixed" son. He contemplates regaining his Korean nationality and undergoing vasectomy. He wishes he could answer the query of why he is naturalized by responding that he had hoped to "convict Japanese crime," but in fact he did it for the sake of his brother's employment: "If it suited my brother, I would have been happy to become an Eskimo" (Lee H. 1975:34, 35). He cannot quite believe in his Japanese wife's lack of prejudice against Koreans and attributes her concrete love ("I love you—Tokio—not because you are Korean or Japanese" [115]) as a product of her idealism [*risō*]. Thoroughly assimilated, Tokio remains imprisoned in the essentialist cage; he believes he is in exile underground. He hopes to end his "exile" as a "tunnel man" by reclaiming his ethnicity and living above ground [*chijō no ningen*] (262). The binary of Korean and Japanese precludes a diasporic identity that he would explore in his later novel, as we saw in the previous chapter.

Both Zainichi and Japanese reinforced the symbolic wall between them. Postwar Zainichi writers, such as Kim Dalsu and Kim Sokpom, used the Japanese language to stoke nationalist, anti-Japanese passions. A sympathetic Japanese critic, in turn, would write that "Zainichi writers' Japanese works . . . are not 'Japanese literature.' In this sense, one cannot but find it insensitive to find the novels and criticisms of Kim Sokpom, Ko Samyon, or Lee Hoesung in the Japanese literature section in bookstores" (Isogai 1979:209–10). In the early twenty-first century, it is just as common to find their work categorized under "foreign literature." The wonder is why anyone would have thought that this form of exclusion or essentialism is more sensitive than the inclusion of Zainichi writers in the realm of Japanese literature. Moreover, even those who explicitly expressed a preference for the Japanese reading of their names found themselves with the Korean pronunciation; thus "Kin Kakuei" is "Kim Hagyon" (Kawamura 2005:46–47). What seems so elusive is the critique of ethnic essentialism, or, simply put, the possibility that Zainichi identity could be between or beyond Korean and Japanese.

THE CUNNING OF RECOGNITION

As early as the 1940s, a third of Koreans in Japan could not speak Korean fluently; and the existence of the second generation by then had prompted some ethnic Koreans to remain in Japan after 1945. It is not surprising, therefore, that Zainichi politics in the immediate postwar years frequently focused on domestic, Japanese issues, ranging from ethnic education to working conditions. By the mid-1950s, however, the primacy of the Cold

War and geopolitics had decisively shifted the Zainichi focus away from Japan to the homeland. Systematically excluded from and disrecognized by Japanese society, the Zainichi population in Japan sought repatriation. As I argued in the previous chapter, exilic identity misrecognized Zainichi experience already by the 1960s and certainly by the 1980s. In the late 1950s, Pak Cheil had insisted that Zainichi returnees to the Koreas would arrive as immigrants, and concrete experience confirmed the gulf between homeland and diaspora. Alienation was the modal response to the experience of actual return. At the same time, as we have seen, Sōren and Mindan were losing their influence over the Zainichi population. Disrecognition and essentialism encountered the inevitable reality of mutual attraction and boundary transgression, evinced most unmistakably by intermarriage and "mixed" offspring. Zainichi identity presented a break from the binary of being Korean or being Japanese: the third way beyond repatriation and assimilation as a distinct category and a viable identity in Japanese life.

The nascent identification as Zainichi can be seen in Zainichi literature. The second-generation Zainichi writer Lee Hoesung, for instance, won the prestigious Akutagawa Prize in 1971 for "Kinuta o utsu onna" [A woman striking the washing board], a depiction of his mother in prewar Japan. The "boom" in Zainichi literature around 1970 instantiates what I call Zainichi ideology, which I elaborate in the following chapter. Although acknowledging the relative autonomy of Zainichi experience, postwar Zainichi literature set the main stage in the Korean peninsula, whether Kim Dalsu's *Genkainada*, Kim Sokpom's *Kazantō*, or Lee Hoesung's *Mihatenu yume*. Although Lee's Akutagawa Prize–winning story is often read as the foundation of a distinctive Zainichi literature (Yamasaki 2003:95–96), there was a decisive forerunner: Kin Kakuei's "Kogoeru kuchi" [The frozen mouth, 1966]. It is a work on Zainichi life by a Zainichi writer that takes place squarely in Japan. In a critical passage, the applied chemistry graduate student describes his commute to his university laboratory as the time to read books on Korea. "Although I am Korean, I still can't understand Korean," says the protagonist, who observes that he cannot "recover" his Korean identity because he was born and reared in Japan so he can at best "awaken" or "acquire" it (Kin 2004:34). At the same time, "No matter how I look Japanese, and feel and live the same way as Japanese, I study in order to realize that I am definitely not Japanese" (34). Neither Japanese nor Korean, his effort to awaken his ethnic self can at best be "ideal" and not "actual feeling" (34). The actual feeling leads away from the question of either/or to the answer of neither.

Pioneering voices, opinions, and events appeared in the 1960s, such as

Kin's story. Perhaps the most sensational and proleptic manifestation, albeit expressed negatively, was the sensational criminal case in 1968, known as the Kim Hiro or Sumatakyō Incident. Kim Hiro [Kin Kirō] shot two Japanese gangsters and then held some eighteen people hostage for nearly four days. When he was given a chance to air his "motives," he spoke to the national media about ethnic discrimination: surely Kim's indictment of Japanese disrecognition reached a larger audience than any prior—and possibly later—Zainichi voice. Kim had dropped out of elementary school after experiencing endless teasing by his classmates as "dirty" and "barbarian"; he was even beaten by his teacher (Kim Hiro 1968:6–7, 1989:15–19). After an unstable life of dead-end jobs and recidivist crimes, he read voraciously, from Greek philosophy to economics, in prison (Abe 2002:18). Relentlessly pursued by yakuza for unpaid loans, Kim decided not only to kill the collectors but also a police officer who had made openly racist statements. Retrospectively, at least, Kim (1989:101) declaimed: "I wanted to appeal the ethnic problem. . . . This was my destiny." Remarkably, he succeeded in coaxing apology for the racist statement from a police chief in front of national television. Later his mother testified at his trial: "I thought that someone had to do something about it. It just happened that my Hiro did it" (Kawata 2005:4). "It" was what I have called disrecognition: the accumulated anger against disrespect and discrimination. Another Zainichi man commented on Kim's action at the time: "He was forced into seeking his liberation by the only method available to him: killing himself" (Suzuki 2007:181).

In Kin Kakuei's 1969 story, "Manazashi no kabe" [The wall of the gaze], the Zainichi protagonist hits the wall of national difference as his Japanese girlfriend leaves him and his professor suggests either emigrating or naturalizing. He comes to realize the pervasiveness of the "gaze." In the Kim Hiro case, "the gaze sprung up across Japan, and never before had it poured into one place, one person" (Kin 2006a:289). He continues: "What was Kin Kirō [Kim Hiro] trying to shoot down? It must be that gaze. If so, then Kin Kirō was pointing the rifle not only at Japanese but also Koreans like me, who incorporate that gaze within" (290). The protagonist concludes that Kim's action was "justified resistance" and compares him favorably to himself; he is "afraid and cowardly flee[s] from the gaze" (290). Kim's mother and Kin's character were not the only people to believe that Kim was attempting to shoot at "the gaze" itself. Kim's defense attorneys stressed the evils of Japanese imperialism and their legacy in the mass media, the police, and indeed Japanese society *tout court:* "This case is an 'ethnic problem' created by the crime against Korea by Japanese state and society" (Kim Hiro Bengodan 1972:15, 289–301). The Kim Hiro Incident inescapably lodged the long-neglected problem of the Zainichi population in the media spotlight. Many Zainichi empathized deeply with Kim's plight (e.g., Kō 2000:81–82). However, both Mindan and Sōren regarded it as a source of shame, revealing the disjuncture between ethnic reality and organizational ideology (Abe 2002:117–19).

In fact, there was a harbinger of the Kim Hiro case: the Komatsugawa Incident. In 1958, the eighteen-year-old Ri Chin'u allegedly raped and killed two women; he was convicted and executed four years later. Although it is unclear whether he was in fact guilty of the crimes, it is clear that he became the Zainichi Bigger Thomas. Arrested on the thirty-fifth anniversary of the post-Kantō earthquake massacre, Ri faced the Japanese police, judiciary, and mass media that had entrenched preconceptions of Korean criminality. Like Kim, he grew up impoverished and suffered discrimination without community support. The prevailing ethnic Korean opinion bemoaned the lack of ethnic education that had presumably led to his crime (Fujishima 1960:32). As in Kim Hiro's case, the main ethnic organizations distanced themselves from the disgraced Korean. Pak Sunam, whose correspondence with Ri became a minor literary sensation, was expelled from Sōren in 1962 because she persisted in communicating with Ri (Nozaki 1994:189–90). He was an autodidact who repeatedly stole works of world literature and pronounced himself, like Camus' Meursault, to be a motiveless murderer, leading a Japanese scholar of French literature to dub him the "Japanese Genet" (Suzuki 2007:58–59, 76).

Ri was the proverbial floating signifier that writers and intellectuals inscribed upon their favored literary works and motifs (cf. Nozaki 1994:79–80). In spite of his conversion to Catholicism and his insistence that neither "poverty" nor "ethnicity" explains his crime (Pak Sunam 1979:39), the Koreanist Hatada Isao's ethnonational reductionism—"We can say that Ri's crime is the microcosm of Zainichi destiny" (Pak Sunam 1979:105)—encapsulated the prevailing opinion. The suicide of Yamamura Masaaki was similarly reduced to his exclusion from both Japanese and Koreans as a naturalized Zainichi, but in his suicide note he explicitly indicted poverty and inequality, "inhuman education," and revolutionary Marxists' "violent rule" (Yamamura 1975:242–43). The impact of these tragic events as "ethnic lessons" would slowly seep out in the course of the 1960s. As a Zainichi man wrote to an ethnic Korean newspaper in 1972: "When the Ri Chin'u incident occurred, I was shocked that my secret had been excavated. I instinctively thought that Ri Chin'u killed a man because he is 'Korean' and he was executed because he was 'Korean' " (Lee Sun Ae 2000:45). Although

Japanese public opinion was not ready to read the Komatsugawa Incident as a consequence of disrecognition, it belatedly became, like the Kim Hiro Incident, a negative expression of Korean powerlessness.

Sensational violence exemplified the hopelessness of the Zainichi situation—no exit—but it would also not be an exaggeration to say that the two cases, a decade apart, shook some Japanese and many Zainichi people into considering and acting on the problematic status of Zainichi in Japanese society. What distinguished the two incidents was the Zainichi and ethnic Japanese mobilization that probably staved off Kim's death sentence. The impact on the Zainichi population was profound. Suh Sung's (1994:56) 1972 testimony during his spy trial highlighted the two cases as "the concentrated expression of the contradiction of the livelihood or reality of Zainichi society." They articulated Zainichi identity, albeit negatively as murderous rage against a society that did not recognize them as legitimate. It is not an accident that the two Zainichi perpetrators were bereft of language and community; neither spoke Korean nor had any sustained ties to an ethnic organization. Their situation recalls the fate of German-speaking Jews who, in the words of Paul Celan (1983:186), had to "go through dreadful deafening, go through the thousand darknesses of death-delivering speech." Ri and Kim both sought to learn Korean in prison. The wayward passions of these souls smoldering in disrecognition stirred the Zainichi population and Japanese society at large, but their individual, criminal acts could not cross the threshold to ethnic acknowledgment and recognition. The more positive articulation of these proleptic passions and cunning anticipations of ethnic recognition had to wait until the 1970s.

Kim Hiro's shooting and kidnapping, as well as the trial that followed, were by no means the only newsworthy event at the time. In 1969, Zainichi high-school students protested their teacher's use of discriminatory language—the teacher had called a student *yotamono* [delinquent]—and in so doing affirmed their Zainichi pride and decided to use Korean names (Kin 1971:38–39). The following year saw Yamamura's suicide. Lee Hoesung (1971:36–38) saw a connection between Kim and Yamamura in the problem of Zainichi oppression.

Most significantly, in 1970, Pak Chonsok sued his employer, Hitachi, for dismissing him after learning of his ethnic background. He won in 1974 (cf. Takenoshita 1996:33). What is remarkable in retrospect is Sōren's hostility to Pak's struggle: Why would a Korean sojourner worry about employment discrimination in Japan? Only those who intended to stay in Japan would support Pak's cause. A Zainichi youth leader angered his elders by arguing that "the place where we are living is here in Japan . . . and we must empha-

size Zainichi" (Satō 1977:50). The youth organization condemned his statement as assimilationist and demanded his resignation. The Hitachi case
opened a decade of legal struggles: the Zainichi equivalent of the civil-
rights years in the United States. As we will see, the Zainichi population
and its supporters achieved a series of striking court victories that restored
the social, civil, and political citizenship rights that they had lost in the
immediate postwar years.

By the late 1960s, then, individual Zainichi were articulating their
grievances as Koreans in Japan. Some found inspiration in the likes of
Frantz Fanon and Malcolm X to illuminate and eradicate ethnic disrecognition (Suh 1998:181). Pak Sunam—Ri Chin'u's correspondent—drew paral-
lels between the struggles of the Algerians in France and those of Zainichi.
Just as Fanon is "half-French," Zainichi are "half-Japanese." Hence, "we
feel that Fanon is a brother" (Pak Sunam 1970:47). She goes on to extend
the comparison of the Zainichi situation to that of black Americans. In
short, she outlines the idea of Zainichi as part of the oppressed "Third
World" (cf. Ko 1998). From a radically different perspective, the civil servant Sakanaka Hidenori (2005a:174) wrote in 1977 that "Koreans are today
legally 'foreigners' but are in fact something like 'semi-Japanese.' In the
future, with the progress of Japanization, they are likely to become something like 'Korean Japanese.' " As early as 1969, the Kyoto University professor Iinuma Jirō (1984:263) had called for a "third way" for ethnic Koreans
in Japan that was neither return (Korea) nor naturalization (Japan), tran-
scending the homogeneous nationalist mind-set. The critical insight,
expressed presciently and profoundly by Kin Kakuei (2006b:553), was that
younger Zainichi by the 1960s had "no ethnic consciousness, ethnic subjectivity to lose"; rather, both Korean and Japanese influences and identities
exist and are inextinguishable but that Zainichi cannot be reduced to either.
Zainichi occupy a special place—"Being on both ends of the gaze, he can
understand it" (Kin 2006a:292–93)—that makes possible "true emancipation." As the Zainichi character in the story concludes: "Born in Japan,
educated in Japan, living in the Japanese environment, and where I will
continue to live, I cannot escape the Japan within myself. I cannot escape
my destiny as someone who is neither Korean nor Japanese, or Korean and
Japanese—Isn't that all right?" (Kin 2006a:292).

These individual harbingers would find collective expressions in the
course of the 1970s. As assimilation advanced, ethnic identity was asserted.
The first generation's concern for homeland politics was superseded by the
second and third generations' interest in Japanese life. It is possible to
bypass disrecognition by disengagement, but recognition can only be won

through engagement. By the 1970s, moreover, there were visible discontents with Mindan's support of the dictatorial regime in the South and Sōren's unreflexive support of North Korea's bureaucratic centralism. In their stead, new social movements and intellectual currents encouraged ethnic mobilization. In response, Mindan, for example, made efforts to advance the interests of the Zainichi population by the mid-1970s (Zai Nihon 1978:35–36), publishing "white papers on discrimination" that promoted rights and benefits for ethnic Koreans in Japan (e.g., Zai Nihon 1979:18–20). Sōren also belatedly paid some attention to the concrete reality of ethnic Korean lives in Japan by the early 1980s (cf. Un 1983:238–40). As we will see in the following chapter, some of the most energetic voices for Zainichi recognition came out of disaffected Sōren members. But these actions could not stem Zainichi desertion from the mainline ethnic organizations and the two Koreas. Many Zainichi saw themselves as independent of and beyond the national division. Lee Hoesung published *Kita de are Minami de are waga sokoku* [Either North or South, my ancestral land] in 1974. In seeking the liberation at once of the individual and the ethnicity from Japan, Suh Kyung Sik (1981:10) echoed Lee's sentiment: "Both South Korea and North Korea are my homeland." By 1978, Pak Sunam (1979:455), who two decades earlier had sought to instill ethnonational consciousness in Ri Chin'u, would write of the "doubleness of [Zainichi] existence": "If we are 'not Japanese,' 'not Korean,' we are 'Japanese' and 'Korean.'" Beyond North and South, neither Korean nor Japanese: therein lies the genesis of Zainichi identity.

A Zainichi graduate student once proposed that Kim Il Sung was a figure out of joint with the march of world history. Far from being the cunning of reason, he had thrown North Korea out of orbit from the dialectical reality of the capitalist world system. It is an intriguing thesis, articulated like a well-read, well-cultured Zainichi intellectual. Whatever its plausibility, it is fair to say that few Zainichi intellectuals in the 1960s predicted the end of homeland orientation, and it is a supreme irony that the brush with North or South Korean reality wrought—cunningly or not—an involution and birth of a new identity. In the following chapter, I explore how the particular manifestation of this cunning—the word in Japanese means "plagiarism" or, put euphemistically, "mimesis"—manifested itself as ethnic self-recognition. Life in Japan seemed like a singular path of desperation and despair for Zainichi, but it in fact disclosed disparate paths of Zainichi affirmation, identification, and even efflorescence.

4. Recognition

In Kaneshiro Kazuki's *Go* (2000), the protagonist, Sugihara, opens the novel with a description of his communist, North Korean father, the Japanese colonization of Korea, and the family's desire to visit Hawaii—a vacation that requires switching their nationality from North Korean to South Korean (and shifting their membership from Sōren to Mindan). The stuff of the novel's first five pages has been recounted countless times by Japanese and Zainichi writers, including in this book, but no one would have imagined that it would make a best-selling novel. Reciting Bruce Springsteen's "Born in the U.S.A."—though observing that Springsteen grew up in a poor family whereas his family is well-off—Sugihara sings his own refrain of "Born in Japan." At once erudite and violent, he is highly individualistic and antiauthoritarian; he is the proverbial nail that should have been hammered in. In the 1960s and 1970s, Zainichi was all seriousness and suffering: as the pejorative slang would have put it, "dark" *[kurai]*. The unbearable burden of Zainichi being traumatized Zainichi life-course and discourse. Instead, Kaneshiro's prose and protagonist exemplify a striking mode of being cool *[kakkoii]* in contemporary Japanese culture.

Kaneshiro's book—made a year later into an acclaimed film—capped decades of Zainichi ethnic ferment in which the question of identity was paramount. Inevitably one reflects at times on existential and ontological questions: "Who am I?" "Where do I come from?" "Where am I going?" Such questions are, as I argued in *Modern Peoplehood* (Lie 2004b:chap.6), essentially irresolvable. Only the dead may aspire to definitiveness, but since the deceased cannot represent themselves, even that aspiration is foreclosed. Any adequate narrative of a life, moreover, demands nothing less than a Victorian triple-decker (and what truly matters often eludes even the longest memoirs or biographies), yet most readers, most of the time, require brevity: vita longa, ars brevis. That questions of identity may be irresolvable may merely make them all the more urgent, and they are especially pressing for people whose place in society is challenged and whose belonging is unsettled. The soul frets in the shadow as it struggles to recognize itself and to be recognized by others. The self invokes collective categories and public discourses even if its ultimate task is to express the private. In the age of modern peoplehood—when membership in an ethnonational group is at once legally mandated and emotionally indispensable—it is not surprising that extant nations should be the principal predicates of identity claims. For Zainichi, it left three plausible possibilities in the postwar period: North Korean, South Korean, or Japanese. The implausibility of return, the obstacle of naturalization, and the naturalness of nationalism made other solutions politically infeasible or conceptually anomalous. As I argued in the previous chapter, Zainichi identity arose as the Zainichi population transcended the division of the homeland and the binary of Korea and Japan.

The inevitable instability and complexity of identity paradoxically generate expressions of ethnic fundamentalism: the notion that one's ethnic background should disclose profound and meaningful truths about oneself. It would be bizarre to believe that one's peoplehood background was irrelevant; the country, the people, and the life produced the self for which any expression cannot possibly expunge them. The condition of disrecognition tempts the disrecognized to reverse the imputed, indubitably pejorative attributes and to crystallize them as the memory of the struggle itself and the essentialist template of recognition. What remains in the first instance is the recollected and rehearsed history of disrecognition and the struggle for emancipation. Furthermore, just as Japanese disrecognition of Koreans portrayed them in the general, the Korean recognition of themselves capture themselves in the general, though the substantive judgments are antipodal. Thus, some Zainichi would articulate a short litany of essential Zainichi-ness, such as the history of enforced migration and the reality of discrimination, which constitute what I call Zainichi ideology: the flip side of Japanese disrecognition and a generalized solution to the question of Zainichi identity.

The quest for a simple and fixed notion—the desire for definitiveness and certitude—is no less common among social scientists. Consider the straitjacket of identity offered in the most elaborate Anglophone social-scientific work on Zainichi: De Vos and Lee (1981:365) claim that Koreans in Japan "tend to feel more conflict about committing themselves to any purpose," but several pages earlier (358) they assert that "Koreans in Japan have responded to their present conditions by an ethnic consolidation not dissimilar . . . to . . . the black American population." Elsewhere (367) they write: "The maintenance of Korean identity invariably implies some conflict over assumption or avoidance of responsibility and guilt." This would apply to virtually any group. Beyond contradictory assertions and banal generalizations, they note (375) that "the family relationships themselves become bonds of aggressive displacement, of mute frustration, and of inescapable ignominy. The family is not a haven but a place of alienation." One may quote the poet Philip Larkin (1988:180)—"They fuck you up, your mum and dad. / They may not mean to, but they do"—as a reminder that family alienation is commonplace, but De Vos and Lee blithely assert its specific attribution to Zainichi.

The condition of possibility of Zainichi identity was the transcendence of the two received binaries: the stark choice between repatriation (exile) or naturalization (assimilation), and the conflicting allegiances to North and South. That is, ethnic Koreans in Japan regarded Japan as home, rather than as a place of exile, and tended to conceive of themselves as a coherent entity. As a form of diasporic nationalism, Zainichi ideology fractured precisely at the point of its crystallization.

ABSTRACT UNIVERSALISM AND ITS DISCONTENTS

Second- and third-generation Zainichi were by most measures Japanese, but the larger society did not recognize them as part of Japanese society. Some Zainichi annulled their exile status by returning to North or South Korea—as we saw in chapter 2—but repatriation was not a viable option for many. Others headed abroad, such as to North America, but that path was limited to the few with resources, skills, or extraordinary will. There was another ready resolution: to transcend ethnonational classification and to claim one's essential humanity.

We can see a number of statements in the 1970s that bridge the nationalist, homeland-oriented discourse of the 1960s and the more explicitly Zainichi-oriented discourse of the 1980s. Pak Chonsok's final testimony at the Hitachi employment discrimination lawsuit concluded that, regardless of the outcome, he was its greatest beneficiary: "Hitachi allowed me to recover my humanity in order to live. . . . As far as I am concerned, I have already won" (Nakahara 1993:33). The Zainichi writer Ko Samyon (1986) narrates his life of suffering under Japanese colonialism and poses abstract questions of the meaning of life and how to live. His answer shifts from

Marxism to Buddhism, but both solutions instantiate abstract and universal thinking. Even when discussing the concrete case of using his Korean, instead of Japanese, name in 1976, Ko could only pronounce grandiosely: "To use one's real, Korean name is very difficult. But today's peace depends on overcoming that very difficulty" (Ko n.d.: 10). Kang Sangjung—the leading Zainichi intellectual in the twenty-first century—did his doctoral thesis in the 1970s on the social theory of Max Weber, in part to make sense of self. Kim Temyong's (2004) study of Zainichi political rights is an exercise in abstract political philosophy. Even earlier, the alleged rapist-murderer Ri Chin'u turned to Christianity for solace and salvation in the late 1950s, while a half-century later Hyon Sunhye (2007) titles her book: "my ancestral land [sokoku] is the world." Examples can easily be multiplied.

The European conception of abstract, universal humanism prevailed in postwar Japan, especially among progressive intellectuals. The cosmopolitan visions of H. G. Wells and Arnold Toynbee, among others, diffused throughout the reading public. Communism was attractive not only because of its egalitarianism but also because of its cosmopolitanism. The widespread enthusiasm for Esperanto and the generalized respect for the United Nations are only two examples of the particular Japanese penchant for the international and the universal. Abstract universalism provided a ready riposte to Japanese particularism. Articulating an abstract vision of species-being either negated particularism altogether or elevated the essentialist mind-set to the loftiest level possible.

Abstract universalism has its place in concrete politics and everyday life. By eliding concrete and particular realities, it can radically change legal and social institutions. The literal application of Article 14 of the Japanese Constitution—"All of the people are equal under the law and there shall be no discrimination in political, economic or social relations because of race, creed, sex, social status or family origin"—would have endowed ethnic Koreans with the rights and provisions for which they had to struggle through lawsuits and lobbying, demonstrations and remonstrations. The effort to enhance the rights and opportunities of the Zainichi population was waged by those committed to protecting human rights or expunging discrimination for everyone. "The struggle to protect the human rights of Zainichi is simultaneously the struggle to protect the human rights and democracy of us Japanese" (Zainichi Chōsenjin 1977:ii). An attempt to provide national pension for ethnic Koreans focused on the illegitimacy of nationality-based discrimination (Zainichi Kankoku—Chōsenjin 1981:31–32). As much as their proponents were likely to slight the complexity of the

Zainichi population, the discourse of rights and antidiscrimination succeeded in dispensing opportunities and provisions for ethnic Koreans.

Nonetheless, the fatal flaw of abstract, universalist reasoning is the elision of concrete particulars. General and generic claims of human rights or antidiscrimination would conflate the situation of Zainichi with that of newly arrived South Korean students or white American executives. The accumulated weight of history—if not quite of Japanese colonialism, then the entrenchment of personal biography in a society of disrecognition—militated against the same solution even for the (presumably) same ethnic group. The option of returning home that was open to the newcomers was not as viable or palatable for Zainichi. To compliment a recent South Korean immigrant for her excellent Japanese would be a generous gesture; to do the same for a third-generation Zainichi would be merely an insult.

It is tempting to bypass all particularistic categories. The politics of ethnic recognition risks reifying ethnic categories. Shouldn't we seek to free ourselves from the alienated categories of peoplehood? In spite of the allures of universalistic ideals and cosmopolitan concerns, they cannot be realized without concrete struggles.

The pursuit of abstract universals hazards empty formalism, which reproduces the discourse of monoethnicity and the phenomena of passive racism. When Japanese students were asked whether they would marry a member of a discriminated group, most claimed that they would. Very few, however, were willing to do so after they were shown a video of pervasive discrimination in Japanese society and the difficulties of intermarriage. Without understanding some of the causes and consequences of past and present discrimination, most people are wont to follow the common sense predicated on the accumulated experiences of inequality and disrecognition. Although they may not actively embrace racist ideas, they lack the ground for countervailing received racist practices. The converse of passive racism is the precarious life of passing. Zainichi who have become Japanese citizens may continue to live in fear of having their Korean ancestry exposed. Although police officers are trained to ignore ascriptive characteristics such as nationality (Bayley 1976:85–86), they frequently harassed Zainichi. However well intentioned, abstract universalism may entrench and perpetuate the abstract particularism that is monoethnic ideology and the concrete particularism that is discriminatory practice.

Well-meaning Japanese, steeped as they may be in the ideology of universal human rights and dignity, reiterate and reenact the discourse and practice of monoethnic Japan. Discussing the 1958 Komatsugawa Incident and the 1968 Kim Hiro Incident, the literary critic Akiyama Shun insistently ignores ethnicity and instead analyzes the crimes—which became sensational because they were committed by ethnic Koreans—in the context of literary criminals in the novels of Camus, Dostoevsky, and Stendhal (Akiyama 2007:102–4). Failing to acknowledge the proverbial elephant in the room doesn't make it go away. As the protagonist in Lee Hoesung's (2005b:ii, 562) novel reacts to the claim that the distinction between Korea and Japan does not matter: "Is it possible for me now to assume a human form without the subjectivity called Korean?" Consider in this regard the shortcomings of the Japanese social sciences. In nearly 700 pages, a volume on contemporary Japanese society has nothing to say about minorities in Japan (Watanabe 1996). A critical overview of Japanese society by the progressive sociologist Mita Munesuke (1996) similarly eschews ethnic concerns. When postmodern and postcolonial scholars revived the issues of nation and ethnicity in the 1980s, some Japanese scholars filled their works with *katakana* [a script used for foreign words] terms, such as *nēshon* and *esunishitī*, but not the indigenous words *kokka* and *minzoku* or with analyses of actually existing Japanese minorities (e.g., Ōsawa 1996). The *reductio ad absurdum* of this mind-set is a book on the multiethnic constitution of Japanese society that fails to mention any group that is not ethnic Japanese (Yamauchi et al. 1991:10).

Disrecognition cannot be overcome merely by appealing to a higher ideal; brute instances of disrespect and discrimination may proliferate and thrive under the rosy glass of pristine ideals. When well-meaning Japanese friends and lovers denied the salience of ethnonational identity, the modal Zainichi response was that it does matter. Idealistic prattle left the ethnic closet intact. As the protagonist in Lee Hoesung's novel *Chijō no seikatsu-sha* [Inhabitants above the ground, 2005] concludes: "There is probably no one who has so perfectly hidden his internal world to himself" (Lee H. 2005b:i, 12). The same claim might have been made by many Zainichi youths, who perforce maintained unbridgeable distance not only to themselves but also to others in the illusory world of abstract universals. Certainly, high-minded ideals were thin gruels to survive and thrive on in an inhospitable environment. As we saw, Yamamura Masaaki, a naturalized Zainichi, embraced Christianity, which promises a universal community, but the faith failed to sustain him, and he eventually committed suicide (Wagatsuma 1981:317–18). Arai Shōkei ascended higher than almost any other Zainichi in the postwar period: the first known naturalized member of the postwar national legislature. As a graduate of the prestigious University of Tokyo and an official in the equally prestigious Ministry of Finance, Arai exemplified the paradigmatic Japanese elite. Yet he could not extricate himself from the rumor of his Korean ancestry or racist innuendos. After a corruption scandal, he killed himself in 1998; most commentators cannot help but connect his suicide to ethnic discrimination and social isolation (Harajiri 1998:113–16; Pak I. 1999:201). As his father remarked, "We are rootless weed. We don't have *Heimat [furusato]*. We don't have ancestral land *[sokoku]*. Therefore, my son loved the Japan that he grew up in. He really loved it" (Pak I. 1999:171). It was, at least in a teleological perspective, an unrequited love.

As alienated and particularistic as ethnic categories may be, we cannot wish them away. Disengagement—for that is what exilic identity or passing implied—did not challenge the culture of disrecognition. Neither universalism nor passing was a viable solution. Zainichi could not simply declaim one's essential humanity or live as Japanese in a society that systematically disrecognized ethnic Koreans in Japan. As I argued in the previous chapter, even haphazard individual actions, such as the crimes of Ri Chin'u and Kim Hiro, stung the conscience of the majority and stirred the soul of the minority. Engagement was necessary for acknowledgment: to shift the cruel radiance of mutual neglect to the warm glow of mutual recognition.

FROM HOMELAND TO DIASPORA: *KIKAN SANZENRI*

Diasporic concerns and identity issues began to supersede homeland affairs and geopolitical topics among ethnic Korean intellectuals in the late 1970s. In rejecting Sōren and Mindan, North and South Korea, *Kikan sanzenri* [Sanzenri quarterly; sanzenri is the traditional measure of the length of the Korean peninsula] shared the motivation of another Zainichi journal, *Madan*, which appeared even earlier in 1973 but lasted only six issues (Honda 1992:23, 144). In 1977, the first scholarly journal devoted to the Zainichi population, *Zainichi Chōsenjinshi kenkyū* [Research on Zainichi history], would publish its inaugural issue. Let me focus, however, on *Kikan sanzenri*, which began publication in 1975 and closed with its fiftieth issue in 1987, as the representative Zainichi journal.

Kikan sanzenri was launched, according to Kim Sokpom (1990:8), in order to "facilitate mutual understanding and solidarity" between Korea and Japan, and it assumed the form of a "general cultural journal" popular in Japan: "Our basic stand was a critique of Sōren's rigidified bureaucratic orientation." Beside Kim, the original editorial committee members were prominent, progressive Zainichi intellectuals: Kang Je'on, Kim Dalsu, Pak Kyongsik, Yun Hakjun, Yi Sinhi, and Yi Chol. In spite of their rupture from Sōren, the journal was largely silent on Sōren and the North Korean regime. It was relentless, however, in its critique of the conservative Japanese, South Korean, and U.S. governments. As the line-up of the premier issue demonstrated—Hidaka Rokurō, Tsurumi Shunsuke, and Wada Haruki—*Kikan sanzenri* aligned itself with progressive Japanese intellectuals. The inaugural issue was a special on the dissident South Korean poet Kim Chi Ha, who at the time was sentenced to death under Park Chung Hee's military dictatorship.

More striking than the absence of articles on North Korea is the paucity of attention to the Korean diaspora in Japan. Pak Kyongsik launched a series on the history of Korean activism in Japan, but this sole contribution was an exception that proved the rule. "Today, 70 percent of Koreans in Japan are second- and third-generation born in Japan. There seems to be among them an orientation toward being 'Koreans in Japan' *[Zainichi Chōsenjin]*: that is, an ethnic minority in Japan. . . . I cannot agree with such a perspective" (Pak Kyongsik 1975:195). Korean activism in Japan for Pak is about Korean people on the peninsula and not about the diasporic population in Japan. He rejects any position that deviates from the ultimate goal of Korean unification. The vast majority of the 200–250 pages per issue was dedicated to studies of ancient Korean culture and history and the political and cultural relationship between Korea and Japan.

The eighth issue (winter 1976) was the first to focus on Zainichi, including reportage on ethnic Korean merchants and an overview of Zainichi history. More noteworthy, however, is a discussion *[zadankai]* among six second-generation Zainichi, ranging in age from 21 to 33 ("Zainichi Nisei" 1976). Their lives instantiate their inevitable immersion in Japanese society. They discuss problems of being Zainichi, not homeland politics. A college student is participating in research on racial prejudice. A physician talks about his decision to use his Korean name. Even when the discussants talk about their visits to South Korea, they identify themselves as Zainichi. The college student notes: "Although I went to Seoul to study in order to become Korean, I was rejected . . . and I came back to Japan" (51). In a similar spirit, the physician says: "My feeling is that people who live in South Korea regard us as guests" (52). The discussion then turns to the topic of discrimination in Japanese society and the gap between their parents' generation and their own. The consensus is that they are neither Korean nor Japanese but Zainichi. Here, then, we find almost all of the topics that animated Zainichi in the 1980s and 1990s. Indeed, two books published in 1977 also pointed to the emergence of linguistically and culturally assimilated Zainichi (Kim Chanjung 1977:chap.2; Miyata 1977:87–98).

The discussants' perspective remained very much a minority view even in that special issue on "Koreans in Japan." Rather, it focused explicitly on Korean cultural and historical topics as well as antigovernment political struggles in South Korea. In the afterword to the special issue, Yi Sinhi (1976) expatiates on the Lockheed scandal and its impact on the Korean peninsula. He even mentions an article on Koreans in China, but the most he can say about the articles on Zainichi is that "the only thing that is certain is that the postwar period has not ended" (Yi 1976:222). Quite clearly, the generational gap was immense. The ontological status of the Korean diaspora in Japan vanished between the journal's editorial focus on the Korean cultural past, the present political imbroglio, and the impending unification of the Korean peninsula. Although one may delight in the glorious reproduction of Chosŏn-period art or the even more ancient and grand achievements of Korean civilization or wax indignant over East Asian geopolitics and South Korean military dictatorship, most readers who were Zainichi were given precious few articles on their distinctive history and culture.

Nonetheless, the readership's enthusiastic response to the first special issue led to another one on the Korean diaspora (no. 12, winter 1977). In the afterword, the editorial board member Kang Je'on (1977a:256) remarks: "After our last special issue on 'Koreans in Japan' . . . many readers expressed their hope that there would be many more special issues on the topic." The second special issue has some telling articles. Satō Katsumi (1977) discusses the 1970 Hitachi employment discrimination case (cf. Iinuma 1983:213–23). The article questions the homeland orientation of Zainichi organizations and points to the nascent contradiction between their goals and those of the rank-and-file members. How is it possible to be born, reared, schooled, and employed in Japan, all the while pretending that they are about to return to their homeland, which few had actually visited and even fewer spoke its language fluently?

Besides the Hitachi case, the 1977 special issue includes articles on Zainichi, discrimination in Japanese society, ethnic Korean pride, and the Japanese welfare system. Paradoxically but predictably, Japanese authors (or at least those with Japanese names) wrote all the Zainichi-related articles. In contrast, the lead article by Kang Je'on (1977b:32) remains on a familiar terrain: "The vast majority of Koreans in Japan are in Japanese society but rather than having relationships with Japanese people their lives are based on deep ethnic ties." He proceeds to criticize those who deviate from the "reality" of ethnic solidarity and the goal of national unification. After two pages excoriating deviations from the editorial line, Kang elaborates on his favored themes of Asian geopolitics and Korean unification. In an article devoted to the Korean presence in Japan, he can only reprise the central concerns of homeland politics.

By the third special issue on Zainichi (no.18, summer 1979), however, the editorial tone shifts. Kang has apparently changed his mind. Claiming that he had bemoaned as early as 1955 the paucity of research on Zainichi activism, he declares his empathy to second- and third-generation Koreans in Japan: "Between the idea and the reality many [second- and third-generation Koreans in Japan] are living with many problems that are not understood by their comrades in the homeland or by first-generation Koreans in Japan" (Kang J. 1979:59). In his conclusion, Kang expresses his hope that the journal will provide more space for members of the younger generation to articulate their feelings and to generate constructive debates about their dual identity.

In the same issue, after observing the demographic shift in the Korean community from a population of Koreans born in Korea to that of Koreans born in Japan, Kim Sokpom describes the struggles of two young Zainichi men. One seeks to become a lawyer without relinquishing his South Korean citizenship, and the other, who had been arrested for burglary, seeks to avoid his deportation. Kim is wary of asserting a minority or diasporic consciousness, however. He observes that the travails of Japanese-born Koreans do not make them part of an ethnic minority. He steadfastly valorizes unification as the ultimate goal of ethnic Koreans. Yet he also goes on to note that one cannot understand Koreans in Japan without understanding the circumstances of their lives in Japan. He asserts that Zainichi is itself a form of unification and underscores the inevitable dialectic between the struggles for rights in Japan and the political agitation for Korean unification.

As Kang's and Kim's 1979 articles suggest, *Kikan sanzenri* had made a significant shift by its fourth year of publication, which was confirmed by the next special issue on Zainichi (no.24, winter 1980). Kang's opening essay touches once again on the inevitable increase in the Japanese-born Koreans and their preference for permanent residency and even naturalization. Although he remains passionately devoted to unification and rebukes the tendency toward assimilation, he stresses the unique existence and perspective of the Korean diaspora in Japan. He finds it "miraculous" that the Zainichi have maintained their ethnic identity in Japan: "Within Japanese society, suffering from all sorts of travail, Koreans have made their livelihood by their own power" (Kang J. 1980:37). By 1981, Yi Sinhi (1981), who had shown very little interest in Zainichi issues, reveals his deep interest in immigration law—a quintessentially diasporic topic—and Zainichi life.

The fourth special issue includes five pieces written by "ordinary" Koreans in Japan. Like the panel discussion in the first special issue, they demonstrate a wide continuum of Zainichi experiences ("Watashi" 1980). Whereas one man describes his *Heimat [furusato]* as the view of Mt. Fuji (an archetypal image of Japan), another expresses his desire to bury his father's bones in his native province in southern Korea. Two women ponder their decision to learn Korean. Another woman hopes to write a history of Korean women. Although they refer to Korean heritage, they also stress their deep roots in Japan. Repatriation and unification are elided as they evince at best weak homeland orientation. They interrogate identity, discrimination, generational conflict, and related ethnic and diasporic issues.

Kikan sanzenri continued to publish many articles by and on Zainichi until it ceased publication in 1987. Yet the most notable fact is the *belatedness* of the journal's interest in diasporic existence and concerns. The linguistic shift—from Korean to Japanese—had been completed at the latest by the mid-1960s. There was obviously no question that it would be written exclusively in Japanese. However much the original editorial board members were interested in ancient Korean civilization or contemporary Asian geopolitics, they were undoubtedly aware of the demographic transition in the ethnic community and the heightened interest in the present and future of Korean lives in Japan. Why then did they bypass diasporic issues at the outset?

The editorial board members maintained homeland orientation and exilic identity. As I argued in chapter 1, the preponderant fact of geopolitics relegated subnational concerns about gender or generation as peripheral and trivial. The political space of Zainichi was restricted to the two ethnic organizations allied with the two regimes. The editorial board members had split from their association with Sōren but they were unable to become a third force. Instead, they were allied with the larger leftist, progressive force in mainstream Japanese society. *Kikan sanzenri* was, in effect, a regionally focused journal that was otherwise indistinguishable from other leftist Japanese journals, such as *Sekai*. Although the editors of *Kikan sanzenri* acknowledged the difficulties of unification, they remained stubbornly committed to it, which justified their focus on geopolitics and homeland affairs.

Enmeshed in Cold War politics, the founders of *Kikan sanzenri* not only valorized geopolitics but also validated the monoethnic ideology of Japan (and of Korea). By preempting ethnic or diasporic politics in Japan, they unwittingly entrenched monoethnic ideology. Yet in part because of the impetus from the readership—many of them second- and third-generation Zainichi—the journal shifted slowly but steadily toward Zainichi issues and concerns. *Kikan sanzenri* thereby unintentionally contributed to the formation of Korean diasporic identity in Japan. Zainichi concerns subsequently would become central in two journals, *Kikan seikyū* and *Horumon bunka*, that began publication in 1989 and 1991, respectively. As descendants of *Kikan sanzenri*, they expressed the diversification and the crystallization of Zainichi identity.

DISCRIMINATED FINGERS AND LOST NAMES

By the early 1980s Zainichi had become a "problem" that was no longer ignored outright or discussed *sotto voce*. As books and articles on Zainichi proliferated, the anti-fingerprinting (or fingerprinting refusal) movement sought to transform the gaze of disrecognition to that of recognition. Recognition entailed not only distinction—the categorical autonomy of Zainichi from Japanese and Koreans—but also connection—the solidarity of diasporic Koreans in Japan. That is, recognition at once cleaved Zainichi from Korea and Japan (repatriation or naturalization) and allowed Zainichi to cleave together. Zainichi movements and discourses transformed the population into a peoplehood identity that was also acknowledged and accepted by Japanese people.

The anti-fingerprinting movement began with a "one-man rebellion" by the Zainichi Tokyo resident Han Chongsok in September 1980. The narrow contention was that forced fingerprinting *[shimon ōnatsu]* during alien registration was a violation of human rights and dignity. The wider concern was the systematic discrimination against Zainichi and other non-ethnic Japanese people in Japan. If Pak Chonsok's suit against Hitachi had opened the possibility of legal struggles to combat disrecognition, then the anti-fingerprinting movement denoted its popular political realization.

For Zainichi and other long-term foreign residents in Japan, a passport was necessary to navigate life within Japan: the Certificate of Alien Registration *[gaitōshō]*. Often reviled as "dog tags," Zainichi noncompliance frequently led to harassment and even arrest by police officers. As one Zainichi man said in the mid-1980s: "One thing I hate most about being Zainichi is the fear of police harassment. If I forget my 'dog tag,' then I am a goner *[hotoke*, or Buddha]." In a scatological scene in Yan Sogiru's *Takushī kyōsōkyoku* [Taxi rhapsody, 1981], a barroom brawl ends in a police arrest. After finding two ethnic Koreans without their certificates, police officers threaten them with arrest and deportation. One of the Zainichi men ponders: "The memory, attentiveness, and behavior themselves of Zainichi are already seen as criminal" (Yan 1987:68). The other merely daubs his fresh defecation over all the police files: Zainichi shit over bureaucratic bullshit.

The certificate was a reminder at once of Zainichi criminality and illegitimacy. The mandatory nature of the "dog tag" and the literally incriminating character of fingerprinting were often at the forefront of Zainichi consciousness as emblems of Japanese disrecognition. The Japanese authorities claimed the authority of science—Henry Faulds had developed the first classificatory system of fingerprinting while working in Japan (Cole 2001:73)—to justify fingerprinting for identification purposes. The inevitable question was why Zainichi needed to be identified beyond the ways in which ethnic Japanese were identified. The all-too-common answer pointed at once to the Japanese presumption of Korean criminality and the Zainichi presumption of Japanese tyranny. Han Chongsok, the "one-man rebel," observed that the Alien Registration Law was "nothing but an instrument to suppress Zainichi" (Han-san ikka 1985:52).

The growing incidence of civil disobedience—refusing to be fingerprinted during alien registration—generated media coverage and even popular debate. As one middle-aged Japanese woman told me at the time: "If Koreans don't like discrimination, then why don't they [fingerprinting refuseniks] go home?" The compelling xenophobic logic had been shared by the mainline ethnic organizations. The acceptance of Zainichi status as foreign explains in large part the general compliance with forced fingerprinting in particular and alien registration law in general. Coming to terms with their present and future in Japan, however, some Zainichi, with others sympathetic to their cause and to general human rights and dignity, engaged in the symbolic and legal struggle to resist the fingerprinting. I attended several rallies to support the fingerprinting refusal movement in the mid-1980s and was struck most by the preponderance of second- and third-generation Zainichi in their twenties and thirties. Most of them said that they were seeking at once to eradicate their shame—being a member of an inferior group or hiding one's ancestry—and to assert their ethnic pride as Zainichi.

The anti-fingerprinting movement generated momentum through the 1980s, gaining the support of the major ethnic organizations. As I noted in chapter 3, Mindan and Sōren tentatively began to engage with diasporic concerns from the 1970s. In the last three months of 1983, Mindan waged a campaign that collected 1.8 million signatures—90 percent of them by ethnic Japanese—protesting the fingerprinting (Ōnuma 1993:277). Sōren also entered the campaign. Eminent Zainichi intellectuals, such as Kim

Sokpom, became "refuseniks." Kim stressed the unification of Korea as the ultimate goal (Kim Sokpom 1993:218), but the momentum of the movement prompted him to participate in a domestic ethnic movement. The emergence of Zainichi concerns in *Kikan sanzenri* discussed above is inextricable from the ferment of Zainichi political activism.

The resistance to fingerprinting was bound up with other means of asserting ethnic existence. As early as the late 1960s there were sporadic initiatives to use ethnic Korean names in Osaka, and individual "comings-out"—to use one's "real name" *[honmyō]* instead of Japanese name *[tsūmei]*—occurred throughout the 1970s (Kim I. 1978:224–27; Maekawa 1981:41). As a 1970s pamphlet stated, "the use of *tsūmei* itself is clearly a form of ethnic discrimination" (Nihon no Gakkō n.d.:3). Arguing against the practical benefits of passing, activists sought not only to promote ethnic pride but also to extirpate discrimination. The "real name" initiative marked the limits of passing in the struggle for recognition. As one man told me, he decided to use his real, Korean name in high school because he wanted to claim pride in his ancestry. Son Puja (2007:162–76) reclaimed her "real name" as she became involved in a Kawasaki group to fight ethnic discrimination. For most ethnic Koreans, "coming out" would occur either at graduation from high school or at college, where ethnic groups and friends, as well as progressive climate, would encourage and support "real name declaration" *[honmyō sengen]*. Another dimension of the "real name declaration" movement was the use of Korean pronunciation. In 1975, a Zainichi minister requested the Korean reading of his Korean name, but NHK, the main television network, refused and used the Japanese reading (Taguchi 1984:160). It was only in 1983 when the South Korean singer Cho Yong-p'il was introduced by that name that NHK had relented from its rigid practice of using the Japanese reading of Chinese characters in Korean names (Taguchi 1984:159).

The "real name" initiative was diffuse and sporadic; its first organizational manifestation appeared belatedly in 1985 when the Association to Take Back Ethnic Name [Minzokumei o Torimodosukai] was formed in Osaka (Ijichi 1994:41, 97). One of its members exemplifies some of the background that spurred Zainichi activists in both the anti-fingerprinting and "real name" movements. Pak Sil was born in Kyoto in 1944. Haunted by discrimination and passing in Japan, he believed that Korea signified inferiority. His sister's job offer was rescinded after her school reported her Korean name to the company. In order to marry his Japanese girlfriend, he was naturalized. Learning about Japanese imperialism, he realized that he had committed a major fault *[ayamachi]* and betrayed his mother. After his child was born, he decided to assert his Korean identity. "Nationality is Japanese, name is Japanese, I didn't know Korean, and I don't know the taste of kimchi. I have nothing in the form of ethnicity" (Pak S. 1990:15). He therefore resolved to learn the Korean language and to participate in Korean cultural activities. Although other Zainichi did not welcome him— he was even accused of being a spy—he participated in the movement to use ethnic names as Japanese. By 1987 he won a court victory to use his Korean name. Pak Sil thereby achieved the hitherto oxymoronic idea of being a Japanese citizen with a Korean name. Similarly, in 1989, Yun Choja, who had grown up with her Japanese mother's name as a Japanese citizen, won the right to use an ethnic name: "If there were no discrimination, my father would have been legally married and I would have my father's surname. . . . Because there was discrimination, I became a 'bastard' [*shiseiji*] and was given Japanese *koseki* [household registry; and effectively nationality]" (Fukuoka and Tsujiyama 1991a:59).

The mid-1980s ethnic political mobilization capped at least a decade's worth of the Zainichi civil rights movement. If Pak's 1970 employment discrimination suit was the first well-publicized use of legal mechanisms to protect and advance Zainichi rights, it was followed by Kim Kyongdok's effort to become an attorney and Kim Hyondon's struggle to receive national pension. There were other, less-heralded attempts to protect and promote ethnic Koreans' rights and benefits in Japan, from the establishment of Seikyūsha in Kawasaki in the 1970s to the rise of the "rights and benefits" movement by Mindan in the late 1970s (Kim Yunjon 2007:70–78; Zai Nihon 1978:18–21). Numerous local initiatives—ranging from Osaka teachers' 1971 proclamation against ethnic discrimination and assimilationist education (Kangaerukai 1971:1) to progressive local authorities' attempts to ensure access to welfare benefits and public housing in the mid-1970s (Hoshino 2005:247–55)—bound concerned Japanese citizens with ethnic Korean individuals and organizations. By the early 1980s, Osaka, among other local authorities, started to hire Korean nationals for civil service positions—a right that was denied immediately after the end of the war. Along with the anti-fingerprinting movement and the effort to use Korean names, some sought to create a Koreatown—emulating Chinatowns and Koreatowns in the United States—in Kawasaki, whereas others sought to win local suffrage rights for Zainichi (Kanai 1997:162). Each step of the way, the Zainichi legal and political struggle for legitimacy and recognition pricked the conscience of ethnic Koreans and ethnic Japanese. Zainichi disrecognition in Japanese public life was clearly in retreat by the 1980s.

ZAINICHI IDEOLOGY

In the context of ethnic ferment, there was something close to a party line that emerged in the 1970s that I call Zainichi ideology. Informed by an internal critique of Sōren ideology, it sought to supplant the ideology that had dominated the Zainichi population in the 1950s and 1960s. The notion that Zainichi constituted a relatively autonomous community was alien to the dominant ethnic organization's homeland orientation, which, as I argued in chapter 2, was a systematic misrecognition of Zainichi actuality. The disjuncture is encapsulated in the question of language. Against Sōren's espousal of the mother tongue, the primary language of the postwar Zainichi population had always been Japanese, as evinced by early postwar ethnic Korean literary periodicals such as *Chōsen bungei* and *Minshu bungei* (cf. Takayanagi 2002:59; Nakane 2004:266–68). The subjugation of literature to politics, which included the question of language, incited some of the earliest resistance to Sōren by the late 1950s, for instance among writers around the journal *Jindare* (Yan 2001:70–72). *Kikan sanzenri* continued in spirit the work of *Jindare*, but these critics' intellectual formation and ethnonational worldview were profoundly shaped by Sōren and would leave their mark in Zainichi ideology. Like its leading proponents, men of the left such as Kim Sokpom (2001) and Lee Hoesung (2002), Zainichi ideology retained a strong link to homeland even as it came to embrace and at times celebrate the Zainichi population's place in Japan.

Zainichi ideology fractured almost from the moment it crystallized not only because of the impossibility of formulating an essentialized identity but also because it was an intellectual construct that faced the withering criticism of rapid obsolescence and ultimate irrelevance. As a product of parthenogenesis—albeit with the long genealogy of Sōren and ex-Sōren intellectuals—it was disengaged not only from the dominant ethnic organizations but also from the experiences and longings of the people who sought to counter Japanese disrecognition, such as those who participated actively in the fingerprinting refusal movement and the ethnic name movement. Zainichi ideologists retained faith in intellectuals as the secret legislators and representatives of the people when it was no longer fashionable or viable to do so in Japanese life.

Let me discuss the work of Yoon Keun Cha, born in 1944, because of its systematic and paradigmatic character. In *"Zainichi" o ikirutowa* [To live as Zainichi, 1992], Yoon locates the appearance of the very term Zainichi in the late 1970s. It "has been recognized as a particular philosophy [*shisō*], demonstrating a young generation's way of living and ideology, including historical meaning" (Yoon 1992:3). As "the historical product of Japanese rule of colonial Korea," that meaning is in a chronicle of vexing events from colonial rule, the division of the homeland, and the Korean War: "Up to today it is unhappiness itself. For the second- and third-generation Zainichi of today, the suffering and the sadness of poverty, losing the family, the inability to meet departed parents again constitute the heartache, which is nothing but 'chagrin' [*kuyashisa*]" (4). As colonial subjects and their descendants, Zainichi belong to the category of oppressed Third World people (cf. Ko 1998:58). Bereft of a stable home and a place of repose, they are also "liminal people" [*kyōkaijin*] (Yoon 1992:5). After criticizing Sōren and the unsavory character of South Korea in the 1960s and 1970s, he bemoans the division not only of the homeland but Zainichi society.

Yoon (60) defines the first generation as those "who spent their childhood in Korea and came to Japan before the defeat of Japan in August 1945. . . . In essence, the major part of their spiritual formation was 'Korea,' and not 'Japan' as 'imperial subject.' " The first generation was defined by "anti-Japanese sentiments of the colonial period" and "strong ethnic consciousness" (63). Reprising the received Zainichi historiography—itself pioneered by intellectuals critical of Sōren—he (71) characterizes Koreans in colonial Japan as being "pushed into the context of absolute discrimination in terms of ethnicity and class . . . [as] low-waged workers at the very bottom of Japanese society." Japan, in short, was "hell" (86). Living in Korean ghettoes [*Chōsenjin buraku*]—he identifies the first-generation as "the period of 'Korean ghetto' " (92)—they longed for ancestral homeland but lived with "discrimination and oppression" (72). The heroic narrative begins, then, from their suffering and "naked labor" and supported by the philosophy [*shisō*] of "work twice or thrice as hard as Japanese, don't give in to discrimination, protect your rights, let's create school, let's unify homeland" (93). For them, "ancestral land [*sokoku*] or ethnicity, *Heimat* [*kokyō*], family were dream and hope. . . . That's all they had" (94). In fact, many equated ethnic organization, especially Sōren, with ethnicity and homeland. Although he acknowledges diversity (65, 77–78)—the Japanized Koreans who supported the Japanese war effort and the entrepreneurially successful Mindan members—he is committed to the singular narrative of exploitation, suffering, and resistance. He can only describe the first-generation Zainichi "who were forced to remain in Japan" as having led lives of serious "suffering in the situation of Japanese political and economic confusion" (79). When he points to the problems of the Zainichi community, such as patriarchy and the dysfunctional family, he is quick to trace their cause to Japanese imperialism (87).

Generational transition began in the early 1970s. The idea of "to live as Zainichi" criticized the first generation's homeland orientation and emerged as a self-conscious appellation in the late 1970s (238). Recognizing that there was no realistic possibility of return in the immediate future but insisting on the impossibility of naturalization, Yoon (1987:196) had earlier advocated a "permanent" status of permanent residency. Neither Japanese nor Korean, Zainichi constitute a relatively autonomous diasporic culture (cf. Kim Sokpom 2004:196). The category of the diaspora is appealing precisely because it points to the possibility of an independent existence. Zainichi ideology, then, is a form of diasporic nationalism.

Yoon (239–40) is acutely conscious of the economic diversity of younger Zainichi and their contrast to the first generation: better educated but largely ignorant of the Korean language, increasingly atomized and fragmented rather than being concentrated in the Korean ghettoes, and much more diverse than the largely monochromatic first generation (cf. Lee B. 2005). He speculates that Zainichi consciousness is based less on genealogy or tradition and more on the "strongly rooted discrimination of Japanese society" (240). "To live as 'Zainichi' is to live in opposition to discrimination" (240), though he again traces its cause to Japanese imperialism (249).

Yoon fears the lure of assimilation, especially for the third-generation. Whether for Lee Yangji (discussed in chapter 2) or Kyō Nobuko (discussed below), ethnicity pales in significance to the self that is common to both Japanese and Koreans (268). By ignoring the essentially historical and political character of Zainichi existence, he argues (268) that the third-generation philosophy strengthens the exclusionary character of Japan. Rather, it is imperative to incorporate the "consciousness of misfortune" [fugū no ishiki]: the population's origins in Japanese imperialism and its destination in Korean unification.

Unification remains the essential goal for Zainichi in particular and Koreans in general (cf. Hyon 1983:168). Some Zainichi intellectuals insist on the category Chōsen as a nationality. As Kim Sokpom (2001:53) argues, unification is the "ultimate task" of Zainichi and the advocacy of Chōsen nationality is an expression of the Zainichi commitment to unified Korea (Kim Sokpom 2001:115). Knowing full well that such a country does not exist, a character in Lee Hoesung's story "Ikitsumodoritsu" admits that it is "simply a sign," but one that seeks to "transcend the era of division [bundan jidai] (Lee H. 2005a:37). The commitment to unification in theory is in turn related to greater ideals that were once associated with Marxism and communism, such as peace and progress. Rather grandiosely, Zainichi ideology strives for the ethnic sublime: the desire for praxis and ultimate universalism.

In summary, Yoon suggests two basic preconditions for being Zainichi: first, "to think about the meaning of being Zainichi, to protect the pride of ethnicity, and strive to gain citizens' rights"; and, second, "to be involved in some way in unification" (14). To be Zainichi means to reflect on Zainichi-ness and to seek unification: to retain historical memory and critique of Japanese imperialism, to sustain oppositional consciousness that is tantamount to anti-Japanese sentiments, and to resist assimilation and naturalization. Zainichi ideology inherited Sōren critique of Japanese imperialism and fervent essentialist ethnonationalism, but rejected its partisan loyalty to the North and homeland orientation.

Yoon's formulation of Zainichi ideology does not command universal assent, but many of his points were reiterated by leading Zainichi intellectuals in the last quarter of the twentieth century. An overview of Zainichi history, for example, discusses the "common consciousness" forged by the historical experience of liberation and independence, the shared desire to repatriate and to build a new country, and the overarching goal of unification (Kim Chanjung 2004a:3). Beyond a consensus on Zainichi historiography—the narrative of forced migration, exploitation and discrimination, and heroic resistance—there are shared political goals. In seeking an alternative beyond repatriation (at least in the short run) and assimilation, the impetus is to create, promote, and protect a distinct Zainichi culture. Sustaining ethnocultural pride means rejecting repatriation and assimilation.

ZAINICHI IDEOLOGY AND ITS DISCONTENTS

Zainichi ideology is a form of diasporic nationalism. Like Japanese or South Korean monoethnic nationalism, it envisions the ethnonational group as homogeneous. Somewhat analogous to Gilles Deleuze and Félix Guattari's (1975:chap.3) characterization of minor literature, diasporic nationalism dwells not only within major or majority nationalism but also accentuates the place of the political and endows each individual utterance with the weight of the collective. It is this conflation of the individual and the collective—ontogeny recapitulating phylogeny—and the inevitably political nature of Zainichi existence that legitimate propounders and protectors of Zainichi identity to prescribe and proscribe Zainichi belief and action.

As an ethnic imperative, Zainichi ideology defines the terms and theories of Zanichi identity. Private meditations necessarily draw on historically and sociologically given categories and concepts. The very prevalence of Zainichi identity rests on the dissemination of Zainichi as a category of both population and thought. There are, then, inevitably ethnic entrepreneurs or identity intellectuals who propose what it means to a representative member of the proposed group. They are *tuteurs* of the people: at once teaching them and protecting them. Inventors and guardians of identity prescribe and proscribe actions and beliefs, even going so far as to judge who belongs in the name of the people. In the case of formal organizations such as Sōren, there were explicit norms and institutional means to mandate conformity. Dissidents were reprimanded and even expelled. In the case of Zainichi ideology, however, there were no formal organizations to articulate beliefs or to supervise behavior. Instead, identity intellectuals spoke and wrote on behalf of their co-ethnics to the mainstream Japanese media and organizations, which in turn purveyed their ideas to the co-ethnic audience. Zainichi ideology was widely discussed and disseminated in informal clubs and groups or by isolated individual readers, most frequently in universities (e.g., Kyō 1987:115; Kang S. 2004:88). The declining hold of the mainline ethnic organizations generated an audience to receive the reformed ideology of Zainichi identity.

In promoting diasporic nationalism, Zainichi ideology erects a prison-house of Zainichi-ness, a collective confinement to ethnic essentialism. Beyond establishing the fundamental pillars of Zainichi identity, it also projects an idealized Zainichi self that mirrors Zainichi historiography: the dialectics of oppression and resistance, poverty and struggle. It also prescribes, like Sōren ideology, cultural nationalism, such as learning Korean language, history, and culture, and retains instinctive suspicion of Japan and discourages assimilation.

Whatever the individual articulation of the ideal Zainichi self, it is clear that many fell short of it. It was something of a common sense among Zainichi in the 1970s and 1980s that there was a natural hierarchy. In one classification, the top are the activists, with a command of Korean; the middle are those with ethnic pride and a knowledge of Zainichi history and ideology; and the bottom are the vast majority, with Japanese names (cf. Kanai 1997:170). In one of Lee Yangji's (1981:167) earliest essays, she writes of "not knowing true poverty, the shame of not knowing." Reminiscent of Simone Weil, Lee in fact confesses her deviation from what she takes to be the prototypical Zainichi experience of poverty and discrimination that she missed as a middle-class, naturalized Japanese girl. Even as Zainichi may have faced harassment from classmates or police officers, the specter of *Panchoppari*—of being incomplete, or failed, Zainichi—weighed heavily, at times forcefully pounded in by bullying fellow Zainichi students at Sōren schools (Shin 2003:55–57). Many Zainichi, in effect, failed to be Korean or Zainichi. Language, as we have seen, was an insurmountable hurdle for many. The second-generation Zainichi Kim Hiro (1968:103), who "speaks Japanese better than Japanese" but did not know any Korean, regarded his "generation" as a "deformity." If the Korean language proved to be an unrealistic parameter of Zainichi-ness, then the critical criteria were the adoption of one's ethnic name and the resistance to naturalization. The presumption that any "decent" Zainichi should use one's Korean name led the critic Takeda Seiji (1983:228) to use a Japanese pseudonym: his act of resistance to Zainichi ideology. Kyō Nobuko (1987:115) found the argument against naturalization—the impossibility of maintaining ethnic Korean, or Zainichi, identity as a Japanese citizen—deeply problematic.

Zainichi ideology valorizes and validates some people at the expense of others. Prewar, pro-Japanese ethnic Koreans are uniformly reviled, as are those who do not condemn the evils of Japanese imperialism. Ethnic Koreans who have become Japanese citizens are also beyond the pale. Just as the postwar ethnic Korean organizations sought to distance themselves from the trials of Ri Chin'u and Kim Hiro, Zainichi ideologists criticize or exclude those who do not fit into their scheme of Zainichi history and identity. The hold of Zainichi ideology can be seen in the received understanding of Zainichi literature, which almost always excludes the author Yasumoto Sueko, even though her *Nianchan* (1958) is the book by a Zainichi writer on Zainichi life that has reached the largest Japanese readership. Japanese literary scholars, to be sure, make a cardinal distinction between "pure" *[jun]* and "popular" *[taishū]* literature; *Nianchan*, if only because of its vast readership, is not really literature in this line of thinking. Yet it is nonetheless surprising to find a systematic effacement of the best-selling postwar book by a Zainichi author. Much the same can be said about Ijūin Shizuka's Bildungsroman *Kaikyō* trilogy [Strait, 1991–2000]. Although peopled by non-Japanese characters and written by a self-identified ethnic Korean, Ijūin's oeuvre is usually excluded from the discussion of Zainichi literature because of its overtly apolitical nature and popular orientation. The mystery writer Rei Ra is similarly excluded from the ambit of Zainichi literature. The valorization of the political and the collective eschewed the stress on the personal and the private: hence, the critical praise for the work of Kim Sokpom and Lee Hoesung over that of Kin Kakuei. Not surprisingly, the champion of Kin's work has been Takeda

Seiji, a self-conscious rebel against Zainichi ideology. Yet those who remained faithful to Sōren, such as Yi Unjik (1967–68) and his epic trilogy on the politics of Korean liberation, are also neglected. Narrow is the gate to Zainichi-ness.

As a form of diasporic nationalism, Zainichi ideology, like Sōren ideology, rejects the category of ethnic minority. Sōren ideology postulated that ethnic Koreans were to repatriate. Zainichi ideology does not share the ideology of return (at least in the short run) but it also rejects Japan as *Heimat*. Indeed, anti-Japanese sentiments may be more fiercely expressed among Zainichi ideologists than Sōren ideologists, presumably because Sōren ideology beckoned Zainichi to look to Korea whereas Zainichi ideology forces Zainichi to consider Japan as a more or less permanent domicile. Recall Kim Sokpom, discussed in chapter 2, who regarded anti-Japanese sentiments as a critical pillar of his life philosophy (cf. Kim Sokpom 2001:48–52). Suh Kyung Sik (2002) characterizes Zainichi as "half" refugees in the title of his book. Elsewhere, he categorizes them as "nation" rather than "ethnicity" (175). Beyond the conceptual confusion, the category of ethnic minority is rejected in order to avoid the incorporation of Zainichi in Japanese society. Yet the ideological resistance faces the recalcitrant reality of cultural assimilation. The similar distance between ideology and reality can be seen in Zainichi ideology's valorization of unification. As we saw in the *Kikan sanzenri* discussions among Zainichi youths, they evinced almost no interest in the issue as early as the 1970s.

The misrecognition characteristic of Zainichi ideology, with its essentialist categories, extends to its genealogy and development. Generational distinctions and transitions are Zainichi clichés, which of course means that the thesis has a grain of truth. Most obviously, first-generation Zainichi with roots to the Korean peninsula—and the mastery of Korean language—are differentiated from second-generation Zainichi without any experience growing up in Korea or having Korean as the natal tongue (cf. Yan 1999:27–28). Yet these schematic classifications obfuscate more than illuminate. Kim Dalsu, born in colonial Korea in 1919, in fact had no choice but to write in Japanese. Kim Sokpom was born only six years later but in Osaka. Though Lee Hoesung and Kin Kakuei are coevals—born in 1935 and 1938, respectively—their attitudes toward ethnic identification could hardly be called alike. Kin, as I argued in the previous chapter, presciently pointed to a position beyond repatriation or naturalization and uncannily illuminated the instability or even the impossibility of solid and stable identity. At the same time, Lee Hoesung sounded nationalist and socialist tunes. Yet one does not necessarily reprise youthful melodies. By the mid-1990s, as we saw in chapter 2, Lee registered completely different notes, singing paeans to diasporic solidarity. A few years later, he became a naturalized South Korean. Yan Sogiru's (2007:85) thinly veiled fictional double muses, "I was born in Japan, a second-generation Zainichi who grew up in Japan," but is baffled to be taken as a first-generation figure. He concedes that perhaps he is close to the first generation, though he does not speak Korean well and feels viscerally different from them. Concrete but fluctuating self-conceptions and the inevitable diversity of the population hew poorly to the line of Zainichi-ness adumbrated by Zainichi ideology.

ZAINICHI IDEOLOGY, ZAINICHI DIVERSITY

Against diversity and dynamism, Zainichi ideology posed a party line that was impervious to deviations and transformations in Zainichi thinking about themselves and their places in Japan. Formulated as it was by Sōren-influenced Zainichi intellectuals, Zainichi ideology reproduced the chasm we saw in *Kikan sanzenri* between its editors and its younger readership. Quite simply, the majority of the Zainichi by the late 1970s did not belong to Sōren; they also had little interest in homeland politics. The modal Zainichi existence by then was not one of pathetic poverty and corrosive disrecognition. Far from being a solidaristic and homogeneous population, Zainichi were separated and diverse.

Ancestry is a rather thin and fragile basis to build an identity and a culture. Hence, the stress remained very much on imagined commonalities, such as the history of enforced migration, the sociology of ethnic discrimination, and the political ideal of unification. Yet a more solid, thick foundation for identification was lacking. In the prewar period, Korean language was the lingua franca among immigrants who lived in relatively isolated communities. In the immediate postwar decades, ethnic organizations, especially Sōren, provided the infrastructure to protect their rights or facilitate sociality and uplift. By the 1970s, however, language or community, religion or culture did not unite ethnic Koreans. Hence, shards of the remembered past and the declining but undeniable reality of discrimination constituted Zainichi solidarity. Yet the path of ex-Sōren intellectuals and movement participants was often orthogonal to that of the silent majority who were neither professional intellectuals nor committed activists. There is more: whereas the Sōren leadership could legitimate, whether through North Korea or itself, its right to represent the membership and at a stretch the Zainichi population, there was no compelling rationale for Zainichi ideologists to represent the Zainichi population. Those who grew up before the war were, with some frequency, unschooled and even illiterate. They may be highly articulate and eloquent but, whether by inclination, habit, or force, they rarely expressed their idiosyncratic outlooks ahead of those of the mainline ethnic organizations. In contrast, those who came of age in the 1960s and later were not only schooled and literate but—sharing in the prevailing Japanese belief in democratic rights and individual dignity—were willing and capable of expressing their own views. They could represent themselves.

Recent Zainichi narratives corroborate the systematic deviation of Zainichi voices from Zainichi ideology. They are exemplary not in the sense of expressing a random or representative sample, or of being the best and the most noble expressions of Zainichi people, but, rather, because they articulate individual experiences without excessive recourse to preconceived categories or received formulas.

Hwang Mingi grew up in a poor area of Osaka notable for a concentration of ethnic Koreans. Living in a tenement house [*nagaya*] in an ethnic enclave, his family and their neighbors experienced a strong sense of community, remarkably devoid of a sense of victimization or of what some social scientists call the culture of poverty. He is critical of poverty tourists, who portray the Korean neighborhood as a site of otherness. Beyond the conglomeration of ethnic Koreans, unlike Chinatown in Yokohama or Harlem in New York, "the town has no special characteristics" (Hwang 1993:5). For him, the area is simply where he grew up and for which he has fond memories.

Hwang nowhere discusses his Korean or Zainichi identity, but his childhood cannot be understood apart from the situation and concern of the Zainichi population. The news of the 1958 Komatsugawa Incident deeply disturbs his father, and affects him and his buddies enough to stop them when they see the image of Ri Chin'u on television in the streets. Teachers in his school appear to know the real (Korean) names of Hwang and his friends, even though they use Japanese names. Although the four "heroes" of his childhood are all ethnic Koreans—"Queen" Misora Hibari (singer), "Emperor" Kaneda Masaichi (baseball star), "Don" Yanagigawa Jirō (a local yakuza boss), and "Japan's brilliant star" Rikidōzan (wrestling champion)—they are not explicitly identified as being of Korean descent (145). It is difficult to discern whether they are heroes because of their Korean ethnicity, or because they are able to succeed in "ordinary" Japanese society in spite of their ethnicity. Certainly, the fact of Korean descent marks the lives of Hwang and his friends. One boyhood acquaintance takes part in the repatriation project, another commits suicide (possibly over the breakup of a relationship, which may have been due to his Korean descent), and yet another joins an ethnic Korean yakuza.

Nonetheless, Zainichi life is immersed in the larger Japanese society. Popular culture references in fact would not have distinguished Hwang and his friends from most other Japanese youths at the time. They constantly talk about the popular superhero series *Gekkō kamen* [Moonlight mask] and Hollywood movies and stars such as Elizabeth Taylor and Audrey Hepburn. Explicitly Korean names and events are "foreign" to them: the North Korean Foreign Minister Nam Il becomes "nameru" [to lick or, as slang, to make fun of]. Even the adoration of violence and the allure of gang life give way to the valorization of the intellect and educational attainment in the context of "the extinction of 'dirtiness' and 'poverty'" in the neighborhood in particular and Japan in general during the era of rapid economic growth (172). From their seemingly unpromising beginnings as juvenile delinquents, some of Hwang's friends become successful: one becomes a medical doctor, Hwang becomes an "intellectual of sorts" (205). As one of his friends tells Hwang (198): "At the funeral, I felt first that I am not Korean [*Chōsenjin*]. And confirmed that I don't want to and couldn't die like my father. . . . I haven't chosen Japan. I merely ceased being Korean [*Kankokujin*]."

Having come of age in the late 1950s, Hwang and his friends are unquestionably Zainichi, even as meditations on Zainichi identity remain peripheral. He claims that he is far from special; he was neither physically powerful nor intellectually brilliant. His childhood is characterized by experiences of boyhood solidarity—jokes and pranks. Growing up in an ethnic neighborhood, he experiences Korean and Japanese people and cultures. Yet when he returns to his hometown, he finds massive changes in the neighborhood, which is replete with "new Zainichi from South Korea and Japanese people with Korean interests" (201). This disappearance of the past is the background of Gen Getsu's "Kage no sumika" [The habitat of shadows, 1999], where the patriarch is one of the few prewar Koreans left and the past is literally crumbling (cf. Ryang 2002:8, 17–18). Yet, as Hwang (206) realizes, what remains are uncertain recollections: "I learned that my memory of place names, personal names, and of the time was almost completely unreliable."

Unlike Hwang, Kyō Nobuko was reared in an affluent Yokohama household. As a child, she had virtually no knowledge of the Korean language, very little familiarity with Korean culture, and little contact with other ethnic Koreans. Celebrating New Year's Day with her ethnic Japanese husband, she can only count the Korean-style rice cake and a diluted form of ancestor worship *[chesa]* as marks of her Koreanness. She cannot, for example, answer elementary questions about Korean culture. She cannot, for that matter, eat "authentic" (i.e., spicy) Korean food.

Kyō cannot but ponder the meaning of being Zainichi (more accurately, *Zainichi Kankokujin*), but in temporally distinct ways. She harbored distinct emotional reactions to her ethnic identity. As a child, she was thrilled to learn that she was a "foreigner," but by the time she reaches fourth grade she reckons: "Perhaps it is a bad thing that I am Korean. Perhaps I should hide it" (Kyō 1987:55). She was never bullied in school, but she used a Japanese name. When her classmate suspects that she may be of Korean descent, she lies about being "mixed-blooded" *[hāfu]*, from a Korean father and Japanese mother. Slightly later, she begins to "avoid and forget" about South Korea and "becomes angry at Japanese" (58). By the time she is in high school, she feels close to but "fears that she would be beaten up" by fellow ethnic Korean high-school students (67). At the University of Tokyo, she uses her Korean name and becomes interested in Korean affairs and culture. However, she is alienated from the prevailing enthusiasm for Marxism, nationalism, and the "deification" of ethnicity. She disagrees with other Zainichi students who advocate unification and condemn assimilation.

Kyō's narrative places her apart from Koreans, Japanese, and Zainichi. She becomes "conscious of the long distance between South Korea and her" when she realizes that "surprisingly, the place name of my grandfather's place of origin has disappeared" (9). She is ignorant of both North and South Korea; both are "foreign countries" (140). She is comfortable in Japan but she can neither shed the past—stories of Japanese misdeeds toward South Koreans that her grandmother told her—nor stop worrying about the future—such as the possibility of worsening Japanese–South Korean relations. In between, her friends drop derogatory comments about Zainichi. She finds herself in trouble when she confronts the authorities without her Certificate of Alien Registration. Her desire to become a teacher is dashed when she realizes that non-Japanese nationals are excluded from the profession. She faces employment discrimination despite her stellar academic record as a graduate of the prestigious Law Faculty at the University of Tokyo. As much as she feels close to her ethnic Japanese husband, she is aware of how ignorant he is—and, by extension, other ethnic Japanese are—about such Zainichi issues as employment discrimination. Yet she cannot identify with other Zainichi students, especially those who are proud of their "ethnicity" *[minzoku]*. One of them exclaims: "I cannot forgive those who naturalize. They are not human beings. They shouldn't live" (115). She is aware that some Zainichi believe that, along with naturalization, "marrying Japanese is to betray ethnicity" (29), but she hesitates only briefly before marrying her Japanese husband.

Kyō's "policy is to live naturally without hiding my Zainichi status" (42). And she insists on the desirability of living "normally" *[futsū]*. "It is not my style to raise my voice in protest or to live quietly without saying anything. I don't pretend to be Japanese, and I don't stress my ethnicity. I want to lead an ordinary life in Japan as Zainichi *[Zainichi Kankokujin]*" (209). She goes so far as to regard her group as a "new species of humanity," despite her alienation from many other Zainichi youths. At one point, she regards the difference in their nationality as something akin to "being tall, looking good in green, having an extroverted personality" (17). Her attempt to downplay ethnic distance or to live "normally" *[futsū]* is problematic. If nothing else, her Tokyo University diploma makes her even more distinct from ordinary Japanese people than the fact of her Korean descent. She nonetheless insists on her identity as a not particularly exceptional individual. As in the title of her book, she is an "ordinary Zainichi," although she considers herself to be quite different from other Zainichi college students.

Yū Miri's 1997 narrative *Mizube no yurikago* [Cradle by the waterside] begins in doubt and ends by affirming the fictive nature of the past. She is born into a family of secrets; she is not sure of her father's age or whether her mother was born in Japan. Her parents' past is a "dark tunnel" that is closed on both ends by "silence" (Yū 1997:18). Her family life, which is a constant theme in her plays and stories, was tempestuous—a violent father, a mother who runs off with another man—but she acknowledges that she was loved by parents, even incurring her sister's envy. She grew up playing with Rika-chan dolls (Japanese Barbie dolls), but her childhood was marked by her exclusion from group life. Other pupils bullied her from early on, the first time in kindergarten when she came with a different hairstyle. In part she blames herself for being unfit for group life. "I was conceited and I thought that I was a chosen person. . . . I thought I was special" (45). At the same time, bullying seems inextricable from her Korean ancestry: "For me, bullying and kimchi are somehow linked" (61).

Yū characterizes herself as a runaway *[tōpōsha]*, as someone who flees not to hide but simply to run away (36). Her adolescence—though common enough among adolescents—is a series of shameful, embarrassing moments and memories. She is ashamed of her aunt, whom one of her friends mistakes for a beggar, as well as the meager lunch she takes to school. She is troubled by her mother taking up a lover and abandoning home for days at a time. Enrolling in a prestigious middle school at her mother's request, she merely yearns to leave. Although she finds friends from time to time, she feels closer to dead writers than to any living people. "I was closer to the dead than to the living. In my bag were books by [the poet] Nakahara Nakaya and [the novelist] Dazai Osamu, and I could only talk easily with the dead. The living inevitably hurt me, but the dead forgave and cured me" (122). She develops a crush on a classmate but is rebuffed: "I don't know what I wanted from her. It was not to become closer or to touch her body or to be touched. Thinking about it now, perhaps I was inviting her to die with me" (127). She "woke up every morning with self-hatred and regret. I didn't know what I hated and regretted but in any case I hated everything. I wanted to cut my ties to family and school and drop out of life" (136). The desire to drop out manifests itself in skipping school, running away from home, and attempting to kill herself. After she is expelled, she contemplates immigrating to the United States.

Yū's memoir is motivated by a long-standing desire to bury her past. When she moves from her elementary school, her homeroom teacher gives her an antique music box and a handkerchief. She buries them, because "I wanted to change, to become a different person. I didn't need souvenirs" (80). Certainly, there are many eminently forgettable memories: a neighbor who molests her, classmates who engage in vicious pranks, and other acts of inhumanity and betrayal. But she also writes in part because she wants to create her own "reality." Joining a theater company, she discovers the "possibility of rewriting my past" (178). She decided to write her memoir while in her twenties because she wanted to "leave herself far behind," to entomb the past (218). She ends on an ambiguous note: "everything is a fact, everything is a lie" (220). Her memoir is a "sedimentation of words" (220).

These narratives are Japanese not only in the (by no means trivial) sense that they are written in Japanese, but also in the deeper sense that they presume broad familiarity with Japanese culture. Precisely because popular-culture names, events, and objects are ephemeral and particular, they provide robust sources of identification with a concrete time and place. Furthermore, they exemplify Japanese cultural repertoire. As I argued in chapter 1, the postwar idea of cultural homogeneity valorized the ideal of normalness or ordinariness [*futsū*], at once an expression of egalitarianism and a rejection of prewar heroics. Kim Hyandoja (1988:3), for example, opens her book by stating that there is "nothing particularly special about my way of living or thinking. . . . I am a particularly ordinary [*goku futsū*] Zainichi." However far apart in their upbringing and outlook, Hwang and

Kyō both regard themselves as not just "ordinary" but "particularly ordinary." Around the time Kyō wrote her recollections, I was at a Tokyo restaurant where my affiliation with the University of Tokyo was mentioned. Middle-aged women in the next table promptly stopped their conversation, turned to me, and then begged me to tutor their children. My fifteen seconds' worth of celebrity expresses the unusually high regard in which that university was held in the postwar era. Hwang's childhood is also anything but "ordinary" for contemporary Japanese people (cf. Fukuoka and Tsujiyama 1991b:5). Only Yū is conscious of her difference and her alienation from group life, but her life is unusual from any perspective.

What in fact unites these three writers beyond their Japanese provenance? The pervasiveness of disrecognition seeps into various spheres of social life. But the reception of discrimination is far from uniform. Neither Hwang nor Kyō mentions being bullied. Although Yū is convinced that bullying and her Korean ancestry are intertwined, she is far from certain that ethnic discrimination is primary. Recall De Vos and Lee's (1981:375) generalization about Zainichi family alienation. Yū appears to be a paradigmatic case. The violent father is an enduring character type in Zainichi literature, but Yū's love for him differentiates him from Kin Kakuei's or Yan Sogiru's patriarchs. But Hwang's and Kyō's narratives do not fit very well into De Vos and Lee's scheme. Kyō's seems deviant precisely in achieving the exalted but rarely realized state of agape among family members.

The structure of biography is biology: a prosaic and predictable trajectory from birth to death. It would be odd indeed not to encounter numerous points of similarity among coevals in the same society. Yet diversity, not uniformity, marks the narratives. Consider the question of ethnic identity. Although Kyō struggles with it, she feels alienated from Zainichi who are passionate about Zainichi causes. Hwang, in contrast, is keenly aware of being Korean, but because he grew up in a Korean neighborhood he does not probe its significance. In a different way, Yū's sense of self literally makes her a character from a play, endowed with certain propensities, such as the desire to flee, but unmarked by her ethnic heritage or Japanese racism.

If we consider the impact of Korean or Japanese culture, then we again find no obvious commonality. In Hwang's world, Korean and Zainichi cultures and events appear here and there. In contrast, Kyō grew up ignorant of Korean and even Zainichi culture. Yū grew up playing with Rika-chan dolls and communicating with dead male Japanese writers. Although almost always described as a Zainichi writer, her literary ancestry betrays almost no Zainichi influence. Diversity also manifests itself in naming preferences. Hwang is a Korean pronunciation of a Korean name. Yū is a Japanese rendition of a Korean name. Kyō Nobuko has a Japanese reading of a Korean surname and a common Japanese first name (though possibly Korean) in Japanese pronunciation. Another woman uses the Korean reading of a Korean surname with a more or less purely Japanese first name: "although my identity is Korean, I am completely different from Koreans in homeland. I am Zainichi. I am almost like a different ethnicity. And I have Japanese nationality" (Fukuoka and Tsujiyama 1991a:45).

Hwang, Kyō, and Yū are Zainichi, but they reveal little commonality. Surely, we can seek their differences in part in their divergent backgrounds: gender, region, class, and so on. These social differences exist alongside different courses and contours of their lives. But this is precisely the point. Beyond the sheer diversity of Zainichi professions and personalities, genders and generations, likes and dislikes, we should not forget that an individual is neither unitary and homogeneous nor stationary and unchanging. Virginia Woolf (1928:278) observes in *Orlando* that "a biography is considered complete if it merely accounts for six or seven selves, whereas a person may well have as many thousand." Although "the conscious self . . . wishes to be nothing but one self . . . 'the true self,'" it cannot squelch distinct moments and conflicting recollections, ambiguities and multiplicities (Woolf 1928:279). Kyō (1990, 2000, 2002) would expend considerable time studying and living in South Korea, and thereafter exploring the distinct trajectories of the Korean diaspora across Asia. Yū would also learn Korean and go on to write novels and stories with strong Korean and Zainichi themes and characters (e.g., Yū 2004). In other words, temporal transformation is commonplace. Kim Kyongdok, who was the first non-Japanese citizen to become an attorney in postwar Japan, wrote when he was thirty-six years old that he was only thirteen years old as a Korean. This is because "I used a pseudonym (Japanese name) until I was twenty-three and pretended to live as a Japanese person" (Kim Kyongdok 2005:56); he was, then, "non-Korean" for the first twenty-three years of his life. Only in college did he come to affirm his ethnic ancestry and identity. After becoming an attorney, he spent over three years studying in South Korea "as the next step to regaining my ethnicity" (Kim Kyongdok 2005:60). Recall Kim Hiro from the previous chapter. It does him no justice to characterize him as a hero of ethnic pride or a criminal of violent sensibility. After 1968, he spent some thirty-two years as a "model" prisoner and seemed to be leading a fulfilling life in Seoul when he committed another violent crime (Abe 2002:194–95). Recidivism notwithstanding, he married again and sought to seek "love" as a way of life (Abe 2002:230). Whatever the truths about Kim

Hiro, it doesn't make much sense to call him essentially this, that, or other.

Zainichi diversity goes well beyond these narratives. Whereas Lee Chongja (1994) articulates Zainichi identity through classical Japanese poetic forms, other Zainichi writers avoid the question altogether. Among the latter, some, such as Ijūin Shizuka, do not hide their Korean descent, while others do. Some Zainichi writers explore the historical legacy of Japanese imperialism (e.g., Yoon 1997), but others wish to transcend the past (e.g., Lee S. 1997:10). Consider music. Some Zainichi eagerly take up traditional Korean music and recite *sinse t'aryong*. Kyō (1987:209) feels that *sinse t'aryong* "that is full of ethnic feelings is not for her," but she would also explore traditional Korean music after her initial meditation on her Zainichi identity. Chon Wolson, a second-generation Zainichi who attended Sōren schools, is an opera singer (Chon 2007), whereas Ryu Yong-gi, a third-generation Zainichi who studied at a seminary, is a hip-hop singer ("Turning Rapanese" 2007). Both experienced discrimination as Zainichi but it would be difficult to generate useful generalizations from their shared background or experience. To say that they are musicians is rendered nearly meaningless by the distance separating the two genres of opera and hip-hop.

The search for the least common denominators of Zainichi identity is futile. Although certain common questions are raised, they are answered in distinct ways. To the extent that there are convergences, they teeter on becoming rather generic to all human beings. Zainichi ideology, like the earlier nationalist allegiance to North or South Korea, proffered an essentialist understanding of the self, such that Kim Dalsu (1981:17) could write: "In my case, experience in literature means, needless to say, experience as Zainichi." The confident "needless to say" appends the brash pronouncement of post-Zainichi self-representations in writers such as Gen Getsu or Kaneshiro Kazuki. Rather, beyond Korean ancestry, what dominates Zainichi writings is the broad background of Japanese society. Viewing the animated manga "Kyojin no hoshi" [The star of the Giants], Shin Sugok (2006:99) experiences a shock of recognition viewing a paradigmatic scene I mentioned earlier—the drunk and violent father overturns the dining table and slaps the protagonist—and wonders whether the family is not in fact Zainichi. Wherever Zainichi turned, there was Japan. Although many commentators see in Zainichi suicides their secret anguish as Zainichi, suicide is much more in the Japanese cultural repertoire than in the Korean. Most encompassing was the language. When the pioneering Zainichi writer Kim Dalsu (1981:17) observes that "experience in literature means, needless to say, experience as Zainichi," he elides the fundamental condition of his authorship: his inescapable reliance on the Japanese language. As the Zainichi poet Kim Sijong (2004:8) remarked: "Japanese—Japanese that is a foreign language—created the foundation of my consciousness."

Paradoxically, the absence of essences does not abjure the necessity of cognition and recognition. Repressing the inevitable questions of identity in a society of disrecognition is liable to generate the revenge of the repressed or, more mundanely, misrecognition and disrecognition. The protagonist of Gen Getsu's *Oshaberina inu* [Talkative dog, 2003] insists, "For me, it doesn't matter 'who I am.'" (Gen 2003a:82). As much as he attempts to be a former Zainichi—though he insists that he is "not 'former' anything" (Gen 2003a:90)—he cannot help but conclude that his impotence is related to his status as a "former" Zainichi. The aforementioned Kim Kyongdok (2005:58) recalls that: "[I] could not comprehend the background of Koreans' poverty and fighting, the illegitimacy of Japanese discrimination. . . . [I] wanted merely to flee from everything Korean." Certainly, the "inferiority complex" of being Korean or Zainichi in Japan is a commonplace recollection among the Zainichi baby boomers.

If we can identify Zainichi essences, they reside in the two terms of their category—Korean descent and Japanese livelihood—and in the persistence of Japanese discrimination that does not allow people of Korean descent to be legitimately Japanese or assume a new form of hybrid identity. The dominant belief in Japanese monoethnicity stipulates that to be Japanese means inevitably to be ethnic Japanese. *Pace* Kyō's title, then, it was impossible to be "ordinary" (Korean) Japanese when she was growing up in the 1960s and 1970s. Given that hybridity and heterogeneity had no place in the dominant Japanese discourse in the postwar period, the fact of Korean descent renders necessary the individual and collective struggles for a viable place and identity in contemporary Japanese society for Zainichi. That Zainichi sometimes struggle together does not mean, however, that there is a simple, static, and homogeneous ethnic identity.

IDENTITY AS DIVERSITY

Why should we expect perhaps a million people of Korean descent in Japan to be homogeneous? What more can we say than that they share the category of Korean descent and their cultural citizenship in Japan? And how important should these factors be in the personal definition of contemporary Zainichi people? How many people would have their epitaph be "Zainichi"?

As we have seen, there was a growing group of Japanese-born Koreans already by the late 1930s. As self-serving and culturally imperialistic as prewar Japanese policies were, efforts to integrate and assimilate ethnic Koreans engendered a cadre who identified themselves as Japanese government officials, military officers, and intellectuals. Class differentiation, not surprisingly, separated the privileged and educated Koreans from their impoverished and illiterate counterparts. Gender and generation, region of origin as well as of destination, fractured the presumed unity of ethnic Korean identity. Whether one considers the length of stay or the vagaries of individual experience, it is bewildering to believe that there should be anything so singular about the Korean experience even during the colonial period. As a youth (around 1940), O Rimjun (1971:22–26) read a Japanese book that depicted virtuous Koreans. He was moved by the story—and could not detect any racial prejudice—but he also empathized deeply with ordinary Japanese people in other stories. It would be facile to consider O as a brainwashed pro-Japanese traitor, but there is no doubt that that category included many ethnic Koreans. The eminent South Korean poet Kim So-un (1983:43, 50) spent some thirty-two years in Japan and recalls "good Japanese people" who redeemed the country for him, despite colonial racism and the dominant anti-Japanese ideology in South Korea of the 1970s and 1980s. O and Kim are hardly a small minority of national traitors and ethnic betrayers.

By the early twenty-first century, there were still significant barriers in terms of employment, marriage, and civic participation for Zainichi. However, it is safe to conclude that they did not constitute a uniformly inferior group. Furthermore, many of them were second-, third-, and even fourth-generation Japanese residents who grew up speaking Japanese, watching Japanese television, playing with Japanese children, attending Japanese schools, and so on, such that virtually the sole source of social differentiation from ethnic Japanese is the fact of Korean descent. Even in the case of those who attended and still identify with the North Korea–affiliated schools and organizations, the overwhelming cultural influence was often no different from that of other Japanese children. As the North Korea orientation of Sōren-affiliated schools waned, the fact of cultural Japaneseness became all the more inescapable (Ryang 1997:198). For every incident of Japanese intolerance and even racism—such as the 1994 Chimachogori Incident, in which female ethnic school pupils' ethnic costumes were slashed—Sōren schools were known and even admired by the Japanese public for their athletic prowess (Uri Hakkyo 2001:108–16, 156–62).

In making sense of a racial, ethnic, or national group—categories of modern peoplehood—one usually looks to language, religion, or custom and culture. Yet Zainichi lacked these elementary bases of distinction from the larger Japanese society by the 1970s. Second-generation Zainichi were Japanese speakers. Although Sōren school graduates knew a great deal of the Korean language, they effectively spoke the Sōren language, thereby distinguishing themselves from both native North and South Koreans. The basic fact, however, was that they were inevitably much more comfortable in wielding their native Japanese-language facility. By the time a new generation of Korean migrants arrived from South Korea in the 1980s, there were no major concatenations of ethnic Koreans where Korean was the lingua franca (cf. Harajiri 1989:127–29).

Religion did not separate Zainichi from ethnic Japanese, either. One may plausibly suggest that Sōren followers practiced a form of secular religion, but in the postwar decades there were many committed Japanese communists who were at once like Sōren communists and unlike other Japanese people. Although Shintō adherents were unlikely to be Zainichi, the major world religions, ranging from Buddhism to Christianity, had faithfuls among both ethnic Korean and ethnic Japanese populations. First-generation Koreans engaged in ethnically distinct Buddhist temples and other ritual practices, but they were clearly on the wane by the 1980s (Hardacre 1984:61–62, 66–67). Prewar ethnic Koreans tended to practice rituals of ancestor worship [chesa] (Harajiri 1989:147–57). Although almost universally practiced by the first generation, the Confucian ritual became vitiated and transformed under successive generations (Yang 2004:120–24). Younger Zainichi either simplified or abandoned *chesa*.

Finally, custom and culture—from food and clothing to material and cultural consumption—poorly differentiated ethnic Koreans from ethnic Japanese. Already by the 1940s, ethnic Koreans' public appearance was similar to their ethnic Japanese counterparts. Ethnic costume was primarily worn by the elderly and women, who tended to stay within the perimeters of ethnic Korean ghettoes. The Zainichi novelist Lee Hoesung wore traditional Korean clothes [hanbok] for the first time in his mid-sixties, in 2001 (Lee H. 2002:384). The propensity to use garlic and chili or to barbecue meat rendered Korean cuisine distinct from the Japanese. The Japanese-born Korean-Canadian writer Ook Chung (2001:63) has the narrator remark: "I understood that I was Korean the day I discovered that I couldn't do without kimchi." Or, as the Zainichi writer Shin Sugok (2006:157) notes, the desire to eat kimchi is "the proof of my grandmother's existence." To be sure, we have already encountered Pak and Kyō, who did not consume kimchi regularly, and it is a common Zainichi experience to find "real" Korean food too "spicy" (e.g., Yan 2006:119, 138). Sagisawa Megumu retrospectively identifies her family's signature dish as a permutation of the Korean *p'ajŏn* (savory pancake): an unacknowledged trace of her hidden Korean ancestry (Sagisawa 2005:92). Yet in the course of the postwar decades there was a striking convergence. Ethnic Koreans adapted to local produce and cuisine; ethnic Japanese, especially after the 1980s, found foreign cuisine delectable. By then, ethnic costume was worn on special occasions and by students attending Sōren schools. Although there were ethnic Korean publications and media, most second-generation Zainichi were weaned on Japanese popular culture. The prevalence of Zainichi stars in sports and music may have generated co-ethnic preferences, but Rikidōzan and Miyako Harumi were representative Japanese celebrities.

The undeniable source of distinction was ancestry, recorded in family registries and official documents, and the readily available marker was name. *Koseki* and *tsūmei* constituted the two weak links in any Zainichi effort to pass as ordinary Japanese. Furthermore, given the pervasive prejudice and discrimination against people of Korean descent in Japan, the fact of Korean descent has a significant impact on Zainichi identity.

Yet ancestry or descent do not pass on as a homogeneous trace. Many Zainichi belong to ethno-political organizations (Gohl 1976:122–31), but many are regionally based, such as for Zainchi people from Chejudo (Ijichi 2000:213–16; cf. Ko 1996:38–46). The relative autonomy of Chejudo identity—certainly distinct culturally from their mainland counterparts—manifests itself frequently in assertions of difference from other Zainichi and Koreans. Regional diversity made mockery of the essentialist claim of Koreanness (cf. So 1993:39–41).

Other social conditions, such as economic or regional background, vary tremendously. What unites Son Masayoshi, Japan's wealthiest man, and a homeless, and socially faceless, Zainichi man? Or consider regional diversity within Japan: a Zainichi man who grew up in Tokyo writes of Zainichi in Osaka as people "who are clearly a different species, an alien cultural group" (Chong 1997:87). When he first went to Ikaino (a Korean area in Osaka), he wondered whether he was still in Japan. Yet Ikaino proclaimed itself to be "Koreatown" in 1987 and a spiritual home for the Zainichi population (Chon A. 2005:304).

The diversity of Zainichi identification also excluded traditionalists who continued to embrace Korean identification and exilic status. Sōren Koreans have long rejected the very label Zainichi. Ko Yon-i (1998:59), who teaches French literature at the Sōren-affiliated Chōsen University, writes: "I reject Japanese people calling me 'Zainichi' [because I am] *essentially* Korean [Chōsenjin]." In contrast, Sagisawa Megumu (2005:162) was not alone in rejecting ethnic identification altogether: "I personally think that ethnicity is fiction." Gen Getsu says in an interview that Zainichi "don't have any identity" and likens it to "floating weed" (Shirai 2007:120). Disidentification from Zainichi identity—perhaps the dominant identification among ethnic Koreans from the 1980s—was commonplace from its very birth.

Thus, ethnicity in and of itself cannot in any sense predict the concrete contours of individual identity. Needless to say, their lives variously reflect the traces of ancestral genes or memes and the persistence of Japanese disrecognition against ethnic Koreans, but it would be difficult to conclude that ethnic ancestry and experience leave consistent marks on individual lives, and provide insights into Zainichi as a singular group. I am skeptical that ethnicity has a determining impact on one's sense of self or personal identity. It is a factor—and it can become the dominant factor for some people at some time—but only one among many. And self-identification may change dramatically over a life course. The usual social-scientific approach—to use social backgrounds or factors as the independent variables and individuals and their identities as the dependent variables—does not work very well. Concrete lives resist simple, reductionist, and essentialist characterizations. Zainichi ideology mischaracterized and misrecognized Zainichi realities.

5. Reconciliation

In the early years of the twenty-first century, South Korean stars illuminated television screens in many Japanese households. In particular, a popular South Korean soap opera, *Fuyu no sonata* [Winter sonata, Kyŏul yŏn'ga, 2002], became by the end of its run in 2004 not only the most watched television show in Japan but also a social phenomenon (Ishida 2007:2–3). Fanatical fans flocked to the filming location in order to catch a glimpse of the star Pae Yong-jun, or Yon-sama, as he was reverently invoked by his ardent fans. Less ambitiously, they snapped up expensive photo books of the charismatic actor. Enthusiasm for South Korean popular culture—variously known as *Kanryu*, *Hanryu*, *Hallyu*, or *K-pop*—was powerful enough to elicit a countervailing movement, *Kenkanryu* [anti-Korean wave]. At the same time, North Korea loomed as a major threat to the Japanese way of life. In particular, the fate of Japanese women kidnapped in the early 1970s and the present danger of North Korean nuclear weapon tests were repeatedly headline news (cf. Ishida 2007:16–18). The North Korean specter haunted the new nationalist agenda of successive prime ministers, Koizumi and Abe. The coverage of the enemy had a lighter side as well. Comic books pilloried the North Korean leader Kim Jong Il's bouffant and elevator shoes, whereas television shows marveled at his conspicuous consumption amidst his subjects' poverty and hunger.

As the existence of *Kenkanryu* and anti-North Korean sentiments attest, Japanese attitudes toward the Koreas and Koreans are at times virulently hostile. Yet the legacy of the colonial past and colonial racism was clearly waning sixty years after the end of Japanese rule. Although there were ethnic Korean superstars in Japan during the postwar period, they left their ethnic origins carefully ensconced in the ethnic closet. In the 2000s, South Korean stars—and some Zainichi figures—were openly and proudly Korean. When Japanese tourism to South Korea took off in the 1960s, one of the primary attractions was sex tourism, bringing countless Japanese men to South Korean prostitutes (Lie 1995). Forty years later, Japanese tourists were much more likely to seek a taste of "authentic" Korean food or to shop for luxury goods. Whereas Japanese elders still recall South Korea as a poor or "developing" country, Japanese youths are more likely to evoke the manifest wealth of Seoul and the allure of South Korean popular culture. By 2001—in anticipation of the new form of *naisen ittai*, the joint hosting of the 2002 World Cup—the Emperor would divulge his ancestry from the Korean peninsula (*Asahi shinbun* 23 December 2001). The World Cup generated surface solidarity and simmering rivalry, but it should be seen as part and parcel of the two countries' rapprochement. It would do considerable injustice to insist on the relentless and recalcitrant nature of Japanese dislike of Korea and Koreans.

Few contemporary Japanese people characterize the Zainichi population in unremittingly negative terms. The long-standing penchant for ethnonational generalizations is losing credibility. The very idea of the essential Korean or Zainichi seems quaint, whether the colonial-era Japanese prejudice that delineated a lazy, dirty, and treacherous people, or the progressive narrative that depicted an exploited, oppressed, and discriminated people. In 1981 Changsoo Lee and George De Vos (1981:363) concluded: "To be known as Korean in Japan today is still to court possible failure in many business or professional careers. It is dangerous economically to 'surface' even after gaining recognition." In spite of remnant poverty and discrimination, we can no longer produce facile generalizations about the impoverished and oppressed Zainichi. Declining, too, is the Zainichi practice of passing as Japanese. Merely a decade after Lee and De Vos's book, the software tycoon Son Masayoshi was at once successful economically and openly "Korean." As we will see, some of the leading intellectuals in contemporary Japan are ethnic Koreans who, in spite of considerable differences in outlook, are routinely identified as Zainichi. In short, Zainichi today inhabit a much more prosaic world. We are also witnessing the rise of the post-Zainichi generation: ethnic Koreans who are ready to embrace their Japaneseness, including Japanese citizenship. The rise of assimilation, naturalization, and Japanization paradoxically generated the assertion of postcolonial identity, primarily as Korean Japanese.

TO BE ZAINICHI IN NORTHEAST ASIA

Kang Sangjung is a renowned intellectual and a professor at the prestigious University of Tokyo (supposedly the first Zainichi to attain this position). He occupies a role in Japanese intellectual and cultural life that is somewhat akin to that held by Edward W. Said, one of Kang's intellectual heroes, in the United States in the 1980s and 1990s. That is, Kang speaks out on a variety of political and cultural issues, is regarded as a man of the left, and retains a great deal of scholarly respect to boot. Rather than discussing his well-known work on nationalism or his frequent intervention in public life, let me focus on his 2004 autobiography, *Zainichi*. Although reproducing Zainichi ideology, including Zainichi historiography, Kang is much more reconciled with Japan. Yet, rather than embracing Japan as *Heimat*, he casts his gaze outward to diasporic networks and Northeast Asia.

Kang was born in 1950 in a Korean ghetto in Kumamoto City in Kyūshū. Most Koreans eked out a precarious living by pig farming or illegal brewing *[doburoku]*. His parents maintained Korean customs and rituals. His mother remained illiterate in both Korean and Japanese and never attained fluency in Japanese. His father first worked in construction and later in scrap recycling. Kang went to Japanese schools using a Japanese pseudonym. In short, Kang's was not an atypical upbringing for a Zainichi child in the 1950s, and he recapitulates the received Zainichi historiography.

Nonetheless, Zainichi diversity is evident in Kang's description of his two "uncles." The "real" uncle was a university-educated military police officer who married a Japanese woman. Because of his loyalty to the Japanese emperor, he sought to kill himself at the end of the war. Dissuaded by Kang's father, he returned to South Korea, became a lawyer, and married a woman from an affluent family. By the time of his brief visit to Japan in 1970, he had expunged his memory as a military police officer and of the Japanese family he had left behind. Unlike his father's younger brother, the other "uncle" was illiterate. Living as an "outlaw" and bereft of family relations, this "uncle" worked and lived with the Kang family after the war. By the time he passed away, he possessed only a few articles of clothing and cigarettes.

Between these contrasting life courses, Kang's childhood memory is at once melancholic and schizophrenic. Lacking a unified homeland, he found it problematic to call Kumamoto or North or South Korea his ancestral homeland *[sokoku]*. He couldn't make sense of the divided Korea or the Zainichi population: "I was very depressed studying history and contemporary society. Society was replete with an invisible climate that rendered being 'Zanichi' as criminal" (Kang S. 2004:62). Negative images of Zainichi—"the trash of history" is one of his terms—"cast a dark shadow" (62, 63). Thus, Japan and Korea became at once the most beloved and the most detested countries. Kang believes that his inability to smile for pho-

tographs and his youthful stuttering are both intimately intertwined with
his problematic identification as Zainichi.

Entering Waseda University, Kang feared the shadow of Zainichi existence and sought to flee it. "Ironically, as Japan[ese life] became brighter,
'Zainichi' seemed to become shrouded in deep darkness" (70). Unable to
talk about his turmoil, he led a lonely life amidst four "worlds": the fading
memory of first-generation Zainichi, the simultaneously attractive and
repellent Tokyo, the newly discovered world of scholarship, and a fellow-
ship of Zainichi students. Against the background of raging student activism, Kang remained "non-poli," or politically indifferent. The 1968 Kim
Hiro Incident made him ambivalent: "the feeling that Kim did well to
spread the existence of 'Zainichi.' However, it deepened the suspicion that
'Zainichi' are 'criminals,' after all" (74).

The major turning point was his 1972 visit to South Korea. "I wanted to
break through the sense of closure so I decided to visit South Korea" (74).
The rigorous interrogation by the immigration authorities—Kang was car-
rying a Japanese magazine with photos of Kim Il Sung—instantly dissipated warm and fuzzy feelings about the homeland. However, the welcome
by his relatives, the contrast between the wealth of his uncle's family and
the prevailing poverty of Seoul, and the wonders of South Korea kindled
his interest in Korea. At Waseda University's Center for Korean Culture,
he explored the roots of Korean problems and the status of Zainichi. He
also discarded his Japanese name and claimed his Korean name. He draws
a stark contrast to another fellow Zainichi student, Yamamura Masaaki,
who committed suicide in 1970 and whom I discussed in chapter 3. Having
been naturalized, Yamamura was excluded from the Center (which was
open only to Korean nationals) and hence could not be accepted by either
Japanese or Koreans. Kang believes that the memory of his interaction with
the first generation of Zainichi provided the paper-thin margin that separated life from death, his fate from Yamamura's. That is, Zainichi meant
life; its denial death. His visit to South Korea, therefore, "meant the discovery of a new self" (88).

Nonetheless, Kang is far from being a paradigmatic Zainichi intellectual. Unlike other Zainichi intellectuals who have focused almost exclusively on Korean and Zainichi topics, Kang's work has only intermittently
dealt with the Koreas and Koreans. His doctoral thesis, for example, was on
the German social theorist Max Weber (though he claims that the pioneering theorist of modernity had suggestive answers for his questions about
Zainichi identity). On television talk shows, he deals with events beyond
the Korean peninsula and the Zainichi population, extending to regional

and global issues. By participating in the national debate on Japan's role in the world, Kang claims that he is seeking to destroy the prevailing image of Zainichi. After returning to Japan from his study in Germany, he had trouble reentering the Zainichi world. "I had breathed too much outside air to return as 'Zainichi.'" (139). He is married to a Japanese woman, for example, and in naming their son, he departed consciously from the traditional Korean practice. Like many ordinary Zainichi, he has deviated from the prescribed practice of the Zainichi ethnic imperative.

Kang's advocacy of Zainichi identity is far from singular. During the anti-fingerprinting movement, he became a minor celebrity by refusing to be fingerprinted. However, faced with the prospect of imprisonment, he complied with the authorities. Against the palpable disappointment of his supporters, he was saved by the sympathetic words of an activist Japanese minister. (The minister later helped him secure a job at a Christian university.) Kang also argues that under current political and economic conditions, the Japanese themselves are becoming more like Zainichi: in effect, the corrosion of social safety nets places the mainstream Japanese population in the same risk-filled state as the Zainichi.

Kang concludes his autobiography by answering why he was born as Zainichi and who Zainichi are. Returning to the Koreas is not a viable solution given the brute fact of linguistic and cultural assimilation in Japan. Yet, unlike Zainichi ideology, Kang is less interested in homeland politics and less inclined to criticize contemporary Japanese society. In a later book (2005:23), he declares that "the Korean peninsula is my 'ancestral land' [sokoku], and Japan is also my 'ancestral land.'" What sustains his Zainichi identity is the memory of the first-generation Zainichi population, and with this memory he steadfastly resists the path of assimilation and naturalization. The task may be difficult, but his memory is "clearly reviving" as he ages (Kang S. 2005:175).

Kang argues that rather than being trapped within Japan, Zainichi should promote diasporic Korean networks and ties to Northeast Asia. In short, Zainichi should be neither Japanese nor Korean but part of the larger Korean diaspora. Like Lee Hoesung's diasporic identification (discussed in chapter 2), Kang seeks to transcend the divided homeland and the choice between repatriation and naturalization. Thus, he takes a major step away from the nationalist focus of Zainichi ideology. "To live in Northeast Asia" is his proposed project and solution (Kang S. 2004:226). Yet Kang is mindful of the brutal colonial relationship, the enforced migration of Koreans to the Japanese archipelago, and the overwhelming poverty and discrimination that greeted the Koreans once in Japan. The capsule history of oppression and resistance constitutes Kang's articulation of Zainichi identity, and therefore his heavy reliance on honoring the memory of the first genera-tion. In this respect, he accepts the critical thrust of Zainichi ideology, however he may depart from it on the primacy of unification or on antipa-thetic attitudes toward Japan.

NOT TO BE ZAINICHI IN JAPAN

If Zainichi identity had to be forged against the centrifugal force that pro-jected the two Koreas as the ultimate homeland of ethnic Koreans in Japan, it faced in turn a powerful centripetal force of assimilation. A representa-tive Zainichi intellectual Kang may be, but he does not represent Zainichi intellectuals. Some reject Zainichi historiography and ideology that stress Korean victimization and Japanese racism. These criticisms inform the nascent post-Zainichi generation. No longer seeking to pass in the ethnic closet, they do not shy away from embracing Japan.

Tei Taikin (Chung Daekyun) was born in 1948 in Iwate Prefecture in northeast Japan. Like Kang, he studied at a prestigious private university (Rikkyō) and abroad (UCLA) and is currently a professor at Tokyo Metropolitan University (if not quite as prestigious as the University of Tokyo, certainly a highly respected institution). Born two years earlier than Kang as second-generation Zainichi, he is also a prominent intellec-tual who speaks out on Zainichi and other issues. Kang and Tei are, socio-logically speaking, virtually identical, but they are poles apart in their perspectives on Zainichi identity. Whereas Kang asserts ethnonational identification, Tei advocates assimilation and naturalization. Kang accepts Zainichi historiography; Tei rejects it. Kang publishes prolifically in pro-gressive magazines; Tei's writings appear in right-of-center outlets.

Is it possible to seek the ideological divergence in family background or personal history? After arriving in Japan in 1922, Tei's father became the first ethnic Korean to author a Japanese-language novel and later became an ardent supporter of the Emperor. Along with Kang's uncle, Tei's father represents a not insignificant population of ethnic Koreans who became Japanese nationalists during the colonial period. After the war's end and mental anguish, Tei's father eventually returned to South Korea in 1960 (Tei and his siblings stayed behind with their mother in Japan). Tei would not see his father again for fifteen years, and unlike Kang, he is ambivalent toward his impoverished and paranoid father. His ethnic Japanese mother, whose dominant identification was as a Christian, reared him as linguisti-cally and culturally Japanese. Far from being proud of his heritage, Tei

(2006:71) was "ashamed of being Korean, and tried to hide it." He was embarrassed by the "poverty" and "ugliness" of other Zainichi, and went so far as to avoid learning anything about Korea. Like Kang, he turned around in college, where he explored his Korean ancestry and Zainichi identity. His long sojourn in the United States (where he studied) and South Korea (where he taught) clarified his lack of identification in any simple way as Korean. Being abroad in fact solidified his sense of belonging to contemporary Japanese society.

Parental or social background is inadequate to make sense of Kang's and Tei's divergent political beliefs. Tei's older brother was long active in a Zainichi organization. His younger sister lodged a 2005 suit that alleged discrimination against the Tokyo metropolitan government for not accepting her application as Zainichi. She was reported after the verdict as stating, "I want to tell the world: don't come to Japan!" (Tei 2006:153). Clearly, having the same parents or growing up together did not generate the same set of response to Zainichi issues. Tei relentlessly criticizes his sister's action ("verbal violence") and her account of the family background and the status of Zainichi.

Tei's position is encapsulated in the title of his 2001 book *Zainichi Kankokujin no shūen* [The end of Zainichi]. He argues that Zainichi lack a sense of belonging to South Korea or of being a foreigner in Japanese society (Tei 2001:14). Having lived and taught in South Korea for fourteen years, he says with some authority that Zainichi people rarely seek to be South Koreans. "Why aren't there people who quit being 'Zainichi' and become 'real' South Koreans?" (18). Furthermore, except for political rights, Zainichi and Japanese are "physically or culturally indistinguishable" (22). The "newcomers," or recent migrants from South Korea, go so far as to reject Zainichi as Koreans (145–47). What sustains the Zainichi status is the taboo on naturalization (55–57), which he does not regard as an act of betrayal (Tei 2006:187).

In contrast to the Zainichi ideology's behest to live as foreign citizens, Tei advocates naturalization. He seeks to sever the past from the present and the Zainichi population from the Korean peninsula. He castigates the victim mentality that harps endlessly on the enforced migration of Koreans to Japan and the ensuing lives of discrimination. Based on his experience abroad, he argues that it is stressful to be a "foreigner" in Japan or Korea and most South Koreans disrespect Zainichi. In contrast, Japanese prejudice and discrimination are in decline, and the rate of intermarriage between Zainichi and Japanese exceeds 80 percent. He blames progressive intellectuals for robbing Zainichi of "life chances." For Tei, being natural-

ized does not mean the end of ties to ancestral land; one may "feel nostalgia" for it. For him, it is a matter of individual choice whether naturalized
Zainichi should repress or express their ethnicity (Tei 2001:193). The birth
of "Korean Japanese" *[Koria-kei Nihonjin]* would not only improve the
status of Zainichi but also contribute to Japanese society (5). A similar
proposal had been made as early as 1997 (Chi 1997), and most forcefully by
Sakanaka Hidenori, the director of the Immigration and Naturalization
Bureau (Sakanaka 2005b:144).

Another source of contrast is North Korea in particular and the Cold
War in general. Tei is highly critical of progressive intellectuals who highlighted South Korea's repressive policies but were silent, if not laudatory,
about North Korea. In so doing, they propped up the authoritarian regime.
Just as Kang bears the mantle of progressive intellectual—his work appears
under the imprint of the progressive publisher Iwanami Shoten and its
longtime flagship journal *Sekai*—Tei publishes in conservative journals,
such as *Bungei shunjū* and *Seiron*.

Tei is far from alone in disputing Kang's role as the representative
Zainichi intellectual. Asakawa Akihiro, born in 1974 in Kobe, is a third-
generation Korean Japanese and a naturalized Japanese who is a specialist
on Australian politics. He lambastes Zainichi ideologues who "stress their
Zainichi" status and use it as a form of "indulgence" to attack others
(Asakawa 2006:34). Asakawa's critique of Kang, especially the autobiography *Zainichi*, is symptomatic of his general critique of Zainichi intellectuals. He provides a searing attack on Kang's claim to speak for or represent
the first-generation Zainichi. He denies that many of them were coerced or
involuntary migrants and denounces Kang's characterization of Zainichi as
a victimized population. Similarly, he chides Kang for being silent on the
disastrous repatriation project. He also defends Japanese governmental
efforts to ameliorate the status of Zainichi. Finally, he relentlessly fulmi-
nates against the solidarity between progressive Zainichi and Japanese
intellectuals. He regrets the way in which progressive networks generated
a good job for Kang, leading ultimately to the University of Tokyo
professorship.

Tei and Asakawa represent a new mode of thinking that emerged in the
2000s. Its post–Cold War perspective accentuates the positive elements of
Zainichi life and Japanese society. In so doing, this line of reasoning exco-
riates Zainichi ideology, which focuses on the colonial past, present discrimination, and the "consciousness of misfortune" (recall Yoon 1992).
Furthermore, it severs Zainichi ties to homeland. That is, Tei and Asakawa
reject all the major tenets of Zainichi ideology. Given their rapprochement

with conservative Japanese opinions, it is tempting to dub them Zainichi "neocons," though it would be more accurate to say that they articulate a post-Zainichi, or Korean-Japanese, worldview.

Chi Tong-wook's 1997 book *Zainichi o yamenasai* [Quit being Zainichi] is probably the earliest explicit articulation of the post-Zainichi perspective. A South Korean journalist in Japan, Chi (1997:18) argues that Zainichi are "superior": "Seeing objectively, it would not be an exaggeration to say that Zainichi are the most superior ethnic minority in the world." Without denying prewar and postwar poverty and discrimination, he is emphatic that Zainichi transcended these obstacles to perform superlatively in a variety of fields, ranging from sports and entertainment to business and academe. What obscured Zainichi achievements is the Japanese propensity to highlight the negative ("minus image") and to bypass ("taboo") Zainichi existence altogether (45, 20). Instead, he suggests broadening the view historically and globally. Rather than focusing on Japanese imperialism, Chi encourages looking into the distant past, to the very roots of Japanese people who hailed from the Korean peninsula. Locating the crucial generational transition in the mid-1970s, he asserts that Japan is the *Heimat* [*kokyō*] for second- and third-generation Zainichi. He is equally critical of North and South Korea for ignoring the fate of Zainichi, as well as the generally discriminatory nature of Japanese society. He is even critical of the Japanese naturalization law that required abandoning one's Korean name. Yet, as aware as he is of the problems of naturalization, he advocates it. In part this position stems from his claim that most diasporic Koreans adopt the nationality of the destination country. Thus, naturalization—to quit being Zainichi—does not imply a betrayal of homeland or ethnicity; but just as much as "ancient Japan was created by Toraijin [from the Korean peninsula]," naturalized Zainichi should also help create the future. To quit being Zainichi is to announce the spiritual independence of Zainichi from the homeland and to choose a life of freedom as "Korean Japanese" (209). Rather than straightforward assimilation to Japan or squelching ties to Korea, Chi beckons Zainichi to be "pioneers" rather than wallowing in the state of homelessness (214–15).

Needless to say, the position that can be summarized as pro-naturalization comprises distinct standpoints. Yet one indisputable strand is a critique of Zainichi ideology that is taken to be pro-North Korean and anti-Japanese. Hence, there is an unholy alliance between the anti-Zainichi intellectuals and the *Kenkanryū* movement. The presumed privileges of Zainichi people are coupled with alleged pro-Korean, anti-Japanese sentiments (e.g., Yamano 2005). An important element, as Chi's argument stresses, is that

Zainichi ideology is a peculiarly Japanese phenomenon that reflects the monoethnic ideology of postwar Japanese society. The new possibilities opened by living or studying abroad—the United States and South Korea for Tei, Australia for Asakawa—underscore the ethnocentrism of Zainichi ideology. Kang's outward focus, however, converges with the post-Zainichi argument in avoiding the trappings of nationalism.

INTELLECTUAL RESOLUTION?

In reviewing two conflicting perspectives, the intellectual temptation is to reconcile them: review the available historical and sociological evidence, assay the logical structure of argumentation, and conclude in a dispassionate, scientific manner. Yet the nature of peoplehood identification resists scientific objectivity and sociological reductionism. Quite simply, it is possible to assert a wide range of claims about one's descent, belonging, and identification (Lie 2004b).

Personal, much less ethnic, identity is far from fixed for even an individual. Kang is not very clear about his youthful sense of ethnic identity, but he did not begin to explore his Korean roots until college. He also used his Japanese name until then. Tei's father was an ardent Japanese nationalist during the colonial period, only to return to Korea and abdicate his Japanese identification. Tei himself spent considerable time doing research on Zainichi identity, later to resist and ultimately to reject it. There are no identity essences over an individual's life course.

Neither is identity reducible to family or social background. Tei's siblings would presumably agree with Kang's description of and prescription for contemporary Zainichi identity. Although Tei grew up in the same family, his deviation is quite manifest. As I noted, Kang and Tei are, sociologically speaking, basically identical. Here I am not denying that there are historically specific generalizations one may make about a group. The societal and historical context of one's life inevitably shapes the horizon of individual destinies. An ethnic Korean could not have become professor at the University of Tokyo in the 1960s. It may even be possible to argue that the socioeconomic constitution of the Zainichi population would make it more likely that the Zainichi population may do worse (or better) on standardized examinations or status attainment. What I am denying is the cogency of group essentialism or sociological reductionism.

Furthermore, history is easily and essentially contested. As much as we strive for objective historiography, the past yields no simple agreements on facts or morals. As we have seen, Kang endorses the Zainichi historiography that delineates a past of exploitation and oppression, struggle and resistance. Tei remains profoundly skeptical about the extent of the generalization and resists the expunction of voluntary will. Kang's memoir endorses Tei's historical perspective insofar as he had an assimilated and privileged family member (his "Korean" uncle). Kang's uncle also reinforces the point about the dynamic transformation one may undergo during one's lifetime; a patriotic Japanese military police officer metamorphoses into an affluent attorney in South Korea. Life of privilege, mainly, but not one that adduces a simple and consistent identity. Certainly political differences do not disappear—along with their vicissitudes even during one's life course, as is evident in the difference between Kang and Tei.

History, moreover, may be academic. As memories fade, any discussion of the sins of colonialism, war guilt, and their postcolonial repercussions are overtaken by present concerns, though distant history may provide incendiary tinder for political conflagration. Postcoloniality is rendered possible by the passing of colonialism as living memory. Kang's recourse to the memory of the first generation is significant because the current reality favors Tei's future orientation. As a second-generation Zainichi in Gen Getsu's haunting story, "Kage no sumika" [The habitat of shadows, 1999], tells a first-generation man: "Our generation—and those after us—cannot achieve a resolution with this country [Japan]. . . . We are—no, I am—so powerless. . . . I am satisfied with maintaining my modest wealth and social position" (Gen 2000a:89).

The present situation—the stuff of economics, politics, and sociology— does not yield an objective and neutral description and evaluation. The successes of Kang and Tei weaken the sociological generalization of the Korean minority as an underclass. It takes a giant leap of faith to classify them as "victims" of Japanese racism or of Japanese society. Yet the eradication of legal barriers or the vitiation of societal prejudice do not necessarily improve one's subjective sense of well-being. What may have been an ordinary event for a Zainichi person in the immediate postwar years—say, an ethnic invective hurled at them—would provoke protest and fury by Kang or Tei today. Paradoxically, the improving lot of a minority group may exacerbate the sense of discrimination and victimization (Lie 2004b: chap.6). It is a common feature of many first- and even second-generation Zainichi that they arose from a broad background of poverty and discrimination. In achieving wealth or fame, the first-generation Zainichi share the memory of poverty and their struggles for mobility and respectability—no different in outline from the vast majority of ethnic Japanese. Zainichi was a race of Horatio Algers and Jude Fawleys (cf. Kim D. 1998:68–72). Present success may very well inflame the perception of past obstacles and injustices inflicted by Japanese society.

Ethnic identity, finally, is as much about the future as about the past or the present. Many discussions of ethnic identity draw on memory and the shared experience as the core constituents. Yet a presumed community of fate is simultaneously a subjunctive community of destiny. "Where should we be?" is the question—Kang answers that Zainichi should live in Northeast Asia among diasporic Koreans, whereas Tei and Asakawa argue that the future of Zainichi is squarely in Japanese society. Each perspective may adduce distinct evidence and arguments, but there is no objective or neutral way to adjudicate which is more cogent or compelling. Needless to say, each individual comes up with her or his conclusion; yet that conclusion is often influenced, at times profoundly, by reading or listening to intellectuals such as Kang and Tei. Legal and economic conditions may change beyond recognition. Tei could not have predicted that he would become a naturalized Japanese citizen in his youth; it is not impossible that Kang may advocate naturalization as the privileged and preferred course of Zainichi in the future. In short, the banal point that the future is uncertain makes any number of claims about ethnic identity more or less plausible, but no particular one definitive.

In short, intellectual resolution is impossible. Given the profoundly prescriptive character of identity assertion, it cannot be reduced to fact or logic, history or sociology. Constituted as it is by memory, politics, and projection, identity choice is fundamentally complex and labile.

THE QUESTION OF NATURALIZATION

What was unthinkable for Sōren ideology and undesirable for Zainichi ideology but encouraged by post-Zainichi ideology is naturalization. As I argued in chapter 3, naturalization remained something of a taboo among the Zainichi population and for much of the 1950s and 1960s the figure fluctuated between the 2,000s and 3,000s. By the early twenty-first century, over 10,000 Zainichi were becoming Japanese citizens every year.

Legal changes facilitated naturalization. The 1985 revision of Japan's nationality laws, as I mentioned in chapter 1, eliminated the patrilineal descent of citizenship, and also the strict adherence to *jus sanguinis* (Sasaki 2006:47–51). In 1987 it became possible to adopt an "ethnic" name as a Japanese national. Thus, Japanese citizenship was compatible, at least legally, with Korean ethnicity.

Naturalization continues to evoke great passion. In the late 1990s Lee

Hoesung decided to shift his "Chōsen" nationality to South Korean. The proximate reasons were his sympathy with the newly democratic South Korea and his antipathy toward the North (he learned that his three cousins who had repatriated to North Korea had died around 1980 after being tortured) (Lee H. 1998:309–11). "There is something strange about living comfortably in Japan as 'exile' or a 'person without nationality'" (Lee H. 1998:314). Kim Sokpom's (1998) response accused Lee of past and present prevarications. Writing directly to Lee, Kim (1998:139–40) argued: "You are not originally a South Korean national. [You are] Zainichi [*Zainichi Chōsenjin*]. . . . Can't you turn your gaze to the suffering of the Zainichi minority [who have Chōsen identification, which is allied with neither North nor South]?" Kim accused Lee of betraying diasporic nationalism and Zainichi ideology. Lee's (1999:268–69) angry response in turn underscores the futility of regarding Zainichi as a "third force" beyond North and South, left and right. Needless to say, naturalization as Japanese would be unthinkable for Lee and Kim. A fundamental pillar of Kim's philosophy, as we saw in chapter 2, is "anti-Japanese." Yet the vicious and involuted debate between Lee and Kim suggests the contemporary irrelevance of Zainichi ideology. After all, the question of nationality for nearly all Zainichi is not about the choice between North, South, and "Chōsen" nationality but whether or not to become a Japanese citizen. Interestingly, Lee continues to reside in Japan presumably because, as he stated when explaining why naturalization was increasing in 2001, "put simply, Japan is easy to live in" (Lee H. 2002:331).

Kim and Lee are exemplary figures of Zainichi ideology. As the nationalist mind-set that precluded the possibility of transnational liaisons and links eroded, so too did the categorical opposition to naturalization. Mindan, for example, dropped its objection to naturalization in the late 1990s (Sasaki 2006:79–80). More significantly, a new generation came of age in which the taboo no longer made intuitive sense. For third-generation Zainichi, the very idea that nationality should be the last redoubt of ethnicity is not as compelling as it was for the previous generations. According to Sasaki Teru (2006:95), the most common reason for naturalization was "for children" (45 percent), followed by "for rights" (21 percent). In Asakawa Akihiro's (2003:140) survey, the intention "to continue to live in Japan" was the primary response, followed by the desire "to give children Japanese nationality." More concretely, naturalization resolved the contradiction between the reality of living in Japan and the inconvenience of being a foreigner. A woman in her twenties who uses a Japanese alias found it strange to be called by her Korean name at a driving school: "After all, I was born in and grew up in Japan. I became naturalized because I . . . intend to continue to reside in Japan" (Asakawa 2003:141). A significant group of Zainichi felt Japanese naturalization merely confirmed their preferred national identity (Sasaki 2006:101). As Kaneko Hiroshi (1996:113) put it: "It's more practical to naturalize. . . . I am a product of Korean blood and culture. . . . I think of myself as Korean Japanese." A strong sense of Korean identity is not necessarily incompatible with naturalization. A man in his forties grew up with a great deal of ethnic pride and used his Korean name at school. Employed by a South Korean bank, he encountered discrimination by South Koreans—"I really dislike South Koreans from the homeland"—and decided to cast his lot with Japan (Asakawa 2003:143). To the extent that there is a modal answer, naturalization expresses a desire to live in Japan. As a woman in her thirties noted: "I thought that it would be better to become naturalized if I were to lead my life in Japan. And my husband is Japanese and what if we have children?" (Asakawa 2003:142). The rise of intermarriage suggests the continuing integration of Zainichi into Japanese life, and naturalization as one of its consequences.

For the post-Zainichi generation, the question of nationality is decoupled from the problematic of Zainichi identity, and the decision to naturalize is a matter of individual choice. The rhetoric of choice paradoxically leaves an uneasy silence on the question of naturalization. As Shirai Miyuki (2007:6) suggests, there are almost no discussions and debates on the rights and wrongs of naturalization. The predominant reason is that the question of naturalization, like that of intermarriage, is the province of individual decision. Given the weakness of Zainichi organizations and the decline of Zainichi ideology, there are precious few institutions or ideas that continue to bind Zainichi to ancestral nationality. As the process has become easier, including the ability to keep many Korean names, the hurdles have lowered on the Japanese side. The pachinko "king," Han Chan'u, became naturalized in 2002 and claims that "nothing changed," not even his name (Shirai 2007:85). It is not surprising that virtually everyone Shirai interviewed could not deny the right of every Zainichi to decide for herself or himself. It was not so long ago that naturalization was tantamount to treason, but as Talleyrand reputedly quipped, treason is a matter of dates, and, one might add, of perspectives.

THE CHANGING JAPANESE IMAGINARY OF KOREA AND KOREANS

If the trend toward naturalization suggests the evisceration of anti-Japanese attitudes among Zainichi, it also implies the decline of colonial racism

and its legacy. Having conquered Korea, the presumption of Japanese superiority was the predominant Japanese attitude toward Korea in the postwar
period. Given the fact of colonialism and the postwar ideology of monoethnicity, one would be tempted to trace an uninterrupted trajectory of
anti-Korean sentiments in Japan. No government, however, colonizes
another because of its dislike for that other; the dislike is almost always
articulated as a sense of superiority. Superiority, in turn, often justifies the
very act of colonization, and the colonized—since they are in some sense
part of the colonizing country—may be inferior but not disliked. People
living in Japan have uttered numerous complimentary comments about
Korean civilization: ancient Japan, after all, imported "advanced" culture
via the Korean peninsula. Even during the colonial era, for every Terauchi
Masatake, the notorious governor of colonial Korea, there was an occasional Yanagi Muneyoshi, a connoisseur of things Korean. As I stressed in
chapter 1, the Japanization effort in the late colonial period provided an
ideological underpinning for a kinder, gentler view of Koreans as people
akin to younger siblings: inevitably inferior, perhaps, but educable and
almost lovable as well. A 1939 survey asked Japanese students to rank in
order of preference fifteen peoples: Koreans ranked fifth, behind Japanese
themselves; two Axis allies, Germans and Italians; and another colonized
people, Manchurians (Tei 1995:3).

The postwar period generated a great deal of ethnic Korean mobilization in Japan, especially in the form of militant workers and black-market
activities, and thereby entrenched the general association of Koreans with
criminality and illegality, violence and insolence. The authorities, as well
as the compliant mass media, projected a bleak picture of ethnic Koreans.
Not surprisingly, by the time the researcher of the 1939 survey reprised
his study in 1949, Koreans were ranked dead last (Tei 1995:3). The prevailing Japanese view of Koreans in the immediate postwar years depicted
them as "dirty, low level of culture, sly, not useful for the economy, make
fun of the Japanese, not good for Japan, bear grudge against Japan, ugly"
(Tei 1995:6). In a late 1970s survey, Koreans were imputed with negative
characteristics, such as sly, rustic, poor, pathetic, and barbaric (Hyon
1983:52–53). The unfair and unfortunate equation of Zainichi with criminal violence was etched in popular memory by the two sensational cases—
the 1958 Komatsugawa Incident and the 1968 Kim Hiro Incident—I discussed in chapter 3. The genealogy of Zainichi violence would be
resurrected from time to time, with suspicions of poverty and patriarchy,
irritability and inscrutability. These unflattering stereotypes would be
perpetuated relatively unscathed during the postwar period.

Given the prevalent conflation of Koreans in the Korean peninsula and ethnic Koreans in Japan, the low regard for South and North Korea merely confirmed the derogatory image of Zainichi. In spite of some avid support for North Korea in the postwar period, anticommunism remained a potent current that rendered Koreans as "threatening" [*kowai*]. As early as the nineteenth century, the rather fanciful portrayal of the Korean peninsula as the "dagger" about to be thrust into the Japanese body politic justified Japanese conquest. The Korean War and the Rhee Line accentuated the negative perception of South Korea among the Japanese public. Furthermore, South Korea, from Rhee Syngman to Park Chung Hee, was autocratic, militaristic, atavistic. The kidnapping of Kim Dae Jung and the missionary incursion of the Unification Church in the 1970s propelled the image of South Korea as a threat to bourgeois comforts and security (cf. Mun 2007:162–64).

Beyond these dark and derogatory images lies a simpler fact: the pervasive Japanese neglect of the Korean peninsula. In the postwar period, Korea was "a country at once near and far" [*chikakute tōi kuni*]. In part the sentiment articulated the geopolitical reality: until the 1965 Normalization Treaty the flow of people and commodities across the Sea of Japan was minimal. In Japan's genuflection to the West, the foreign referred above all to the United States and to lesser extent to European countries. For a good two decades after 1945, the only Japanese university to offer a course of study in Korean was Tenri University (Hatada 1969:78–79), and it largely served Japanese police officers and security officials (Hagiwara 1998:57–58). The study of Korean history and culture was almost nonexistent (Yoon 1990:102–3, 1997:201–5). Although books and articles on the Koreas and even the Zainichi population appeared, few depicted the quotidian livelihood of South or North Koreans or the Zainichi population. It is only in the mid-1980s—in anticipation of the 1988 Seoul Olympics—that Sekikawa Natsuo (1984b) and Yomota Inuhiko (1984) provided pioneering accounts of contemporary South Korean life that went beyond geopolitics and ideological conflicts to portray Koreans as "ordinary" people. The general ignorance about the Korean peninsula extended to the Zainichi population as well. As an early work on Zainichi noted: "Ignorance, lack of consciousness, discrimination, and prejudice are overflowing in the everyday life of Japanese people" (Satō 1971:24; cf. Zainichi Chōsenjin 1977:2).

The fundamental fact about Japanese attitudes toward Korea and Koreans was therefore *ignorance*. A 1979 study showed that most Japanese lacked elementary knowledge of Zainichi history, such as the post-Kantō earthquake massacre (Uchiyama 1982:12–13). In another survey conducted a decade later, one in five Japanese did not know that Japan had colonized Korea (*Asahi shinbun* 8 January 1991). Prejudice is learned; racism is a form of social knowledge. Therefore, it should not be surprising that pejorative sentiments deepened with more education in the postwar era (cf. Hatada 1969:72). Undoubtedly, colonial-era knowledge persisted in the postwar period, but by the turn of the century the memory of the colonial era was squarely in the realm of history. Negative attitudes toward Korea frequently seized on shards of geopolitical knowledge: the devastations of the Korean War, the military dictatorship in South Korea, the communist dictatorship in North Korea, and the presumed poverty of the two Koreas.

The phenomenal popularity of *Fuyu no sonata* ironically demonstrates the Japanese public's abysmal ignorance about South Korea. According to the sociologist Mōri Yoshitaka's (2004:42) interviews, fanatical fans were surprised that South Koreans do not usually don their ethnic clothing or that they are technologically advanced. A woman in her forties disliked South Korea because her husband had gone there on a *kisaeng* (call girls masquerading as Chosŏn-era courtesans) tour (Hirata 2004:60). That is, South Korea was assumed to somehow lag behind Japan in gender relations. Similarly, a woman in her thirties went to South Korea as a student but found the country "behind" Japan. The soap opera, however, showed that South Koreans lived no differently from Japanese, eating for example at fashionable restaurants (Mōri 2004:43). That is, the world of the soap opera was denuded of Koreanness. In sensing similarities, the few differences became interesting and even charming, including the thick tangle of family relations that had become unusual in Japanese life (Hirata 2004:65–66).

The status of an ethnic group is correlated to the standing of its home country. While South Korea was consistently one of the most disliked countries among Japanese people in the 1960s, by the early 1980s roughly 20 percent "disliked" and 10 percent "liked" South Korea; by 1999, favorable sentiments exceeded unfavorable ones (Terasawa 2002:149). From the 1988 Seoul Olympics to the 2002 World Cup, sports kindled Japanese interest in South Korea. Along with growing tourism, Korean food became a "boom." By 2000, kimchi was the most-produced pickle in Japan, far exceeding the more traditional *takuan* (Chon D. 2005:319). Ogura Kizō (2005:56–68) proposes a "Copernican revolution [in the Japanese image of Koreans] as cool, powerful, exotic, and romantic" (Ogura 2005:56–68). The generally positive image of South Korea buoyed the prevailing Japanese perception of Zainichi. It is not an accident that the first prime-time television drama to feature a Zainichi character aired in 2004—*Tokyo wankei* [Tokyo bayview]—at the height of the *Fuyu no sonata* boom. The 1993 release of the film *Tsuki wa dotchi ni deteiru* [Where is the moon rising] had revived Zainichi in the Japanese popular media (Henshūbu 1995:13). Since the film received the Kinema Junpō award in 1994, three others with very strong Zainichi ties have garnered the prestigious prize: *Go* (2001) in 2002, *Patchigi!* (2004) in 2006, and *Fura gāru* [Hula girls, 2006] in 2007.

Favorable sentiments toward Korea, Koreans, and Zainichi did not arise *de novo* in the 1980s. There were Korea sympathizers from the colonial period, but the initial stirrings in the postwar period date from the early 1960s, exemplified by the establishment of Nihon Chōsen Kenkyūjo [Japan Center of Korean Studies] and Zainichi Chōsenjin no Jinken o Mamorukai [The Association to Protect the Rights of Zainichi]. These in turn owe a great deal to the mass-media coverage of the 1958 Komatsugawa Incident (as much as it enforced negative stereotypes about Zainichi criminality) and the late 1950s repatriation project (cf. Takayanagi 1995:56–59). Both incidents drew attention to the plight of individual Zainichi—along with the bestseller *Nianchan* (1958)—but the repatriation project in particular led the Japanese mass media to convey "candid descriptions of the adverse living conditions of Koreans in Japan" (Lee Changsoo 1981:102; see Rōdōsha Ruporutāju Shūdan 1959). Sakanaka Hidenori (2005b:146–47) recalls the shock of discovering the "hidden 'Japan' " while working as a low-level civil servant in the Immigration and Naturalization Bureau's Osaka office. He had believed that "foreigners" denoted Westerners but experienced a "culture shock" when he realized that "99 percent" of them were Zainichi. He learned the "ferocity of Japanese society's anti-Korean discrimination" that necessitated "passing" and even occluding one's ethnic status to children: "I felt strong anger against the existence of horrible discrimination against Koreans" (Sakanaka 2005b:148). Sakanaka is hardly alone. A society of disrecognition—as much as "good" Japanese existed during the colonial period—produced ethnic Japanese who sympathized with the Zainichi population. The actress Kuroda Fukumi (1995:9) became an "expert" on Korea in the 1980s because of her "anger against 'Zainichi discrimination.' " However supercilious or superficial the views and commitments of some of them may have been, the possibility of Zainichi recognition and reconciliation depended on the righteous ethnic Japanese population. More prosaically, there were indisputable bonds and relationships between members of the two groups. In a mid-1980s survey, less than a quarter of Zainichi respondents claimed to have no close Japanese friends (Kanagawa-kennai 1986:120–23). Although one may interpret the number to signify ethnic distance, many ethnic Koreans had established close ties to ethnic Japanese people.

Anti-Korean sentiments, to be sure, are openly articulated in contemporary Japan. The manga *Kenkanryū* seeks to redress what the author sees as a dangerously anti-Japanese sentiment among both Korean and Japanese media and intellectuals (Yamano 2005). Its phenomenal popularity should not, however, be equated with colonial and postcolonial racism. The author claims to be "basically attracted to South Korea" (Yamano 2006:231). His anti-Korean views are informed by knowledge of Zainichi history and sociology. It is a far cry from several decades ago, when ignorance and insouciance, if not an outright sense of superiority, dominated the Japanese perception of Zainichi and Koreans. More to the point, it is a backlash against the predominance of favorable sentiments about Koreans and Zainichi. When the playwright Tsuka Kōhei (1990) wrote openly about his Korean ancestry, I was struck that several people—some Zainichi but others not—disparaged his effort to escape the ethnic closet. They suggested moreover that Tsuka had done so in order to call attention to himself—a Japanese vice—in order to resuscitate his sagging popularity. In fact, after 1990 or so, I heard repeated criticisms of Zainichi writers precisely for being open about their Korean ancestry. Rather than being a stigmatized status, Zainichi transformed into a privileged position for some. The critic Ri Kenji (2007:25) was told by an ethnic Japanese fellow graduate student: "I am envious that you are Zainichi. If I were born as Korean, my research would have received more attention." Far from being a heroic figure taking part in a political struggle of ethnic recognition or a probing author engaged in ethnic exploration, they were at times dismissed for attempting to "sell" their ethnicity.

The indisputably greater stock of knowledge that Japanese people gained about the Koreas and Korean history and culture applies to the Zainichi population as well. At times the knowledge accentuated the acknowledgment of similarity. For example, persistent patterns of gender discrimination, especially the legacy of patriarchy and patrilineality, do not differentiate Koreans from Japanese as much as unite them (Chon 1993:50–55). Familiarity may breed contempt, but it also breeds familiarity; the devil you know is reputedly better than the one you don't. It is easy to criticize the superficial nature of contemporary Japanese political correctness, but it is far better to have political correctness if one wishes to minimize verbal assaults and employment discrimination (cf. Iwabuchi 2000:60). Essentialized or misrecognized though they may be, Zainichi and South Koreans are no longer objects of derision and dismissal.

In general, the decline of monoethnic ideology opened up possibilities for ethnic recognition. By the turn of the millennium, active and vocal organizations of minority groups refuted Japanese monoethnicity. When I began working on my book *Multiethnic Japan* in the late 1980s, several people quipped that the title was either an oxymoron or the topic of a very short essay. By the time the book was published in 2001, some people said that I was stating the obvious: a common enough sociological sin, to be sure, but an indisputable indication of change. In this context, Zainichi identity is accorded a degree of legitimacy and respect that would have been unimaginable even in the mid-1980s.

RECONCILIATION WITHOUT RESTITUTION, ACCOMMODATION WITHOUT ATONEMENT

The escalating esteem of South Korea—though North Korea remained a country to fear and parody—occurred in tandem with the decline of ethnic discrimination. The Japanese government's effort to be in line with the "advanced" countries—as well as in response to pressures from human rights and antidiscrimination groups—extirpated outright policies of discrimination. Social movements contributed to raising Japanese consciousness about societal evil. The efflorescence of subpolitics—the rights of women, the disabled, minorities, and other subnational groups—elicited a cultural shift against prejudice and discrimination. Japanese people became conscious of, as well as personally engaged with, Zainichi people. By the late 1980s, discrimination [*sabetsu*] had become a dirty word.

Japan's ratification of the Universal Declaration of Human Rights in 1979 and the International Refugee Convention and Protocol in 1981 enshrined human rights and eviscerated racial, ethnic, and national discrimination in Japanese government policy. The first major measure was to open public university professorships to foreigners in 1982, followed by postal work in 1984 and nursing in 1986 (Nakahara 1993:65–69). Although both national and local authorities continued to restrict foreigners from public-sector employment, open discrimination has been in retreat since the 1980s. By 1991, the permanent residency [*tokubetsu eijū*] status was granted to almost all the Zainichi population, and by 1993 fingerprinting was abolished for permanent residents during alien registration (Kang C. 1994:162, 116). In theory at least, Zainichi as "settled aliens" [*teijū gaikokujin*] are "guaranteed almost the same rights as [Japanese] nationals" (Kondo 2001:9).

The declining force of systematic discrimination engendered efforts to incorporate the Zainichi population. Beyond lowering the hurdles for naturalization and dismantling legal bases of exclusion, the most visible act of recognition was suffrage rights in local elections. After the 1995 Japanese Supreme Court ruling on the constitutionality of local suffrage for noncitizens, the Zainichi right to vote in local elections spread across the nation. Sōren steadfastly maintains the mutually exclusive character of Koreans and Japanese and argues that the former should not meddle in the latter's affairs. Araki Kazuhiro (1997:64) voices the same logic: "If [Koreans] would like suffrage, then they should become Japanese citizens." This essentialist, binary logic perceives nationality, citizenship, and rights therein as fundamentally indivisible. In fact, however, there is nothing indivisible or inevitable in the relationship between citizenship and suffrage. As there are numerous nationals and citizens who did not exercise the right to vote (most women until the twentieth century), foreigners have cast votes in various places and times (Lie 2004b:132–33, 166). The significance of the local suffrage movement highlights the advances made by the Zainichi population as well as the limits of Zainichi ideology: to gain the ultimate mark of belonging (the right to vote) without actually belonging (resistance to naturalization) (cf. Kang S. 1994:39–43).

The decline in ethnic exclusion was accompanied by the economic integration of the Zainichi population. The general equation of ethnic Koreans with poverty was pronounced in the immediate postwar decade; Pak Cheil (1957:137) highlighted "impoverishment" as one of the two dominant characterizations of ethnic Koreans in Japan. More than three decades later, a 1991 study by a Zainichi group surveyed the employment situation in the Osaka area (Zainichi Kōrai Rōdōsha Renmei 1992). Self-employment (at nearly three times the frequency of Japanese) and working for fellow Zainichi (over 50 percent) characterized the sample. Forty percent experienced employment discrimination. Yet what is striking from this potentially grim portrait is the transformation from the immediate postwar decades. The majority claimed to have faced no employment discrimination when the reflexive refrain in the 1960s was that Koreans could not work in mainstream occupations. Fully half of the respondents claimed to use their ethnic Korean names. Along with the rapid enrichment of Japanese society, many Zainichi experienced structural and individual mobility. While the proportion of laborers was 21 percent in 1964, it had shrunk to 4 percent by 1984, even as the proportion of white-collar workers increased (clerical, 7 to 22 percent; merchandising, 14 to 21 percent; services, 2 to 7 percent) (Pak I. 2005b:277). Educational and employment gaps between ethnic Japanese and ethnic Koreans had narrowed considerably by the 1980s (Fukuoka and Kim 1997:27–28). Already by the mid-1980s, the proportion of ethnic Koreans in medical and scientific fields was twice that of the ethnic Japanese population (Nakahara 1993:9). At the time, there were an estimated 10,000 Zainichi with a total asset of 100 million yen or more (Pak I. 2005b:277). In a 2002 survey, 11 percent of respondents claimed an annual income of 10 million yen or more (Pak I. 2005b:284). Eleven of the twenty-four wealthiest Japanese are Zainichi (Miyatsuka 2006:96). Intraethnic inequality seems more pronounced than interethnic inequality after the 1980s (cf. Shōya and Nakayama 1997:81–91).

A persistent obstacle to Zainichi-Japanese reconciliation remains the ruling party and government bureaucracy's unwillingness to apologize and to make amends. The official line is that the 1965 Normalization Treaty resolved all the relevant issues, including colonial crimes. Yet no serious effort has been made to atone for historical injustices and mistakes, from the colonization of Korea itself to the systematic exclusion of Zainichi from Japanese public life until the 1980s (Wada 1985:7). Each protest, such as the anti-fingerprinting movement of the mid-1980s or the *ianfu* [wartime Korean sex workers] restitution movement, encounters a recalcitrant ruling party and a constitutionally conservative government bureaucracy. Instead, what steals the media attention is the revanchist right, from Prime Minister Koizumi's attendance at Yasukuni Shrine to honor Japan's war heroes to Kobayashi Yoshinori's manga screeds and *netto uyoku* [the Web-based ultranationalists].

Kenkanryū advocates exemplify a politics of pride and envy. They frequently take pride in Japan and resent its secondary status in world affairs, especially its inferiority against the victims of Japanese aggression. They also reveal *ressentiment* that rejects the empowerment of a minority. Their critical ire focuses on the progressives who harp on Japanese war guilt and Zainichi figures who criticize Japan. Engaged in ad hoc attacks—"crazy" is one of the many vitriolic adjectives hurled at Yū Miri by Ōtsuki Takahiro (2006:60)—the anti-Korean/Zainichi faction bemoans privileges meted to Zainichi, blames the progressive media and intellectuals, and endorses patriotic pride (cf. Ino 2006). That some of the most vociferous critics of Kang, Yū, and other critical Zainichi should be Zainichi themselves should not be surprising: think of African Americans who revile affirmative action policies and criticize black intellectuals. The self-described "third-generation Zainichi" Arai Kazuma (2006:11), for example, resurrects the essentialist binary and suggests that "if [Zainichi] want to engage deeply in Japan then they should do so by becoming Japanese nationals." In rejecting outright the possibility of complexity and hybridity, he also accepts right-wing historiography and merely turns Japanese "exclusion" of or "discrimination" against Zainichi into Zainichi "just deserts" (Arai 2006:231).

We should not underestimate the popular appeal of the nationalist right or *Kenkanryū*, but we should also not equate them with Japanese popular opinion. Neither should we efface the growing popular acknowledgment and acceptance of the Zainichi population because of official reluctance to atone, much less restitute, for colonial crimes and postcolonial mistreatments, as terrible as it is.

AUGURIES OF THE POST-ZAINICHI GENERATION

Since Kim Saryan in the colonial period, many ethnic Koreans writing in Japanese gained a significant following. If Kim Dalsu, Kim Sokpom, and Lee Hoesung were representative Zainichi writers in the postwar period, the emergence of Lee Yangji in the 1980s and Yū Miri in the 1990s went well past the older generation's male- and Cold War–centered narratives. By the 1990s, the classic problematic of Zainichi—the product of colonialism, capitalism, and racism—was fading in significance along with Zainichi ideology. Instead, Zainichi writings anticipated the post-Zainichi generation and Korean-Japanese identity.

Yan Sogiru's novel *Yoru no kawa o watare* [Cross the river of night, 1990] depicts Shinjuku nightlife. Although there are recollections of past struggles—the ethnic school he attended, the Japanese government's "suppression and discrimination," and ethnic Japanese harassment and violence against ethnic Koreans (Yan 1990:147–53)—the novel is anything but a chronicle of past discrimination. Rather, the focus is very much on the gambling, prostitution, and drugs that constitute the main characters' struggles. For them, "Japanese banks and Zainichi banks are the same" (Yan 1990:27). The changing Tokyo nightlife means that "foreigners" no longer refer automatically to ethnic Koreans, as Chinese and Filipina women are "taking over" Zainichi clubs and prostitution rings. It is a new Zainichi world of transnational flows of money and people and transethnic interactions and encounters.

A similar sensitivity is clear in Yan's recollection of his father, *Chi to hone* [Blood and bone, 1998]. Taking place in a Korean ghetto in colonial-era Japan, one might very well have expected an indictment of Japanese racism. Instead, it depicts the savage fury of the father's will to power. He beats and rapes his wife, threatens and thwacks business associates, openly takes a Japanese mistress: in short, he is a despicable figure. The power of the drama revolves around one man's life; its unvarnished visualizations of patriarchy and power take the story far beyond the province of Zainichi history. As much as the novel and the 2003 film explore the particular context of Zainichi characters, their deft examination allows its appeal to spread beyond the ethnic audience.

Tsuka Kōhei's *Musume ni kataru sokoku* [Ancestral land narrated to my daughter, 1990] is an epistolary reportage of the playwright's participation in staging one of his plays in South Korea. Born in 1948, he grew up in an era of "ferocious discrimination": "When I was a child, [South] Korea was definitely not a country that I could be proud of. Rather, I wanted to hide it" (Tsuka 1990:29, 31). Although married to a Japanese woman, Tsuka steadfastly refuses to become naturalized. At one point, he suggests that his action would be "socially important," but realizes later that if he were to naturalize other Zainichi may be emboldened to follow his example (42, 65). Although prejudice against Koreans has waned in Japan, he is aware of the lurking xenophobic and racist sentiments. Yet he does not feel compelled to write on explicitly Zainichi themes, such as "enforced migration," or to take part in Zainichi political activities, such as the fingerprinting refusal movement. Talking to a Zainichi businessman in his fifties, the discussion inevitably turns to the horrors of the early years and the unimaginable improvements in recent years. The businessman conveys his shock that his daughter's Japanese friend would like to wear her Korean costume: "What happened to the humiliating era when we continued to be discriminated against and our resentments grew? What was that about?" (63–64). Tsuka's "patriotic" feelings for South Korea are dashed when he is criticized upon arrival in Seoul for not knowing Korean (83–85). Beyond his linguistic limitation, his mode of living, as for the Zainichi writers I discussed in chapter 2, is thoroughly Japanese. He cannot, for example, join his South Korean actors in consuming dog meat. He is taken aback that the physical manifestation of sexual frustration in South Korea is an itchy ear, not a bloody nose as in Japan (130–31). He concludes that his ancestral land is his daughter's beauty, his wife's kindness, and "the passion of papa's love for mama" (180).

These three works from the early 1990s demonstrate the fracturing of Zainichi identity and the loosening grasp of homeland orientation and Zainichi ideology. A critical departure from Sōren or Zainichi ideology is the acceptance of Japan as home.

Consider other contemporary Zainichi life narratives. Shigeyama Sadako suffered poverty and prejudice, but remained so proud of her Korean ancestry that she refuses to become naturalized. Yet she intends to die as a second-generation Zainichi in Japan: "I can say with pride that 'blood is Korean' and 'heart is Japanese'" (Shigeyama 2006:313). As a self-described "third-generation Zainichi" Lee Seijaku (1997:10) readily claims dual belonging: "As my South Korean father's daughter I am a South Korean national, but because I was born and reared in Japan, I am also Japanese." Chon Jan's poem, "Falling in Love with Japanese," ends: "Falling in love with Japanese / I was able to love / My Korea and the Other's Japan / As Zainichi I was able to love / The other's Korea and my Japan / I called myself, anew, *saram* [human being in Korean]" (Morita and Sagawa 2005:358).

Kyō Nobuko (2002:301) recalls that there used to be only two solutions: "complete assimilation as Japanese or ethnic consciousness as Korean." In spite of her efforts to pursue the latter course, in the end she finds that, "my simple sensibility was that I was neither Japanese nor Korean" (Kyō 2002:302). This is the dilemma from which Zainichi identity, as well as Zainichi ideology, emerged. Yet by the turn of the century, many Zainichi were rejecting the solution of diasporic nationalism. Zainichi ideology remained too beholden to the tragic past and to homeland; its prescriptive and restrictive dictates did not find a receptive audience who wished to represent themselves individually. Thus, Korean-Japanese identity emerged: an identity that in turn was something of a nonidentity. The received vocabulary of blood and nation, ethnicity and purity, no longer made sense: "I don't really understand the meaning of having the same blood" (Lee S. 1997:90). Kaneshiro's protagonist champions individual freedom and revels in the floating signifier that is ethnicity. "I intend to rebel against the ethnicity to which I belong" (Kaneshiro 2000:25); "I will one day erase the national boundary line" (217). As Sugihara quotes his father: "no soy Coreano, ni soy Japonés, yo soy desarraigado" [I am not Korean, not Japanese, I am deracinated]. Escaping the trap of essentialism results in rejecting the trap of identity: "I am not Zainichi, South Korean, North Korean, or Mongoloid. Please don't push me into a narrow corner. I am I. No, I don't like that I am I. I was to be liberated from being myself" (234). However inchoate and incomplete, Zainichi experienced emancipation from colonial domination and postcolonial disrecognition.

ASSIMILATION AND ASSERTION

The postcolonial period has not ended insofar as reconciliation and restitution have not occurred. Neither North Korea nor Sōren has disappeared, contrary to every expectation. Zainichi ideology itself is undoubtedly in decline but still has many adherents. Some Zainichi, who were born, reared, and expect to be buried in Japan, are determined to go to their grave with their Chōsen, North Korean, or South Korean nationality intact. Nonetheless, representative Zainichi groups are no longer Sōren and Mindan, but newly formed associations, such as Ryōchikai, established in 1996, to promote convivial society *[kyōsei shakai]* for Zainichi and Japanese. The sheer diversity of Zainichi, as exemplified in Ryōchikai's (1997) book *100 nin no Zainichi Korian* [One hundred Zainichi], resists a solidarity based on sameness or even similarity. In accepting Japan as "home" and distancing themselves from the Koreas, they are no longer in thrall of the mainline ethnic organizations or the straitjacket of Zainichi ideology.

Ethnic solidarity has become less compelling also because of the "newcomers" from South Korea. The postwar period never totally closed the influx from the Korean peninsula: legal and illegal entries continued. Saitō Hiroko (1994:17–18) illegally entered Japan in 1965 to pursue her romance; she was far from alone. In a mid-1980s survey of Kanagawa Prefecture, 18 percent of ethnic Koreans came to Japan after 1945, and over 10 percent after 1972 (Kanagawa-kennai 1986:14–15). What was distinct by the 1990s, however, was that the newcomers formed their own networks, rather than being integrated into the existing Zainichi communities. Already by 1989, there was a periodical, *Kankokujin seikatsu jōhō,* which catered to recent immigrants from South Korea. They added distinct layers of diversity among ethnic Koreans in Japanese society. Gen Getsu's *Ibutsu* [Foreign object, 2005] depicts the exclusionary and even racist sentiment of a third-generation Zainichi protagonist, Ikeyama, against ethnic Korean "newcomers" from South Korea and China. Often "invited" by longtime residents though illegal, they have replenished and transformed the declining population of Zainichi in the multiethnic city that is Osaka. Yet Ikeyama finds that "culture and language are different"; the newcomers are an "eyesore" (Gen 2005:153, 150; cf. Gen 2007:59–60). Yang Tae-hoon (2007:132, 17), the self-professed "new first-generation Zainichi," finds Tokyo to be a wonderful place to live but the Zainichi population puzzling. However atypical Ikeyama and Yang may be, Zainichi and the "newcomers" hardly constitute a homogeneous group. Social distance among "Koreans" reveals the false promise of ethnic solidarity and therefore the implausibility of Zainichi ideology.

None of the pillars of Zainichi ideology, then, remains robust: anti-Japanese sentiments have weakened, homeland orientation is in decline, unification is no longer a paramount political goal, and the categorical resistance to intermarriage and naturalization has withered away. In short, the end of Zainichi ideology is nigh. Symptomatically, rather than the rigorous party line during the heydays of Sōren or even of Zainichi ideology, Zainichi criticisms of Zainichi society abound. Pak Hwami (2000:29) bemoans the persistence of "feudal" gender and family relations and urges Zainichi to acknowledge the legitimacy of anger, autonomy, and individuality. Pe Ginban (2000:59) laments that social welfare has been "left behind" and that there are no associations to aid the disabled in Zainichi society, unlike the larger Japanese society. By 2007 the naturalized Zainichi attorney Pae Hun was saying that "It is all right if [Zainichi] should disappear" (Shirai 2007:28). Sakanaka Hidenori's (2005a:185) argument from the late 1970s seems prescient: "Sometime in the first half of the twenty-first century, Zainichi will become perfectly assimilated into Japanese society . . . we will not be able to see their shape in Japanese society." Does the declining influence of Zainichi ideology mean the decline of ethnic identity and the disappearance of Zainichi?

Just as much as essentialist thinking is misleading, discrimination and identity are not mechanical, objective variables. The eclipse of institutional racism or legal discrimination does not necessarily extirpate the subjective experience of prejudice or discrimination. While the physical lynching of African Americans was far too common in the postbellum United States, the charge of racism then was almost certainly less frequent than today, when symbolic slights can easily provoke righteous indignation. To put it polemically, Jews in Germany did not cry "anti-Semitism" during the Shoah, but their descendants will not hesitate to make the accusation when graffiti disgrace Jewish graves. Being profoundly symbolic, ethnic honor and ethnic identification may very well be enhanced even as structural discrimination recedes (Lie 2004b:258–63). Harajiri Hideki (1998:174) counters the claim that many Zainichi are not discriminated against by noting that "the problem lies with those who say that they are 'not discriminated against.'" There is little doubt that pejorative characterizations and ethnic epithets filled everyday conversation among Japanese people before and after 1945. Yet the rare public utterances of previously common locutions such as *Senjin* or *Daisankokujin* became noxious vesicants by the turn of the century (cf. Kure 2007:25–28). Experiences of racism or discrimination are ultimately subjective interpretations.

As we have seen, assimilation was discussed as early as the 1930s. Whether one picks up a book on Zainichi written in 1957, 1967, 1971, 1978, or 1993, it is taken to be a master trend affecting the population (Pak Cheil 1957:131, Mitchell 1967:159–60, Ri 1971:398–99, Kim I. 1978:183–86,

Fukuoka 1993:52). Furthermore, the received definition of Zainichi as Korean nationals residing in Japan provides the sole source of Zainichi demographics. As naturalization proceeds, the Zainichi population seems to be in terminal decline. If we regard Zainichi to include Japanese citizens with Korean ancestry, then the population figure is surely increasing. Naturalization and assimilation, in other words, do not inevitably imply the end of Zainichi. Instead, identity assertion is compatible with educational and employment integration. When ethnicity ceased to be a structural feature that determined individual opportunities and trajectories, it emerged as a symbolic locus of identity formation. The paradox of structural integration and cultural differentiation can be resolved by considering the capacity and consciousness of a minority group. When ethnic Koreans were indisputably a lower-status group during the colonial period, few Koreans had the opportunities or resources to articulate an identity. To the extent that some did—as we saw in chapter 1—they did so as assimilated Japanese. By the end of the twentieth century, and in spite of the persistence of interethnic income and educational inequality, many ethnic Koreans had the positions from which to speak out and the intellectual resources with which to articulate the message. The changes were overlaid with the enhanced sensitivity to slights as ethnic Koreans ascended the status hierarchy. That is, whereas ethnic epithets may have been merely an accompaniment of physical blows during the colonial period, they stung more sensitive souls reared in the belief in human rights and dignity.

In the early twenty-first century, Zainichi identity, if not Zainichi ideology, remains vibrant. Moreover, Zainichi ethnic assertion is far from uniform, as we can see from diverse attitudes toward ethnic education and reproduction. As we saw in the previous chapter, Kim Kyongdok, the first non-Japanese national to become an attorney *[bengoshi]* in Japan in 1979, had effaced his ethnic identity for the first twenty-three years of his life. Yet because he believes that "Zainichi Koreans must take back the Korean language that had been stolen by ethnic discrimination," he continues to speak in less-than-perfect Korean (Kim Kyongdok 2006:15), even as his South Korean wife tries to talk in Japanese. In spite of his explicit commitment to promoting ethnic consciousness, he has not in fact told his children, who converse in Japanese, about the past or the present of Zainichi (Kim Kyongdok 2006:18).

Kanemura Yoshiaki is a well-known baseball player who became a television commentator. Having "naturally accepted" his third-generation Zainchi status, he hopes to inculcate the same "Zainichi spirit"—which he often equates with the "hungry spirit" denoting a diligent life—to his children. Having experienced ethnic jeering and discrimination, he responded by redoubling his effort (Kanemura 2004:85–86). Although he and his wife tell their children about their Zainichi status, they are indistinguishable from other Japanese people (253). Kanemura stresses the universal nature of human life and looks forward to a time in which twenty-first-century youths will regard the problem of Zainichi as "smaller than snot" (254).

Yi Chinmi (2006), a "2.5 generation" Zainichi married to a Japanese man, also makes very little effort at ethnic education. Her two daughters can say simple greetings and write their names in Korean. "Our daughters have never been to South Korea and they cannot speak Korean. They cannot eat spicy food and they don't have a particular pride as Korean" (Yi C. 2006:36). Unlike Kim Kyongdok's children, they don't even support South Korean teams. Yi believes furthermore that Zainichi women should marry Japanese men. Yet the two girls identify themselves as Korean [*Kankokujin*] and use their Korean names to attend Japanese school. They are "openly [*akkerakan*] doing 'Korean'" (Yi C. 2006:37).

Kim Yong (2006) sends his children to a Sōren school but finds it hard to sit through the singing of a song honoring Kim Il Sung and remains skeptical about the North Korean ideology inculcation [*shisō kyōiku*]. He sends them to Korean school for "very small reasons," such as being able to take kimchi in school lunch and to play with ethnic Koreans while speaking "poor" Korean (Kim Yong 2006:82–83). Another parent who chose an ethnic Korean school told me that Japanese public schools are ethnic Japanese schools. Hence, as an ethnic Korean, she felt more comfortable with an ethnic Korean school.

Yi Kisun (2006) chose Japanese school for his two daughters. When they lived in South Korea, he also sent them to Japanese school where their younger daughter was bullied by other South Koreans because she was "Japanese." She was in turn bullied as a Korean when she returned to Japan. Yi is skeptical about ethnic education and valorizes "human education" [*ningen kyōiku*], believing that ability to think ethically, for example, is far superior to the value of patriarchy common to Japan and South Korea (Yi K. 2006:120).

Iwamoto Mitsuo (2000), born in 1960, attended Japanese public schools and experienced a fair amount of anti-Korean prejudice in the course of his life. As a child he would go to bed wishing that "when I wake up, perhaps I will be Japanese," and dream that he was "really Japanese," but inevitably he would wake up sighing that he was still Korean (Iwamoto 2000:70). A trip to North Korea left him cold. Listening to anti-American slogans, he thought, "This is stupid. Whatever you say about the United States or

Japan, both are inseparable for us who live in Japan" (110). He eventually married a Japanese woman, became naturalized, got divorced, and gained South Korean nationality. Long ashamed of being Korean, in his forties he can more or less openly declare, "I was [South] Korean until recently, but I am now doing Japanese. However, I may become [South] Korean again. Oh, I was doing North Korean in the past" (216). As the verb *doing* suggests, he is relatively secure that his individuality can be decoupled from nationality and name: "I don't need to brood over who I am. My freedom is to live as Zainichi" (219). Although the book is titled "Zainichi who want to be Japanese," his desire is not to naturalize but rather to live in Japan, "living through crying and laughing" (220).

As Iwamoto's case suggests, naturalization does not mean the expunction of Korean ethnicity, but rather its continuation and even accentuation. Arai Eiichi, the self-proclaimed Korean-Japanese singer, embarked on his search for his roots as he was contemplating naturalization. The search transmogrified into his epic song "Chonhā e no michi" [The road to Chonhā, 1985]. Yi Jon'yan (1985:55) studied Korean history and Zainichi literature after naturalization. Whereas he had used his Japanese alias, after naturalization he uses his Korean name—now ironically his *tsūmei*. Asakawa's survey of naturalized Zainichi suggests that naturalization may in fact sustain and even enhance Korean identification. One woman in her sixties discusses how her sister began to learn Korean after naturalization; another woman in her fifties claims that her Korean "blood" is manifesting itself in her interest in things Korean; a man in his forties is conscious of the fact that his "root is [South] Korea"; a man in his fifties remarks, "Whatever the nationality, I think of myself as [South] Korean after I became naturalized"; and a woman in her twenties who is a fourth-generation Zainichi says, "Even though I became naturalized I merely gained Japanese nationality and in reality there is no change in the fact that I am [South] Korean" (Asakawa 2003:170–72). Naturalization implied neither betrayal nor Japanization.

The plausibility of Korean-Japanese identification can be seen in the adoption of ethnic Korean names. Whereas 85 percent of Korean children attending Japanese schools used *tsūmei* in 1979, the figure dropped to 65 percent by 1989 (Kyoto Daigaku 1990). Interestingly, the major reason—cited by 62 percent of the surveyed parents in 1989—for using a Japanese name is because "there is no particular need" to assert Koreanness. Yi Kisun (2000:20) writes: "For the first generation, *tsūmei* was theater. However, for the second generation that had to perform theater from birth, theater itself is life. . . . For the second generation, *tsūmei* is real name."

The resistance to using one's real name reveals the internalized discrimination against Koreans in the Zainichi psyche; using one's real name is a cure for the mental illness engendered by Japanese discrimination against Koreans (Yi K. 2000:22). The protagonist of Kaneshiro's *Go* (2000:23) does not resist the Japanese school officials' desire for him to use a Japanese name because he was bullied by teachers in his ethnic Korean schools as a "betrayer" after he had decided to switch to a Japanese school. The Zainichi historian Kim Yondal (2002:103) concluded: "I think it would be fine to have several names. I do not think that name must be something ethnic." There was clearly a sea change in the Zainichi "defense" of ethnicity by the 1990s.

Zainichi voices differ widely, but many accept their ethnic ancestry as readily as their permanent residence in Japan. The possibility of "ordinary" Zainichi becomes a realistic option. In these straightforward assertions and embrace of Korean ancestry lies the possibility of "Korean Japanese" identity that transcends the limitations set forth in Zainichi ideology (cf. Tai 2004:366–67; Sasaki 2006:20–25).

THE RECOVERY OF MULTIETHNIC JAPAN: LAUGHTER AND LOVE

The dark decades of disrecognition had given way to the crepuscular light of mutual recognition and nascent reconciliation by the turn of the twenty-first century. Both ethnic Japanese and ethnic Koreans recollected the monoethnic past and recast it as multiethnic. In so doing, the thematic of laughter and love superseded those of pathos and struggle that had clouded the postwar period. Yet another, albeit often neglected, dimension of recognition surfaced: the murky mixture of achievement and gratitude that strives toward acceptance and agape.

Two of the most popular Japanese movies of the 2000s, *Go* (2001) and *Patchigi!* (2005), feature Zainichi characters. *Patchigi!* takes place in the 1960s: a guitar-strumming ethnic Japanese student falls in love at first sight with a girl at an ethnic Korean school. Her brother is a boss among ethnic Korean high-school students, constantly fighting a gang of ethnic Japanese students. In a stereotypical '60s trope, love conquers all in the end, to the tune of Japanese and Korean folk songs. The movie's subtitle in English is "We shall overcome someday," and its promotional phrase is "The world can be changed by love" (Lee B. 2007:27). In spite of obstacles, the Korean siblings both end up with ethnic Japanese lovers. What reveals the movie's twenty-first-century production is its undertone of humor: even violence is funny. *Patchigi!* is set up like *West Side Story,* but the viewer is given neither interethnic conflict nor doomed romance. Saccharine, perhaps, but the bitterness is gone.

In spite of remnant racism, many Zainichi people lead comfortable and confident lives. The straightforward belief in their good fortune to be in Japan—long a repressed sentiment—became openly articulated by the 1990s (Kōtō Zainichi 1995:219–21; Fukuoka and Kim 1997:67–68). It is the context in which younger Zainichi, such as the protagonist in Kaneshiro's *Go,* can dismiss discriminatory Japanese people as "ignorant, weak, and pathetic" (Kaneshiro 2000:91; cf. Gu 2002:122). Alternatively, Kanemoto J. Noritsugu (2007:148) identifies his roots as Korean and finds it fitting for a "metrosexual" like him to be interested in a Korean cuisine that promises beauty.

Zainichi narratives in the age of reconciliation are perforce, in however muted a form, triumphalist, because material enrichment and weakening discrimination are indisputable. However much Zainichi ideologists indict Japanese society, the worst crimes were committed in the past. Physical lynching and cultural strangulation are distant, though constantly revived, memories; even desperate poverty and open racism are the stuff of infantile memories for Zainichi people. Shin Sugok (2006:241–42) casts her life as a master-slave dialectic: "I was discriminated from society because of being Korean, excluded from public services because I didn't have citizenship, and therefore forced into a condition of poverty, and discriminated against because of poverty." Yet her servitude allowed her to see through the "master" society and regain dignity. In spite of growing up amid poverty and discrimination, then, her dream is to "be born again as Zainichi [*Zainichi Chōsenjin*]." Kim Kyongdok (2005:57) describes his childhood in what can only be called Dickensian fashion: "A man [*ajoshi*] has been drinking [*shōchū,* Japanese vodka] since the morning and is in a drunken stupor on the roadside . . . . A woman [*ajumoni*] passes him by, pulling a cart and collecting leftovers from various houses for feeding pigs. . . . Couples fight in Korean, the angry man overturns the cart . . . dispersing the accumulated leftovers on the road. . . . Japanese passers-by glance coldly, avoiding the fighting couple." Yet Kim, as we saw, embraces his Korean identity. These memories are possible only for a dwindling number of Zainichi who came of age before the Tokyo Olympics.

What the representations of laughter and love exemplify are the possibilities of reconciliation beyond the assimilation of ethnic Koreans into Japanese society or the assertion of ethnic Korean consciousness. Since the 1990s, conviviality [*kyōsei*] has become the buzzword among well-meaning

Japanese people who seek mutual recognition and reconciliation (cf. Kim Yunjon 2007:162–66). The awareness of multiethnic Japan renders Zainichi recognition mainstream, and makes possible a perspective beyond the narrow Zainichi-Japanese relationship. Kaneshiro Kazuki (2001) can therefore write a novel that includes Filipino-Japanese and Zainichi characters and yet appeal to the ethnic Japanese population. Simultaneously, it calls for Zainichi to go beyond its received identity as an oppressed group to recognize its privileges and potential complicity in sustaining disrecognition against others. Kim Chongmi, born in 1976, attended ethnic Korean schools and did not really think about discrimination until she encountered Sakurai Toshio, a leper and poet. Her "pride was hurt" when she acknowledged her "unconscious discrimination" against the disfigured Sakura (Kim Chongmi 2002:52, 57). The acknowledgment of nonessential Zainichi, such as the disabled, led to movements and discourses to advocate their rights and welfare (Iinuma 1989, Kon 1993). Rather than focusing exclusively on ethnic Koreans—across Asia and even around the world—Zainichi recognition and empowerment pose an ethical challenge not to reconstruct the wall and recast the gaze of disrecognition against people who now occupy the unenviable positions that their forebears once suffered.

RECAPITULATION

After colonizing Korea and striving to assimilate Koreans, Japanese society systematically disrecognized ethnic Koreans who remained in Japan after the end of the war. Having been told that they were Japanese in blood and spirit, almost overnight they were apprised of the colonial illusions and their incorrigibly Korean nature. Colonial hierarchy and postcolonial domination cast ethnic Koreans as at once the inferior and Other. Not only were Zainichi receptacles of aspersions and animadversions—everything that was inferior to and different from the ethnic Japanese majority—but they should also not have been there. Living under de facto apartheid, ethnic Koreans did not even have the luxury of having the master race acknowledge their precarious place in Japanese society. Between 1952 and 1985, the legal reality and prevailing common sense projected Japan as a monoethnic society. Especially in the darkest decades of disrecognition—1950s and 1960s—the plaintive wails of Zainichi children pierced the inner recesses of Zainichi psyches and households. They were virtually Japanese; they were definitely not Japanese. How many cried that they wanted to die? How many blamed their parents for giving them birth?

Even as Zainichi were tethered to Japan—undergoing one of the most rapid spurts of economic growth in world history precisely during the darkest decades for ethnic Koreans—they learned at once to loathe their actual home and to love their "real" home. Ethnic organizations, especially Sōren, provided ideological and infrastructural support for co-ethnics. Sōren ideology, a permutation of the North Korean state ideology, promised return. It is not an accident that youths drenched in Sōren rhetoric looked to and loved the future: for the individual, return to homeland; for the collective, unification and utopia. The repatriation project, like the North Korean regime in general, turned out to be a fiasco, even a catastrophe. Disappointed in the dream of Sōren and North Korea, the Zainichi gaze shifted, especially after the 1965 Normalization Treaty, to South Korea. Yet the autocratic polity promised far less than the North, and the concrete reality of the South divulged distance and distrust. Disappointed in their divided and distant homelands, they gradually also lost their enthusiasm for the ethnic organizations that were their temporary asylums in Japan. Passing provided the master identity and the privileged path. The only hopes of worldly success seemed to reside in sports and music. By the late 1960s—exemplified by the Kim Hiro Incident—the Zainichi situation appeared desperate. They were trapped in Japan, they seemed destined to be the underclass, and they remained disrecognized.

Nonetheless, as the early 1970s victory of Pak Chonsok's employment discrimination lawsuit indicated, Zainichi individuals, along with concerned ethnic Japanese, had begun to engage in a politics of acknowledgment and acceptance, recognition and redemption. Zainichi ideology superseded Sōren ideology in finding a place for ethnic Koreans in Japanese society. Sustaining some of the politics and psychology of postwar, postcolonial struggles, Zainichi ideology remained instinctively anti-Japanese and homeland oriented. Yet it also provided a widely disseminated understanding of what it meant to be and to behave as Zainichi. During the 1970s and 1980s, discourses and movements of Zainichi recognition overturned much of the legal, institutional, and ideological apparatuses of disrecognition. Regaining much of the economic, civil, and social rights that they had lost between 1945 and 1952, Zainichi carved a legitimate and respected place in Japanese society. The very success of the population fractured any credible unitary ethnic identity; Zainichi ideology no longer made sense for differentiated Zainichi lives.

By the early twenty-first century, there were hints of reconciliation between the Zainichi population and Japanese government and society. In a way, one may very well understand reconciliation in its negative sense:

resignation. Yet it is possible to detect its positive articulation: mutual acknowledgment and acceptance. Just as much as Japanese society transformed profoundly, ethnic Koreans transfigured equally dramatically. The idea of multicultural Japan and the identity of Korean Japanese are inextricably intertwined and suggest one possible outcome of the modern Korean-Japanese entanglements.

6. Reflections

Kim Chung-myong's *Migiwa no tami* [People of Migiwa, 2000] expands the narrow historical and geographical focus on Zainichi to project a panoramic portrait of the people of Migiwa in the ninth century. In tracing the Buddhist monk Ennin's sojourn to seek knowledge on the Asian continent, Kim chronicles the prehistory of Korean-Japanese relations. Migiwa refers to seaborne people whose canvas of operation stretched from western to eastern Asia. From his voyages and conversations, especially with Ibn Zaid of Arabia, Chō Hokō, the leader of Migiwa, learns "that he is responsible for the eastern edge of world trade. Simultaneously, he began to think that he would like to see its entirety. . . . Compared to [it], the goings-on within Silla Kingdom [in the southeastern Korean peninsula] seemed like a tempest in a teacup" (Kim Chung-myong 2006:195). In contradistinction to the landlocked people—who constructed a legal state, status hierarchy, property rights, and the consequent distinctions and discriminations based on wealth, gender, and ethnonational belonging—the people of the sea are without government or hierarchy, gender or ethnic discrimination, territoriality or propriety. A "Japanese" ship includes many sailors from the Korean peninsula, one of the captains is a woman, and knowledge heeds no national boundaries. Neither North nor South, essentialized Korea or homogeneous Japan, exists for the particular people and period.

Nearly twelve centuries later, across the vast ocean that Chō Hokō barely glimpsed, two ethnic Korean women are driving through the melee of the 1992 Los Angeles riots. Intractable ethnic tensions permeate Kim Masumi's story, "Moeru Sōka" [The burning grass house, 1997]. Denizens of South Central Los Angeles hurl ethnic slurs and exude racial hatred. Yet what is more striking is the depth of incomprehension between the two people of the same ethnonational group. The Korean immigrant to the United States, Miryon, dismisses the naturalized (or soon-to-be naturalized) Zainichi Ryōko as someone who has forsaken both homeland and ethnicity. Ryōko cannot speak Korean and is repeatedly mistaken, by fellow ethnic Koreans as well as by everyone else, for Japanese. She cannot explain or declare her identity, even to an elderly Korean woman who tells her: "Long ago, a woman from my neighboring village was forcefully taken to your country [Japan] right before her wedding" (Kim Masumi 2004:154). Even her friend Miryon cannot understand "the ambiguity of [her] consciousness" that is very much part of her Japanese upbringing (114–15). A black man wants to wreak violence on Koreans, but Miryon tells him: "[Ryōko] is Japanese. No question. And I am a pure Korean" (170). Ryōko wonders whether Miryon's claim is a "proof of friendship": "I am wrapped around in friendship like pure cotton. However, doesn't the pure wool contain within it innumerable needles?" (172).

In the early twenty-first century, we live with well-entrenched categories of peoplehood. One is, or should be, Japanese, Korean, or perhaps even Zainichi. Yet the continuous influx and efflux of bodies across national borders, or the efflorescence of subpolitics and subnational identities, threaten to make mockery of established categories and identities. We have come to appreciate, in however tentative ways, the decline of a world in which national boundaries were clear-cut and national belongings were deemed at once essential and homogeneous. Belatedly, then, our world once again approximates the hurly-burly, transgressive world of Chō Hokō, even as it remains strewn with shards and occasional explosions of ethnonational tensions and conflicts, misunderstandings and mirecognitions. This concluding chapter presents theoretical, personal, and comparative reflections in order to situate this study of Zainichi identity.

DIASPORIC NATIONALISM

Let me consider the larger regional and global forces that the discussion of Zainichi identity has raised by focusing on something particular but central to diasporic Koreans: "The Song of Arirang," the Korean national folksong. Its mournful melody accompanies the incantatory refrain of Arirang: "Arirang, Arirang, Arariyo / Going over Arirang Hill / My love who has left / Won't be able to go very far." Said to exemplify the elegiac soul of the Korean people, it expresses *han* or *ressentiment* or even *Schadenfreude*. Arirang is probably a place-name but we are not sure of the exact place (cf. Chon 2008:21–24). What we know is that many Koreans regard the song as an encapsulation of the national essence, an expression of the ethnic soul. This is no less true in North Korea than in South Korea. What we also know is that the canonical version hails from the Kyŏnggi region, and it became a national song after the appearance of the eponymous 1926 film directed by Na Un-gyu (cf. McCann 1979). Rather than a quasi-natural entity, presumably coeval with the Korean people, the song spread across the nation along with national identity.

Nationalism is an ideology that asserts an isomorphism between a people—often thought of as a racial or an ethnic group who share common descent and contemporary commonality—and a territory. That is, geographical boundaries in principle define the nation. The chief criterion of membership is involuntary yet inclusionary; common descent guarantees belonging regardless of moral worth, native intelligence, or personal achievement. It is the place—when one must be from, or go, somewhere— they have to take you in. Like home, it seems natural and eternal, ineffable and lovable.

Nonetheless, if there is any academic consensus in studies of nationalism, then it is its modernity as a political ideology and as a form of popular identity. In *Modern Peoplehood* (Lie 2004b), I argued that national identity *qua* popular identity is a product and predicate of modern state formation. On the one hand, modern polity achieves cultural integration through mass schooling, military conscription, mass media, and other developments of national-level networks and institutions. In so doing, political belonging—state or national identity—supersedes both the supranational (e.g., civilizational or religious) and the infranational (e.g., village or regional). On the other, status integration transforms the masses into nationals and incorporates them into the high tradition of the nobility. Rather than hierarchal status, such as peasants and nobles, individuals assume status equality as fellow nationals. The twin processes of cultural and status integration transmogrify a population—an external attribution or an analytical category—into a people—an internal conviction or a self-reflexive identity.

In spite of the patina of antiquity and continuity, popular peoplehood identity was a belated, modern phenomenon, and Korea was no exception. For the idea of being a Korean was foreign to much of the population living on the Korean peninsula before the twentieth century. The low level of popular national identification in Chosŏn Dynasty Korea should not be surprising in a polity that had only 330 magistrates for 10 million inhabitants (Lie 1998:177). The traditional state did not have a bureaucracy capable of disseminating or instilling popular national consciousness. Lacking a national educational system or a standing national army, premodern Korea had underdeveloped national-level transportation, communication, and commercial networks and infrastructures. As late as the end of Japanese colonial rule, the dissemination of radio amounted to fewer than four sets per 100 households, and the sole Korean-language newspaper published fewer than 2 copies per 100 Koreans (Miyata 1985:14–16). Just as significantly, strict status divisions sharply separated the population into qualitatively distinct categories of people. The court literati had a protonational or proto-Korean consciousness but that identification was denied to the vast majority of the population. Not only were the cultural horizons of the landlocked masses largely limited to subnational—and often intensely local—identifications, they were also qualitatively different kinds of people from the *yangban* [the ruling stratum]. In other words, the weakness of cultural and status integration reserved Korea as an elite identity without a mass following or popular allegiance (cf. Sin 1987). The contrast to contemporary South Korea is striking. By the late 1980s the South Korean state commanded nearly a million people in the military and the police, and another half-million in local governments (Lie 1998:176–78). It had well-developed national systems of education, communication, and transportation. Status integration was so successful that one of the hallmarks of South Korea was said to be its radical egalitarianism. In short, nationalism is a powerful presence in contemporary South Korea (Shin G. 2006). Much the same can be said, at least in this regard, about North Korea.

Thus, the belated canonization of "The Song of Arirang" as a national folksong should not be surprising. In the climactic scene of the 1926 film—now presumed irretrievably lost, an apt state for a foundational cultural artifact—the Japanese police arraign the protagonist and accompany him over Arirang Hill (cf. Mun 1929). Given the particular historical context of the film and the song, it almost begs to be an allegory of Japanese colonial oppression and Korean popular resistance. I shall return to this theme—the coeval emergence of anticolonial resistance and popular nationalism—but first let me stress a slightly different theme from this same scene: exile, migration, and diaspora.

Diaspora—literally, the scattering of seeds—usually refers to the Jewish Diaspora, to the exiled adherents of Judaism after the destruction of the Second Temple. Whereas religion was the basis of premodern Jewish identification, the modern notion highlights peoplehood grouping. That is, modern Jewish identity is based on common descent and common belonging. What made it diasporic is deviation from the nationalist norm—the idea of one nation, one people, one country—such that the Jews were, until the establishment of the Israeli state, a people without a country. After the formation of Israel, the self-identified people of Jewish origin and therefore potential members of the Israeli state lived largely outside of the territory and thereby as diasporic Jews. In the case of Korea, the spread of people-hood identification was coeval with the consciousness of diasporic identity. It is precisely when people who live in the Korean peninsula identified themselves as racial, ethnic, or national Koreans that the notion of diasporic Koreans emerged. Diaspora in this modern sense refers to a people who live outside of their nation: deviants from the standpoint of national belonging and nationalist ideology. Diasporic peoples are resident aliens, immigrants, ethnonational minorities, or long-term foreign residents who constitute the host nation's Other because they belong to their homeland not only conceptually but literally.

The theme of population movement beckons us to see the Korean prisoner in the film as exemplifying not only the iron fist of Japanese rule but also the widespread uprooting of the peasantry. The colonial period unleashed convulsive movements ranging from the enforced conscription of female sex soldiers to the expulsion of the peasantry. At least a tenth of the Korean population resided outside of the colonial territory by 1944 (Grajdanzev 1944:81). Colonial modernity entailed large-scale intra- and international migration. The colonial period was the origin not only of popular national identity but also of the Korean diaspora, dispersing the colonial subjects to China and the Soviet Union in the west and to Japan and the Americas in the east. Precisely when national identity was spreading widely, the very bodies to which these categories and identities were assigned were being uprooted. These movements also coincided with the heightened state surveillance that in turn reinforced the sense of national borders and belongings (Nishinarita 1997:167–75). While people had moved without the heavy burden of categories and identities or the fortified obstacles of borderlines and checkpoints, they encountered a world of passports and identity papers (cf. Torpey 2000). Just as the Japanese state meticulously carried out cadastral surveys and population registers, they also participated in recruiting, sometimes by brute force, Koreans to work in Japan (Pak Kyongsik 1965; Underwood 2006).

From these initial observations I propose theses on diasporic nationalism. *Diasporic nationalism* is a paradoxical term. Nationalism by definition minimizes the significance of diaspora; everyone should live in their homeland, their nation. If there are people outside of the nation, then it is either temporary or by dint of unnatural, unfortunate, or at least unusual circumstances. Hence, the ideological temptation of diaspora is to fuse with the nation and nationalism that simultaneously denies or at least questions their existence. My contention is that diaspora is crucial and in many ways is constitutive of the nation and nationalism. Far from being a centrifugal outpouring of people from homeland, the reality also includes a centripetal intrusion of people from the diaspora. The involution of people and ideas into the nation—that is, the role of the diaspora—is critical for the formation of the nation and nationalism. In short, diaspora, nationalism, and diasporic nationalism are coeval ideas. In the cases of the Japanese archipelago and the Korean peninsula, they emerged in the nineteenth century.

The Nationalist Marginalization of Diaspora

The nation-state is the privileged unit of analysis in the human sciences. Given the pervasive power of the modern state and the popular dissemination of peoplehood identity, it seems natural and necessary that we should make sense of the world in terms of nations. Who can deny the intuitive force of Joseph de Maistre's quip that he has never met a humanity in general but only French, Germans, and so on (cf. Lie 2004b:129). Yet the nationalist frame sets a narrow horizon for our vision of the past and the future and marginalizes the significance of transnational, regional, and global forces. It also denigrates the domain of diaspora.

The regnant view of the nation-state presumes the isomorphism of territoriality and peoplehood. Put simply, nationals in principle live within the borders of the nation-state. Exceptions are few, such as diplomats, students, traders, travelers, and occasionally tragic figures such as refugees and exiles. Furthermore, the object of the human sciences is society or nation in which explanatory primacy is given to internal factors. There is a tendency to regard society or nation as a homogeneous entity, at once autochthonous and autotelic. International society is a society of societies, a world with the same order of entities. Non-national historiography and social science are therefore at best the comparison of reified entities that downplay non-national or transnational factors (Shaw 2000:27–30).

In this line of reasoning, diaspora is a minor phenomenon, largely described and explained by the language of international migration. As exemplified in the long-dominant historiography of U.S. immigration, migration entails an entelechy, or an immanent development (e.g., Handlin 1973). In the master narrative of immigration, people uproot themselves from their country of origin and reroot themselves in the country of destination, leading ultimately to assimilation. The sojourn is singular and linear—the fundamental rupture is the international crossing—and it transforms immigrants into assimilated and naturalized citizens. An individual is, in this sense, a member of one nation or another. The liminal status is temporary, at once insignificant and suspicious.

The master narrative is articulated in a minor key. Even in the United States—a country associated above all with immigration—the significance of immigration was minimized even in the twentieth century. Oscar Handlin famously sought to write a history of immigration and ended up writing a history of the United States *tout court*, thereby helping to establish the centrality of immigration in U.S. historiography. Other national historiography lags far behind, however. France is a country of immigrants, as Gérard Noiriel (1988), among others, has convincingly demonstrated, but Fernand Braudel, who certainly knew better, ignored the past of migration in his *L'identité de la France* [The identity of France, 1986]. By downplaying past population movement, present-day ethnic diversity is also minimized. Instead the nationalist and essentialist vision of France limns it as timeless and homogeneous. The second-generation Maghrebi immigrants, or the Beurs, remain the principal exception, but, again, as very much a *minor* phenomenon. In spite of being a "continent of immigration," the idea of "Fortress Europe" remains resonant not just in France but all over Europe (Bade 2003:276).

Similarly, the ideology of monoethnic Japan, as I argued in chapter 1, excises the tremendous diversity and dynamism that characterized the history of the Japanese archipelago, admitting at best a small group of Koreans and Chinese in contemporary Japanese society. Korean nationalist historiography, whether of North or South, has also squelched dynamism and diversity, as well as heterogeneity and hybridity. Except for the mythistory of Korean origins—where the origin of the Korean people is sometimes traced to present-day Manchuria—the dominant historiography presents an essentialist entity encapsulated within present-day political borders and encompassing the pure descendants of the Korean race. The received view admits only a small number—a mere trickle—of Koreans who have left the homeland. Symptomatically, the few available scholarly works on these populations are on Koreans (who happen to be) residing in other nation-states.

Nationalist assumptions, as we saw, pervaded not only the vast majority of ethnic Japanese but also ethnic Koreans in postwar Japan. Sōren ideology perceived the Korean diasporic population in Japan as a marginal and temporary phenomenon. Homeland orientation in turn envisioned ethnic organizations such as Sōren as peripheral and ephemeral. It is not surprising that Zainichi people developed something akin to a Zainichi inferiority complex vis-à-vis homeland Koreans. Ethnic cleansing was desired by both the Japanese government and the Zainichi population.

Nationalist historiography and social science minimize the scale and salience of population movements across national borders. They tend to delineate a simple and singular trajectory of homogeneous migration that misses the multiple and complex circuits of individuals and the differentiated and heterogeneous category of people. In challenging the nationalist view, we can excavate the empirical complexity of the migratory flux. This is true not only in a crude demographic sense but also in apprehending non-national or transnational realities, whether in terms of complex trajectories or social differentiation (Cohen 1998; Hoerder 2002). Far from being a modern phenomenon, movements of people come as close as any other phenomena to being transhistorical. This generalization certainly holds true for premodern East Asian polities. Rather than being "closed," regional (eastern or southeastern Asia) and transregional (to Europe and beyond) movements of traders and missionaries occurred (e.g., Arano 1988).

Quite simply, the sheer number of diasporic Koreans is immense. At the end of the Japanese colonial period, the Korean subjects living in the Japanese archipelago numbered over 2 million. Following the far-flung Japanese empire, thousands of Koreans reached Southeast Asia and the Pacific islands. At the same time, there were millions in China and the Soviet Union. In the post–World War II era, especially after 1965, over a million South Koreans migrated to the Americas, primarily the United States. There were also notable outflows to Europe and Australasia. In short, Koreans became a global presence. Yet these numbers merely scratch the surface. As I noted, Japanese rule and capitalist commercialization hastened the rural exodus, literally uprooting millions of peasants from their villages. Though dismissed as internal displacement, the shock of movement was profound and constituted (internal) diaspora. The establishment of the two Koreas engendered another diaspora of sorts for millions of Koreans, spawning enduring memories of displacement as families were divided and individuals dislocated from their hometowns. The Korean War generated not only mass deaths but also massive displacement. The topsy-turvy world of twentieth-century Korea cannot be understood apart from population movement, and in the twenty-first century there are sizable ethnic Korean populations across the world (cf. Yun 2004; Koh Chung 2007).

The numbers tell only one dimension of the story, however. As I have emphasized, the master migration narrative fits at best a small minority of diasporic Koreans. Even in highly aggregated terms, the mixture of historical contingencies and macrosociological forces has resulted in highly complex patterns. Even within the relatively simple story of South Korean immigration to the United States, some began their sojourns in Brazil or Argentina, others as diasporic Koreans in China or Japan. Stalin's dictatorial rule accounts in large part for the surprisingly large number of Koreans in Kazakhstan. Peasants who had crossed what to them was meaningless space found themselves under the thrall of the dictator who considered them a security risk and therefore banished them to Central Asia (Khazanov 1995).

Finally, we cannot neglect social differentiation. After all, the dissemination of popular national identity *qua* Korean is largely an achievement of the twentieth century. Precolonial Korea was a highly stratified society in which the landlords and the nobility distinguished themselves from the peasants and other subjects. Even for South Korean immigrants to the United States in the 1970s—when South Korea had become a hypernationalist country—their motivations for movement and social background are inextricable. Far from the presumption of the homogeneous Korean, we find, for example, an overrepresentation of already displaced—internal diasporic—Koreans, such as refugees from North Korea or the discriminated denizens of the Chŏlla provinces.

The first thesis is thus a call to capture the complex reality of diasporic Koreans, whose significance has been systematically minimized by the nationalist mind-set. Yet there is a great deal more at stake than merely challenging the marginalization.

Diasporic Intervention

The nationalist neglect of migration accords with the etymological root of diaspora: the spreading of seeds from a particular place of origin. Rather than relying on the lexical root, however, let us consider the original, or the Jewish, Diaspora. The origins of Judaism and Jewish people are shrouded in mythistory but we can be safe in assuming that there was no original Jewish nation. Judaism probably began as a slave religion in ancient Egypt (Gottwald 1979). To be Jewish meant to be Judaic, or followers of the Jewish religion (Cohen 1999). On a much more solid historical ground, we know that the Diaspora—with the unintended assistance of Nazi atrocity—facilitated the creation of the state of Israel. Notwithstanding the existence of Yishuv—itself a product of a diaspora within the Diaspora—it is not the nation-state that gave rise to the Diaspora but rather the Diaspora that gave rise to the nation-state (Sternhell 1998).

Needless to say, the instance of the Diaspora and Israel may be unique in the particulars, but would we be so far off the mark to say that it is something of a paradigmatic case? Even in the invincible terrain of internal, homeland nationalism, the significance of diaspora broadly conceived cannot be denied. For example, no one would point to the English or British diaspora as the source of English or British nationalism, but Paul Langford's 1989 study of English identity stresses the signal salience of expatriates as the source of English identity and the discourse of Englishness. In Germany—the first land of nationalism according to Isaiah Berlin (1980: 350)—the influential initial articulation of *Deutschtum* was by Herder, who in the contemporary language of peoplehood was born in Poland and worked in Latvia. That is, a man at the extreme periphery of the German sphere of cultural influence first proposed the modern vocabulary of peoplehood in general and Germanness in particular.

In the case of Korea—though usually not known as a country of massive migration—the diaspora played a significant—indeed, constitutive—role in the development of Korean nationalism and the nation-state(s). Korean nationalism was diasporic nationalism both as an imaginary and as an institution.

Recall that the genealogy of the modern Korean nation is largely coeval with Japanese colonialism. Diasporic Koreans dreamed of an independent Korea and the epic struggles for independent Korea principally occurred outside of the Korean peninsula. Christian-influenced and Japanese-educated intellectuals in Japan initiated the March First Movement of 1919, the beginning of the anticolonial independence movement. Its immediate impact affected diasporic Koreans, leading for example to the formation of the Korean National Congress in Vladivostok the same year when an estimated half-million Koreans resided in Manchuria and Siberia (Wada 1989).

To be sure, the initial inklings of Korean nationalism long predated the March First Movement, but my argument holds. The oft-claimed father of Korean nationalism, Sŏ Chae-p'il, was instrumental in the formation of the Independence Club and the newspaper *The Independence*—both crucial to the formation of Korean national consciousness. Far from being a traditional, Confucian gentleman, he was U.S. educated and a U.S. citizen with the Anglophonic name of Philip Jaisohn. Much the same story could be told about Sŏ's successor, Yun Ch'i-ho. The cultural crucible in which the idea of the modern Korean nation and subjectivity were forged was constituted by a bricolage of diverse and heterogeneous influences. What is certain is that it was by no means a pure internal product.

The Korean national imaginary is hybrid and usually of external provenance whether we look to literature or history. Han Yong-un transformed Korean Buddhism and Korean literature; his revolutionary influence cannot be told apart from the indelible impact of his Japanese sojourn. Two giants of modern Korean literature, Yi Kwang-su and Yi Sang, were profoundly influenced by Japanese literature, Japanese-inflected European literature, and, above all, the modernity that they experienced in Tokyo. Exilic literary imagination, discussed in chapter 2, is also diasporic imagination. The nationalist historiography of Pak Un-sik or Sin Ch'ae-ho is inextricable from the Japanese backdrop of their intellectual development. As hypernationalist as they may have been—an indelible lesson of modern Japanese historiography—their efforts to locate the Korean nation led them away from the Korean peninsula into the tundra of Siberia and Manchuria. The construction of pure internality ironically relied on the external that ultimately displaced internal territoriality on the external (cf. Eckert 1999, Schmid 2002).

Beyond the constitution of the nationalist imaginary—the lineaments of national culture as contemporary South Koreans understand them—lie the concrete institutions and movements of Korean nationalism. What unites the hagiographic reconstruction of North and South Korea—they agree on little else—is the centrality of anticolonial, diasporic struggles. In the case of the North, Kim Il Sung's guerrilla wars in Manchuria were central to the myth of the North Korean state (Wada 1992). Kim San—the emblematic revolutionary hero delineated in Nym Wales's *Song of Ariran* (1941)— fought alongside the Chinese Communists in Manchuria. As I have mentioned, diasporic Koreans, especially Zainichi, regard *Song of Ariran* as something like the Bible (Hyon 2007:28). Be that as it may, in the case of the South, the peregrinations of Syngman Rhee [Yi Sŭng-man] in Shanghai, Hawaii, and elsewhere played a prominent part in the story of Liberation. The power elite of the Shanghai Provisional Government laid the political foundation of contemporary South Korea. The prime minister was Rhee, whose principal adult language was English, as befit a man with a Ph.D. from Princeton and an Austrian wife. The all-important Minister of Home Affairs—an important post in the Imperial Japanese government—was An Ch'ang-ho, who settled in Los Angeles, and the Minister of Foreign Affairs was Kim Kyu-sik, who was reared by the missionary Horace Underwood in Seoul but spent much of his life in Paris, Shanghai, and elsewhere.

In more macrosociological language, the inevitable significance of geopolitics (especially but not restricted to colonized societies) and the European origin of the language and conception of modern politics (the nation, above all) heighten the importance of the external and the diasporic. Anticolonial, nationalist movements are almost always forged and led by those formed in the colonial metropolis and are framed under the influence of and reaction to colonial ideals. The very idea of nationalism was imbibed in the belly of the beast by, for example, Ho Chih Minh and Léopold Sédar Senghor in Paris. Ho and Senghor, to be sure, may not be "diasporic" but the impact of external influences cannot be gainsaid.

The central and constitutive role of the diaspora went well beyond the struggles for national liberation. The single most important personality behind the making of contemporary South Korea was Park Chung Hee. Park's vision for South Korea was deeply influenced by the Japan he experienced through his military training. The stress on military discipline, infrastructural development, and heavy industries all emulated the example of imperial Japan.

In this regard, the rapid economic development of South Korea in the 1960s is often explained by purely internal factors, whether the Confucian work ethic or the strong state. The South Korean takeoff cannot be fully explained without appreciating the impact of diasporic and external factors. For example, one of the leading export items of the 1960s was hair and hair products, which relied heavily on diasporic networks. At the same time, South Korea's export-oriented light industrialization was made possible by producing relatively low-capital- and low-technology-intensive items that had been manufactured in Japan. By importing the machinery, market, and know-how of the Japanese textile and other industries—mediated disproportionately through Japanese-educated South Koreans and diasporic Koreans in Japan—the South Korean economy made the initial strides in its industrialization efforts. One cannot discount the diasporic experience, principally in colonial Japan, of governmental and business leaders who engineered the "miracle on the Han" (Lie 1998:60–61).

Diasporic nationalism is nationalism *tout court* for many postcolonial societies. The idea of the nation is imagined and lived in the language and context of the colonizers, dialectically transforming colonial universalism into anticolonial nationalism. In the epistemic and political transformation, diaspora plays a central and constitutive role.

Negative and Positive Pathways

The nationalist marginalization of diaspora obfuscates the reality that the diasporic and transnational perspective can illuminate. There are two possible conclusions.

A negative lesson would be to expand the parameters of national reification and incorporate the diaspora in the nationalist narrative. That is, we can expand the essentialism of the nation to that of the diasporic nation. This is in fact one of the more recent political-cultural moves by the South Korean government. The explicit agenda is to rally diasporic Koreans around the flag of South Korea in order to prolong the Cold War by other means, promote transnational commercial ties in Paraguay or Kazakhstan, and enhance domestic electoral support and solidarity. Alternatively, the negative solution is to propose a minority nationalism, or diasporic nationalism, for the minority population.

A curious manifestation of this form of diasporic nationalism was for the South Korean government to name Nam June Paik one of Korea's ten cultural treasures. Paik was born in colonial Korea (to a notoriously collaborationist merchant family) but was educated in Japan, where he was influenced above all by Marx and Schoenberg and actively aligned himself with North Korea. After his association with Fluxus, he became a pioneering performance artist—in collaboration with Charlotte Moorman and others—and an influential visual and installation artist. What is the essence of Paik's Koreanness that makes him one of Korea's ten cultural treasures? He was of course born in Korea—though part of Japan then—and once noted his artistic debt to two avant-garde Korean writers, Chong Chi-yong and Kim Ki-nim. Yet, perhaps not surprisingly, they were both schooled in Japan and deeply influenced by Japanese-inflected modernism. Paik's diasporic existence is not something that can be reduced to his Koreanness or even his diasporic Koreanness.

Zainichi ideology was minority nationalism for the Korean diasporic population in Japan. As a form of diasporic nationalism, it shared the preconceptions of majority nationalism, both Japanese and Korean. The assumption of homogeneity provided a prescriptive identification for the diasporic population. In recalling the tragedy of Japanese colonialism and its postcolonial legacy, Zainichi ideology sought essential commonalities among the population, even claiming that the Zainichi population was a repository of rare and unique experiences: "Zainichi are absolutely a minority wherever they are in the world" (Hwang 2007:15). Thus, even fellow Korean "newcomers" are perceived as distinct from Zainichi. Yet the solidarity of oppression and memory misrecognizes the concrete situation of the actually diverse Zainichi population.

The positive conclusion would be to consider diasporic nationalism as diasporic through and through (though not as an essence), and something that cannot be reduced to a primordial national essence. Theoretically, we should resist the Hegelian temptation to find essences and cast off the nineteenth-century legacy of nationalist historiography and social science. We need to drop the blinders entailed in the immanent, internalist mode of understanding and explanation that has dominated the twentieth-century human sciences. In the case of Korean nationalism, we should resist the curious conflation of the claims made by nationalist movements that unwittingly rehash nationalist narratives. It is not merely the imaginary and the institution of the nation that cannot be sought within the present-day Korean nation(s). Scholars sometimes even slight what was so obvious to the principals: the significance of geopolitics or the paramount powers of Western nations that made diasporic politics so central to colonial and post-colonial societies.

The non-nationalist and non-essentialist approach allows us to shed, or at least provide the condition of possibility of shedding, certain blinders that have occluded our view of the past and present. Consider once again the famous scene in *Song of Arirang* in which the Japanese police take a farmer over Arirang Hill. The proximate cause of his arrest and his exile—that is, his crime—was that he had murdered a landlord. Far from being an anticolonial narrative, it can be read as plain, old-fashioned class struggle or, more accurately, peasant struggle.

Hardheaded empiricists often mock the inchoate concepts of diaspora, transnationalism, and so on, but they often remain trapped in the equally grandiose, albeit successful and therefore naturalized, categories and concepts of nationalism and nationalist history and social science. Take as a seemingly impregnable case the nationalist trappings of modern African-American or black thought. W. E. B. Du Bois's *The Souls of Black Folk* has by now become the indisputable classic of black, indeed American, thought. It is often read as a nationalist account, replete as its pages are with black spirituals or folk-songs. Yet a proper appreciation of Du Bois's canonical work requires us to appreciate the influence of German Romanticism. This should not be surprising for someone immersed in modern German thought, if only by dint of his study in Berlin. After all, the idea of "double consciousness" is but another articulation of that famous line about "zwei Seelen in einer Brust" from Goethe's *Faust*. The German idea of the folksong as an expression of the *Volk* inspired the Japanese bureaucrats in colonial Korea to produce the first compilation of Korean folksongs in 1912. Again, this should not be surprising because of the German-drenched education of the bureaucrats at the imperial universities. Some Kamikaze pilots—the suicide bombers par excellence—scribbled in their farewell letters not about the glories of the Emperor, Shintō, and the Japanese nation but rather the philosophical conundrums of Marx, Nietzsche, and Heidegger (cf. Ohnuki-Tierney 2002: 192–93).

Put another way, the roots of diaspora should not be exclusively located in a primordial, bounded space. To take the African-American example again, Alex Haley (1976) famously traced his roots to Kunte Kinte; in the realm of the arts, Henry Louis Gates Jr. (1988) linked contemporary African-American literature to the oral culture of western Africa. Yet such nationalistic readings obfuscate external and diasporic influences (Gilroy 1993). As Ishmael Reed (1989:227)—ironically the author of the final work discussed in Gates's study of African-American literary genealogy—once remarked: "If Alex Haley had traced his father's bloodline, he would have traveled twelve generations back to, not Gambia, but Ireland." Although Koreans often pride themselves on their racial purity, such claims are ultimately hollow, made possible only by expunging external and diasporic experiences.

What I am proposing is a form of super-empiricism. Rather than relying on reified nineteenth-century categories and concepts, we should take seriously the concrete transnational peregrinations of human beings who have long been unbound by the institution of national borders or the imaginary of the nation. As Adorno might have said, the national is false. The recalcitrant reality of complexities and contradictions of human life requires us not to rely on abstract universals but concrete particulars and then—and only then—concrete universals.

My proposal poses a challenge to the usual way of doing things in the human sciences. It has never been clear to me why the realm of imagination should be severed from the realm of institutions or that political economic, social, and cultural phenomena can so easily be separated even for analytical purposes. I am certain that we can no longer be content to call ourselves area specialists, whether of Korea or Kenya, or ethnic studies, whether of Korean Americans or African Americans. We must alas become at once interdisciplinary and transdisciplinary, do area studies and ethnic studies, in order to make sense of the world within which we live.

Returning to "The Song of Arirang," its plaintive lyric and plangent tune somehow evoke memories of home, but it is, in fact, send-off music: a song of departure. The protagonist's father in Ook Chung's *Kimchi* (2001) loved the song but insisted that there was no return, only new departure. This is somehow fitting for an author, born in Japan to ethnic Korean parents, who migrated to Canada and writes in French. The negative articulation of diasporic nationalism, such as Zainichi ideology, would have little place for him as he returns, as he in fact did for a spell, to Japan. The positive expression opens an expansive understanding not only of the itinerant personality but also the very nature of the world in which we live.

ACADEMIC REFLECTIONS

For a deracinated, cosmopolitan intellectual—an object of self-pity and self-importance, and therefore of ridicule—it is easy to forge a book out of the variegated materials that lie in the libraries or lurk in the Web and even occasionally to listen, *viva voce,* to rambling recollections and reflections. Documents frequently exemplify the bureaucratic in all its pejorative connotations, written records are often self-serving apologia or ideological pap, and oral narratives are at times painful palavers: eye-glazing and mind-numbing. Confronting the world that is confounding and contradictory, the beguiling temptation is to make sense of the booming and buzzing confusion by a theoretical fiat. That is of course what scientists or scholars are supposed to do: analyze the inchoate, simplify the complexity, cleanse the mess. This task, whether understood as mimetic, artistic, or scientific, cannot but end, at least to the satisfaction of the author, in an order, especially so for a self-styled theorist. One might even aspire to achieve a view from nowhere, to find the hidden laws, and possibly to peer into the future.

As much as I appreciate the bedeviling difficulties and the occasional triumphs of the human sciences, I can only sadly say that too often the aspirations amount to nothing more than hubris. For how can we know better than the very people who lived through it all: pangs and wonders of birth and growth; delights and despairs of family and friends; falling in, falling out, or improbably staying in love; triumphs and tragedies at playground, school, or work; predictabilities at once of continuity, change, and contingency; and getting and spending and eating and defecating: the humdrum endurance and experience of everyday life in all its pettiness and grandeur. Historians and ethnographers will rightly stress the insights afforded in retrospect or to an outsider, the possibility of comparisons to other times and places, the training in sorting facts and analyzing them: that is, the very apparatus of modern, scientific scholarship. Philosophers and theorists, Immanuel Kant or Joan Scott, will insist that theoretical presuppositions are inherent in any actual or recollected experience. Reading deeply the recondite texts of Hegel, Husserl, and Heidegger, or mastering assiduously the intricacies of technology and methodology, they must somehow do something more to the necessarily ignorant and ill-equipped minds and masses, documents and data. As scholars and scientists, we cannot but think that our work is supererogatory.

The crystal ball or the computer screen is invariably opaque. This is true both at the individual and the collective level. Recall Kang Sangjung and Tei Taikin from the previous chapter. Would it have occurred to anyone in

Kang's family or Kang himself when he was collecting scraps with his "uncle" that he would end up as a professor at the University of Tokyo? Could the intellectuals and scholars cited in this book predict that someone like Kang might ascend the pinnacle of Japanese academic and intellectual life? When did Tei envision the possibility that he would end up studying in the United States or teaching in South Korea? Or that he would return to Japan as a professor at a major university? Beyond the vagaries of individual lives, who would have thought that the Korean minority would persist as a vibrant presence in Japan a half-century after the end of World War II? Who foresaw legal victories and legislative improvements? Or that ordinary Japanese people would be spellbound by South Korean movies and soap operas? Retrospectively we can begin to make sense of the dramatic transformations. Yet we should resist the intellectual temptation to hunt for deep and deterministic causes that may in turn be able to make sense of the future. What we should learn are the limitations of facile sociological generalizations, whether to assume a singular identity in a population or to reduce identity to history and sociology.

Carolyn Kay Steedman's *Landscape for a Good Woman* (1987) captures the excitement of scholarship and politics and theory that her teachers, especially E. P. Thompson, offered. Yet a Marxism that was profoundly male-centric failed to make sense of people like her working mother. The disjuncture between what her teacher's theory told her and what her mother's stories told her is something that she could not bridge easily. And the problem is in fact much deeper. In what sense can we say that class as an analytic category makes sense either of the individual or the collective? Doesn't it merely wreak violence on the very people that it is supposed to illuminate, instruct, and inspire?

Perhaps we should query instead the urge to encapsulate the Other—although the same urge may be found in the effort to essentialize one's own group or oneself—into a simple and static receptacle. The search for certainty in something as complex, confused, and changing as identity seems misplaced. The endeavor, which probably belongs more properly in the realm of the aesthetic or the spiritual, finds social scientists out of their depth, though seduced as they might be by the goal and deluded as they might be about their effectiveness. Gustave Flaubert (1993:180) was right to emphasize our limitations: "Whereas the truth is that fullness of soul can sometimes overflow in utter vapidity of language, for none of us can ever express the exact measure of his needs or his thoughts or his sorrows; and human speech is like a cracked kettle on which we tap crude rhythms for bears to dance to, while we long to make music that will melt the stars."

These concerns underlie my sometimes heavy reliance on personal narratives. They are, in some sense, the way in which identities are constituted and constructed. The philosopher Mark Johnson (1993:11) argues: "Narrative is not just an explanatory device, but is actually constitutive of the way we experience things." They offer, at the least, a rich repository of the ways in which people make sense of themselves, which are, after all, the very stuff of identity. Novelists and memoirists, most impressively, attempt to capture a life—a sense of the self—out of a welter of historical residues, social backgrounds, personal experiences, and considered reflections by narrating: we are *Homo narrans*. This is especially so in the modern Japanese literary context where the "I novel" *[watakushi shōsetsu]* has been a dominant genre, as influential as Dostoevsky in shaping the Zainichi literary canon (cf. Akiyama 2006:8). It is no secret that Kim Sokpom and Lee Hoesung, Yan Sogiru and Yū Miri all draw heavily on personal experiences in their ostensibly fictive work, sometimes reproducing verbatim their putatively nonfictional narratives.

One may nonetheless harness the passion of science in order to emulate the precision of poetry. The human sciences will best achieve their purposes when we cultivate the best impulses and practices in science and literature, theory and evidence, abstractions and particulars, categories and experiences. Or so I would like to think that I have achieved in this and other books. This is of course not the place to expatiate at length on the issues I raised in this brief excursus. I merely hope to signal that even a study so delimited—perhaps a million people over a half-century—cannot bypass these bedeviling questions that accompany any attempt to represent other peoples, other times.

COMPARATIVE CODA

I have lived in Japan on and off for nearly a decade, but I don't regard myself as Zainichi or even a diasporic Korean in Japan. I was born in South Korea and moved to and lived with my family in Tokyo when I was a child, but my father had a semi-diplomatic posting, and we had no known relatives in Japan. The entire rationale of our stay in Japan seemed to be about avoiding the inconvenience of life in South Korea, be it premodern facilities or noisome relatives, and to be able to bear the material riches and technological wonders of Japan back to South Korea in regular, short trips home. The recipients—the largely appreciative relatives—were at once impressed by "the clever Japanese" but quick to recall their treachery, violence, and cruelty. My maternal grandfather diligently shaved—so as not to look Japanese, he said—but gladly used the Japanese-made shaver. More exuberantly, he delighted in conversing in Japanese. This state of affairs is but a small example of the profound ways in which Japan shaped Korea— most obviously during the colonial period but for many decades thereafter. We cannot possibly understand colonial and postcolonial societies without capturing the uneasy mix of repulsion and attraction, moments of rejection and longing and belonging.

Unfortunately for my youthful self, South Korea didn't provide much of a home: a place of repose and nostalgia, comforts and commensality, longing and love. My annual visit to South Korea when I was growing up in Japan was to a very strange land. Seoul in the 1960s, as Kang Sangjung found in his first visit in the early 1970s, was a city of shocking poverty and inequality: truly pathetic beggars roamed—and fortunate were those who were able to amble—the streets next to overworked oxen pulling rickety carts. Grilled grasshoppers and melting ice cream were the desserts of choice. My spoken Korean deteriorated rapidly over the years, taking on Japanese intonation and pronunciation that incurred the wrath of distant relatives and random passers-by. Most of my elder relatives—both maternal and paternal grandfather, for example—spoke Japanese fluently. When I was with my maternal grandfather's friends, I took their Japanese facility for granted and was struck by their use of archaic terms and turns of phrase, such as using the colonial-era appellation *Keijō* for Seoul. Seoul was infinitely preferable to my putative ancestral homeland [*kokyō* or *kohyang*] south of Seoul. In retrospect, the endless rice paddies and the pristine ocean nearby must have made my paternal grandfather's village a model of pastoral beauty, but it merely looked like sticks to my childhood self. Walking around one of the mountains, my paternal grandfather told me that our Japanese surname—the Japanese colonial government had mandated an ethnic Japanese name by 1940—was Matsuyama, for the mountain [*yama*] with many pine trees [*matsu*]. My father's sole recollection of the colonial period occurred at that moment: the Japanese authorities made him and his schoolmates squeeze oil out of the pine trees. Be that as it may, I thought at the time that no civilized person could possibly live there, in such godforsaken wilderness, so far away from civilization. Mercilessly ridiculed as I was by my sociological observation, my father deployed this knowledge thereafter to threaten me with banishment to my *Heimat*, which readily rectified my truancy in adolescence.

My primary childhood memory of Tokyo, however, was the banal Zainichi experience of being bullied at school. I had been going to a Catholic school—referred to as an American school—but I couldn't speak English and I found the sisters and the students strange. After repeated and relentless requests, I was allowed to go to a Japanese public school. I went by the Japanese pronunciation of the Chinese characters used in my Korean name: Ri Zaikun, as I was known then. I was often teased and even beaten up. In my first-grade transcript, my primary teacher remarks that my Japanese pronunciation is "rapidly improving," but I don't recall being teased for the deviant way in which I enunciated Japanese words. The cause, as best as I can reconstruct, was my "funny" name. The fact of Koreanness was evoked rarely. In retrospect, however, there were other reasons to pick on me. I was intellectually and socially precocious; mothers of the very children who slugged me would praise me and express their desire to get the filth in my fingernail so that they could steep it and serve as tea to their sons. Were some of my peers envious? Like Yū Miri's tormentors (1997:86), did they find me arrogant or conceited? Or perhaps they resented the ways in which my clothing and mannerisms signaled my bourgeois upbringing (I was, alas, a particular Japanese character type: *botchan*). I have a group picture of an outing [*ensoku*] in which all the classmates are in some sort of blue uniform; I stand out for my azure sweater. I was well above average in height but I was at times awkward and probably effeminate. Or perhaps it is simply misplaced sensibility? Yū Miri becomes tearful as she faces an ostensibly insensitive bureaucrat and tells her, "You are being mean." The clerk, however, responds, "Why do I have to be mean to you? I have read every book you have written" (Yū 2007b:721). In any case, I cannot at all be sure four decades hence exactly how frequently I was teased and bullied. I do know, however, that my classmates repeatedly elected me as a class officer. To be sure, Yamamura Masaaki (1975:14) was teased and bullied—called "Chōsen"—but repeatedly elected to be a class officer in elementary school and even a student body president in middle school: "I like school. . . . I had a sense of superiority." Yet he burned himself to death. My brother, a year below me at the same school, claims that he was never teased or bullied.

Nonetheless, I never thought of myself as Zainichi. Yet shared infantile memories are the stuff out of which nostalgia and intimations of roots emanate. When I was fourteen I was part of a diasporic Korean youth delegation from the United States. I don't recall feeling a great deal of identification with my fellow Korean Americans—Ohio or Oklahoma were extremely alien for someone growing up in Hawaii—but I felt a great sense of familiarity—really, relief—with a group of Zainichi students who were in Seoul at the same time. Perhaps it was the shared experience of Japanese popular culture or perhaps it was the sense of not fitting in with my group.

Or perhaps they found me exotic and I relished speaking Japanese for the first time in many years. Over a decade later I spent a year in Japan. Although I participated on the fringes of the anti-fingerprinting movement, I couldn't dive into it. In part it was due to my intoxication with high theory but it was in part also due to my ineffable distance from second- and third-generation Zainichi activists. I had obviously lived away from Japan for the past fifteen years or so but the passage of time understates the divergence in background, experience, and identity of Zainichi and *Zaibei* [Korean Americans].

The received wisdom suggests that Zainichi and Zaibei are at least different and even possibly antipodal in character. To put the contrast polemically, Zainichi are oppressed, despised minority in Japan, whereas Korean Americans are a successful, model minority in the United States (cf. Abelmann and Lie 1995:165–70). Pak Sunam (1970), among others, argued that Zainichi are like African Americans; Korean Americans are Asian Americans, the model minority. Representative Zainichi are, in this line of thinking, music and sports stars in the way that's true for African Americans. Representative Korean Americans are, in contrast, well-educated and in prestigious professions.

If we accept the prevailing Zainichi historiography and the model minority narrative, the divergent fate of Zainichi and Zaibei stems from the involuntary character of Zainichi migration and the voluntary nature of Zaibei migration. Zainichi historiography, as we have seen, highlights enforced migration *[kyōsei renkō]* with the broad background of Japanese imperial and capitalist expansion that led to expropriation of the peasantry. In short, it is a chronicle of exploitation and discrimination, occasional resistance, and eventual emancipation. In contrast, the received narrative of Korean immigration to the United States is cast in the dominant U.S. immigration scheme. In order to avoid poverty and autocracy, Koreans pursued opportunities in the United States. In addition, ethnic Koreans had no intention of residing permanently in Japan. They were, rather, temporary *[dekasegi]* workers who regarded Korea as their natural home. In contrast, ethnic Koreans who went to the United States expected to settle there, hoping to become U.S. citizens. The contrast goes deeper. Like many involuntary migrants in world history, Koreans who were forcibly relocated by rapacious Japanese people had hailed predominantly from the impoverished, rural peasantry. In contrast, Korean Americans—at least the majority who arrived after the 1965 immigration reform—were disproportionately well-educated and middle-class, if not even elite, in origin. That is, Zainichi came from the bottom rungs of colonial Korea; Zaibei hailed from the middle, if not the upper, strata of postcolonial South Korea.

If the history and sociology of migration demonstrate remarkable contrasts between Zainichi and Zaibei, then the nature of destination country differed as well. Colonial-era Japan was a society of ethnoracial hierarchy, exclusion, and discrimination. Ethnic Koreans were not only treated poorly at work and secluded in ghettoes, but they were also disrecognized by the larger population. In contrast, diasporic Koreans found in the United States a land of freedom and equal opportunity. They were integrated into mainstream society in terms of work and residence; they were treated more or less as equals, and even recognized as Americans. In short, the conventional wisdom has Japan as a horrid place for ethnic Koreans, and the United States as a welcoming home.

Furthermore, ethnic Koreans in Japan faced an implacable Japanese opposition to ethnic assertion. Beginning in the colonial period, ethnic Koreans faced Japanization. That is, ethnic Koreans were unable to speak Korean or to employ ethnic names. Physiological similarities made possible the phenomenon of *passing*, which in turn led Zainichi to become "invisible" in Japanese society. In contrast, diasporic Koreans faced less pressure to Americanize. There were no efforts to strip them of their ethnic language or names. Because of their physical distinction from the dominant European population, there was no possibility of passing, which ironically forced them to be open about their ethnic ancestry and identity. In summary, Zainichi were forced to pass as Japanese, being discredited as Koreans; Zaibei were allowed to be proudly Korean.

In part because of the foregoing sources of contrast, the two populations demonstrated distinct characteristics. *Politically*, Zainichi were oppositional, predominantly allied with North Korea and the postwar progressive Japanese intellectuals. In contrast, Korean Americans were conservative, allied with South Korea and the anticommunist elements in the United States. In terms of the Cold War, Zainichi were part of the communist bloc, whereas Zaibei were part of the capitalist bloc. *Economically*, Zainichi were overwhelmingly poor and faced serious obstacles to mainstream and professional employment. Not only did their educational attainment fall behind that of the larger population, but they also came to be concentrated in the non-educationally-credentialed service sector, such as scrap recycling, restaurant and pachinko-parlor ownership, and entertainment industries. In contrast, Zaibei were disproportionately affluent and well-educated, finding success in prestigious professions. *Sociologically*, Zainichi exemplified a high level of ethnic solidarity in the form of ethnic organizations, especially Sōren or Chongryun and to a lesser extent Mindan. They identified themselves as Koreans long after the possibility of return receded. In contrast, Korean Americans are presumed to be much more individualistic, readily identify themselves as Americans or Asian Americans, and regard the United States as a permanent home. *Ideologically,* Zainichi remain implacably anti-Japanese and obsessed about historical wrongs and injustices. They resist naturalization and Japanization. In contrast, Zaibei are broadly pro-American and resolutely forward-looking. They embrace U.S. citizenship and Americanization. In short, Zainichi remain alien elements in Japan; Zaibei are integrated into the United States.

I am skeptical of the received contrast. Rather, considerable convergences in fate and present reality characterize the two populations. As I have argued, Zainichi historiography exaggerates the involuntary character of Korean immigration to Japan, the uneducated and impoverished background of Korean migrants, and their homeland orientation. It is a general truth of immigrants—except of course involuntary migrants, such as slaves—that they require at once the capacity and the will, thereby excluding the least informed and the most impoverished people. As I have shown (Abelmann and Lie 1995:75–77), the high educational and economic attainment of Korean immigrants to the United States has been exaggerated. Correspondingly, just as we can see the permanent-residency orientation of ethnic Koreans in Japan from the 1930s, we can also see not only the ideology but the actuality of return among Korean Americans at least since the 1980s. Differences are matters of degree rather than kind: quantitative, not qualitative.

It would be foolhardy to underestimate the ferocity of disrecognition—from physical lynching to symbolic violence—of Japanese people and government against ethnic Koreans from the colonial period to the present. Yet we should not underestimate the extent of recognition and even reconciliation of Japanese society with the Zainichi population. There are no systematic data on the frequency of racist comments and treatments, but I am not at all sure that the present situation of Zainichi is much worse than that of Zaibei. The incidence of racial slurs, bullying, and even physical violence occurs in both countries; yet, in part because of the prevalence of passing in Japan (and the presumption of racial isomorphism and cultural similarity) and the stubborn survival of white supremacy in the United States, the sense of security may be higher in Japan than in the United States.

Furthermore, the force of cultural conformity is powerful in both host countries and it would be a mistake to regard the United States as a paragon of ethnic tolerance and Japan as its antithesis. The pressure for Anglo conformity is strong in the United States, for example, in naming practices. Similarly, in spite of the existence of a viable purgatory of permanent resident status—the so-called green card—the place of an alien is far from comfortable. The United States is a nation of immigrants and a land of multiculturalism, but the situation of ethnic Koreans in the United States is hardly the flip side of that of ethnic Koreans in Japan. In urban areas in Japan today, it is common for ethnic Japanese people to eat kimchi or watch South Korean soap operas; either activity would be highly unusual for non-ethnic Koreans in the United States.

Therefore, the broad characteristics, far from being antipodal, show some remarkable convergences. *Politically*, it is simply false that Zainichi are disproportionately pro-communist, pro-North Korea, or leftist. If nothing else, the articulate voices of what might be called "neocon" Zainichi, such as Tei Taikin or Asakawa Akihiro, falsify the presumption of Zainichi political uniformity. Similarly, it is not necessarily true that Korean Americans are predominantly anticommunist and conservative. In general, overgeneralization is a persistent flaw in the analyses of both groups. *Economically*, we should not exaggerate the educational and occupational disadvantages of Zainichi and the respective successes of Korean Americans. Recent surveys show considerable improvements in educational and income attainment of Zainichi; we know that Korean Americans, despite the commonsense assumptions, do not fare any better than the U.S. average. Any Zainichi can cite Son Masayoshi as one of the richest Japanese or Lotte as a major conglomerate; very few Korean Americans will be able to name a rich Korean American or a major Korean-American corporation. *Sociologically*, given the decline of the mainline ethnic organizations, Zainichi strike me as having very weak ethnic solidarity. This is in contrast to Korean Americans, who are organized extensively by Christian churches and ethnic Korean associations [*Han'inhoe*]. The diversity in Zainichi identification is no different from that of Zaibei senses of belonging. To reprise, then, robust sociological generalizations are far and few between for both groups. *Ideologically*, I am not at all sure that the conventional wisdom is in any way true. Most Zainichi I have interviewed professed great attachment to Japanese society and culture in a way that is rare to find articulated among Korean Americans. It is the thematic of Korean-American literature to dwell on the past—such as Japanese colonization of Korea in general or the problematic of *ianfu* in particular (see *A Gesture Life* by Chang-Rae Lee or *Comfort Woman* by Nora Keller). One doesn't find the same sort of obsession in the best-selling novels of Yū Miri or Kaneshiro Kazuki. Furthermore, the post-Zainichi generation readily embraces the idea of Korean-Japanese identity. The identification as Korean American is surprisingly rare among Korean Americans: much more common is the self-identification as "Korean."

The overarching assumption that Zainichi have suffered and failed in Japan whereas Zaibei have prospered and succeeded in the United States is problematic. Continuing with the example of literature, though there have been several Akutagawa Prize winners among Zainichi authors, none to my knowledge has received the American equivalent, such as a Pulitzer Prize or a National Book Award. For that matter, most Japanese can name numerous eminent Zainichi cultural figures in a variety of fields. Most Korean Americans—let alone Americans—would be hard-pressed to name one. What was ironically in part a product of employment discrimination has created a situation for Zainichi today that would be the envy of many Zaibei: it is shocking for young Korean Americans to realize that some of the greatest sports or popular-music stars in Japan are ethnic Koreans. Even in the staid academic world, Kang Sangjung, among others, commands renown in a way that no Korean-American academic can begin to match.

Thus, the conventional wisdom that contrasts Zainichi with Zaibei is misleading: Zainichi are not so impoverished, unaccepted, and miserable in Japan; Zaibei are not so affluent, accepted, and comfortable in the United States. I am not denying that there are profound differences in historical experiences and contemporary realities. Furthermore, there are factors—such as the length of the diasporic experience and the relative size of the population—that make the comparison more complicated than either the conventional wisdom or my truncated analysis might suggest. Be that as it may, we should rethink the received wisdom of Zainichi and Zaibei, past and present.

TOKYO, AUTUMN 2007

The soap opera *Tokyo wankei* [Tokyo bayview, 2004] is noteworthy not only because it was the first prime-time television show to feature Zainichi protagonists. Subtitled "Destiny of Love," it depicts two generations of love between Zainichi women and Japanese men. The earlier generation's passionate romance was extinguished by physical and ethnic obstacles. Fortuitously, their respective children also fall in love: presumably permanently this time around. Whereas the metaphoric gulf between the earlier couple was the Sea of Japan, it is merely the Tokyo Bay for the present generation (both men boast that they will swim across the water; the son's claim, in spite of the pollution, is an exercise in rhetorical modesty). Beyond the narrowing gap, the gulf is not merely ethnic but also class-based: the Zainichi woman hails from an affluent family; the Japanese man from a rural, farming household who works as a forklift operator. His rival in love is a wealthy Zainichi; he dons a luxurious watch worn by the Pae Yong-jun character in *Fuyu no sonata* [Winter sonata]. As absurd as the plot is— though the course of true love never does run smoothly and the melodramatic imagination has its irrational rhythm—the backdrop of the drama would not have sustained Japanese, or for that matter Zainichi, credulity not so long ago. The suspension of disbelief depends on a climate of plausibility; by the early twenty-first century it was credible to feature a wealthy Zainichi family, and the Zainichi-Japanese relationship was a topic of potentially mass appeal.

The ordinary appearance and reception of Zainichi in contemporary Japanese society suggest Zainichi recognition and Japanese-Zainichi reconciliation. Whereas *Chōsen* was a derogatory term, *Koria* is by and large neutral. There continues to be a preponderance of Zainichi sports stars. Opening a daily one morning, I noticed Zainichi figures on the Japanese national soccer team and a tournament of Go masters. It is also hard to miss the relatively rare but nonetheless noteworthy appearance in print and on television of ethnic Koreans presenting themselves with ethnic Korean names. Bookstores display stacks of books by Kaneshiro Kazuki or Yū Miri, as well as a book by a Zainichi conductor discussing Beethoven's symphonies.

Needless to say, this moment of reconciliation is not the endpoint to which Zainchi and Japanese have ineluctably been heading. Neither can one assume that comity will be permanent. One generation's reconciliation or emancipation cannot guarantee everlasting reconciliation or emancipation. Perhaps nothing focuses the mind and braces the spirit more than the sheer fact of the Shoah. Its tragic inscrutability is enhanced, rather than diminished, by the symbiotic character of the German-Jewish experience (Lie 2004b:chap.5). Even the nascent Nazis and the ardent Zionists did not see the "Final Solution" as the terminus of social accommodation and cultural assimilation of Germany Jewry in the Weimar Republic. Most Jews spoke German and adopted German customs, the rate of intermarriage was high and rising, and more than a few intellectuals foresaw the end of Jewish identity in Germany. Yet it is equally true that in 1945 no one prophesied the revival of the Jewish community in Germany by the early twenty-first century. Walter Benjamin's gnostic claim that the past isn't free from present and future struggles has become an academic cliché, but we shouldn't forget that the past can only be apprehended in the present, which in turn is worthwhile only as it ushers in a more desirable future. It's a pity that we cannot confidently prognosticate a utopian future or believe somehow that intellectual struggles over historiography or ideology matter deeply. It's also a pity that the critical spirit in these uncertain times should be involuted toward disputatious scholasticism or disengaged critique. Without denying the dark clouds of the past or the future, however, we should also look up at the patches of bright blue sky and behold the beauty that has yet to come into the world.

References

Abe Motoharu. 2002. *Kin Kirō no shinjitsu.* Tokyo: Nihon Tosho Kankōkai.
Abelmann, Nancy, and John Lie. 1995. *Blue Dreams: Korean Americans and the Los Angeles Riots.* Cambridge, Mass.: Harvard University Press.
Aciman, André. 2000. *False Papers: Essays on Exile and Memory.* New York: Farrar Straus Giroux.
Adorno, Theodor W. [1951] 1997. *Gesammelte Schriften,* vol. 4: *Minima moralia.* Frankfurt am Main: Suhrkamp.
Akiyama Shun. 2006. *Watakushi shōsetsu to iu jinsei.* Tokyo: Shinchōsha.
———. [1967] 2007. *Naibu no ningen no hanzai.* Tokyo: Kōdansha.
Aoki Atsuko. 2005. "Kikoku jigyō ni okeru 'Nihonjin tsuma' o megutte." In Sōji Takasaki and Junjin Pak, eds., *Kikoku undō to wa nandattanoka,* 121–44. Tokyo: Heibonsha.
Arai Kazuma. 2006. *Zainichi Korian—za—sādo.* Tokyo: Ōkura Shuppan.
Araki Kazuhiro. 1997. *Zainichi Kankoku—Chōsenjin no sanseiken yōkyū o tadasu.* Tokyo: Gendai Koria Kenkyūjo.
Arano Yasunori. 1988. *Kinsei Nihon to Higashi Ajia.* Tokyo: Tokyo Daigaku Shuppankai.
Arendt, Hannah. 1978. *The Jew as Pariah: Jewish Identity and Politics in the Modern Age.* New York: Grove Press.
Asakawa Akihiro. 2003. *Zainichi gaikokujin to kikaseido.* Tokyo: Shinkansha.
———. 2006. *"Zainichi"ron no uso.* Tokyo: PHP.
Bade, Klaus J. 2003. *Migration in European History.* Translated by Allison Brown. Oxford: Blackwell.
Bayley, David H. 1976. *Force of Order: Police Behavior in Japan and the United States.* Berkeley: University of California Press.
Berger, John. 1984. *And Our Faces, My Heart, Brief as Photos.* London: Writers and Readers.
Berlin, Isaiah. 1980. *Against the Current: Essays in the History of Ideas.* Ed. Henry Hardy. New York: Viking.

Bestor, Theodore C. 1989. *Neighborhood Tokyo*. Stanford, Calif.: Stanford University Press.

———. 2004. *Tsukiji: The Fish Market at the Center of the World*. Berkeley: University of California Press.

Braudel, Fernand. 1986. *L'identité de la France*. 2 vols. Paris: Flammarion.

Brodsky, Joseph. 1988. "The Condition We Call Exile." *New York Review of Books*. http://www.nybooks.com/articles/4548 (retrieved 7/7/08).

Carey, Peter. 2005. *Wrong about Japan*. New York: Knopf.

Cavalli-Sforza, Luigi Luca, and Francesco Cavalli-Sforza. [1993] 1995. *The Great Human Diasporas: The History of Diversity and Evolution*. Translated by Sarah Thorne. Reading, Mass.: Addison-Wesley.

Celan, Paul. [1958] 1983. "Ansprache anlässlich der Entgegennahme des Literaturpreises der Freier Hansestadt Bremen." In Paul Celan, *Gesammelte Werke*, vol. 3, 185–86. Frankfurt am Main: Suhrkamp.

Chan Dōsiki. 1966. *Aru Zainichi Chōsenjin no kiroku*. Tokyo: Dōseisha.

Chan Jonsu. 1989. *Zainichi 60 nen—jiritsu to teikō*. Tokyo: Shakai Hyōronsha.

Chan Myonsu. 1991. *Uragirareta rakudo*. Tokyo: Kōdansha.

———. 1995. "Kikoku senjō no 'kenkin kōsaku.'" *Bessatsu Takarajima* 221:118–28.

Chapman, David. 2008. *Zainichi Korean Identity and Ethnicity*. London: Routledge.

Chaudhuri, Nirad C. [1951] 1989. *The Autobiography of an Unknown Indian*. Reading, Mass.: Addison-Wesley.

Chauncey, George. 1994. *Gay New York: Gender, Urban Culture, and the Making of the Gay Male World, 1890–1940*. New York: Basic.

Che Sogi. 2004. *Zainichi no genfūkei*. Tokyo: Akashi Shoten.

Chi Tong-Wook. 1997. *Zainichi o yamenasai*. Tokyo: Za Masada.

Choe Chan Hwa. 1978. "Ōmura shūyōjo to iu tokoro." In Chan Hwa Choe, ed., *Papa o kaeshite!*, 227–58. Tokyo: Fūbaisha.

Chon Ayon. 2005. "Rojiura kara hasshin suru bunka." In Fujiwara Shoten Henshūbu, ed., *Rekishi no naka no "Zainichi,"* 303–17. Tokyo: Fujiwara Shoten.

Chon Deyon. 2005. "Nihon no shokubunka to 'Zainichi.'" In Fujiwara Shoten Henshūbu, ed., *Rekishi no naka no "Zainichi,"* 318–34. Tokyo: Fujiwara Shoten.

Chon Sunpak [Chŏng, Sŭng-bak]. 1994. "Tonsha no bannin." In Sunpak Chon, *Chon Sunpak chosakushū*, vol. 6, 73–91. Tokyo: Shinkansha.

Chon Wolson. 2007. *Kaikyō no aria*. Tokyo: Shōgakkan.

———. 2008. *Kinjirareta uta*. Tokyo: Chūō Kōronsha.

Chon Yonha. 1993. "'Zainichi' to ie seido." *Horumon bunka* 4:41–55.

Chong, Ayong. 1997. "Tokyo-kei Chōsenjin ga mita! konnamon arimasuka in Osaka." *Horumon bunka* 7:86–95.

Chong Jaejung. 2006. *Kim Dae Jung kyūshutsu undō shoshi*. Tokyo: Gendai Jinbunsha.

Chung, Ook. 2001. *Kimchi*. Paris: Le Serpent à Plumes.

Cohen, Robin, ed. 1998. *The Cambridge Guide to International Migration.* Cambridge: Cambridge University Press.

Cohen, Shaye J. D. 1999. *The Beginnings of Jewishness: Boundaries, Varieties, Uncertainties.* Berkeley: University of California Press.

Cole, Simon A. 2001. *Suspect Identities: A History of Fingerprinting and Criminal Identification.* Cambridge, Mass.: Harvard University Press.

De Vos, George, and Changsoo Lee. 1981. "Conclusions: The Maintenance of a Korean Ethnic Identity in Japan." In Changsoo Lee and George De Vos, eds., *Koreans in Japan: Ethnic Conflict and Accommodation,* 354–83. Berkeley: University of California Press.

Deleuze, Gilles, and Félix Guattari. 1975. *Kafka.* Paris: Minuit.

Denoon, Donald, Mark Hudson, Gavan McCormack, and Tessa Morris-Suzuki, eds. 1997. *Multicultural Japan: Palaeolithic to Postmodern.* Cambridge: Cambridge University Press.

Dore, R. P. [1958] 1999. *City Life in Japan: A Study of a Tokyo Ward.* Richmond, U.K.: Japan Library.

Dower, John W. 1999. *Embracing Defeat: Japan in the Wake of World War II.* New York: Norton.

Duus, Peter. 1995. *The Abacus and the Sword: The Japanese Penetration of Korea, 1895–1910.* Berkeley: University of California Press.

Eckert, Carter J. 1999. "Epilogue: Exorcising Hegel's Ghosts: Toward a Postnationalist Historiography of Korea." In Gi-Wook Shin and Michael Robinson, eds., *Colonial Modernity in Korea,* 363–78. Cambridge, Mass.: Harvard University Press.

Field, Norma. 1996. "Texts of Childhood in Inter-Nationalizing Japan." In Laura García-Moreno and Peter C. Pfeiffer, eds., *Text and Nation: Cross-Disciplinary Essays on Cultural and National Identities,* 143–72. Columbia, S.C.: Camden House.

Fitzpatrick, Sheila. 1999. *Everyday Stalinism: Ordinary Life in Extraordinary Times; Soviet Russia in the 1930s.* New York: Oxford University Press.

Flaubert, Gustave. [1857] 1993. *Madame Bovary.* Translated by Francis Steegmuller. New York: Knopf.

Fujishima Udai. 1960. *Nihon no minzoku undō.* Tokyo: Kōbunsha.

Fujiwara Tei. [1949] 2002. *Nagareru hoshi wa ikiteiru.* Tokyo: Chūō Kōronsha.

Fukazawa Kai. [1992] 2006. "Yoru no kodomo." In Jirō Isogai and Kazuo Kuroko, eds., *"Zainichi" bungaku zenshū,* vol. 14, 5–101. Tokyo: Bensei Shuppan.

Fukuoka Yasunori. 1993. *Zainichi Kankoku—Chōsenjin.* Tokyo: Chūō Kōronsha.

Fukuoka Yasunori and Myung-Soo Kim. 1997. *Zainichi Kankokujin seinen no seikatsu to ishiki.* Tokyo: Tokyo Daigaku Shuppankai.

Fukuoka Yasunori and Yukiko Tsujiyama. 1991a. *Hontō no watashi o motomete.* Tokyo: Shinkansha.

―――. 1991b. *Dōka to ika no hazamade.* Tokyo: Shinkansha.

Fukuoka Yasunori, Hiroaki Yoshii, Atsushi Sakurai, Shūsaku Ejima, Haruhiko

Kanegae, and Michihiko Noguchi, eds. 1987. *Hisabetsu no bunka, hansabetsu no ikizama.* Tokyo: Akashi Shoten.

Gaimushō Ajiakyoku Hokutō Ajiaka. 1969. *Kita Chōsen gaikyō.* Tokyo: Gaimushō Ajiakyoku Hokutō Ajiaka.

Gates, Henry Louis, Jr. 1988. *The Signifying Monkey: A Theory of Afro-American Literary Criticism.* New York: Oxford University Press.

Gellner, Ernest. 1983. *Nations and Nationalism.* Oxford: Blackwell.

Gen Getsu. [1999] 2000a. "Kage no sumika." In Getsu Gen, *Kage no sumika,* 5–96. Tokyo: Bungei Shunjū.

———. 2000b. *Warui uwasa.* Tokyo: Bungei Shunjū.

———. 2003a. *Oshaberina inu.* Tokyo: Bungei Shunjū.

———. 2003b. "Unga." In Getsu Gen, *Jakuya,* 129–53. Tokyo: Kōdansha.

———. 2005. *Ibutsu.* Tokyo: Kōdansha.

———. 2007. *Kenzoku.* Tokyo: Kōdansha.

Gilroy, Paul. 1993. *The Black Atlantic: Modernity and Double Consciousness.* Cambridge, Mass.: Harvard University Press.

Goffman, Erving. [1963] 1974. *Stigma: Notes on the Management of Spoiled Identity.* New York: Jason Aronson.

Gohl, Gerhard. 1976. *Die koreanische Minderheit in Japan als Fall einer "politisch-ethnischen" Minderheitengruppe.* Wiesbaden, Germany: Harrassowitz.

Gornick, Vivian. 1977. *The Romance of American Communism.* New York: Basic.

Gottwald, Norman K. 1979. *The Tribes of Yahweh: A Sociology of the Religion of Liberated Israel, 1250–1050 B.C.E.* New York: Orbis Books.

Grajdanzev, Andrew J. 1944. *Modern Korea: A Study of Social and Economic Changes under Japanese Rule.* New York: Institute of Pacific Affairs.

Gu Mitsunori. 2007. *Yakiniku shōsetsu purukogi.* Tokyo: Shōgakkan.

Gu Sūyon. 2002. *Gūzen ni mo saiaku na shōnen.* Tokyo: Kadokawa Haruki Jimusho.

Hagiwara Ryō. 1998. *Kita Chōsen ni kieta tomo to watashi no monogatari.* Tokyo: Bungei Shunjū.

Haley, Alex. 1976. *Roots.* Garden City, N.Y.: Doubleday.

Han Doksu. [1972] 1980. "Kin Nissei shuseki ni yoru kaigai kyōhō mondai no kagayakashii kaiketsu." In Chōsen Daigakkō, ed., *Zainichi Chōsenjin undō ni kansuru shuyō ronbunshū,* 23–43. Tokyo: Shiryō Henshū Iinkai.

———. 1986. *Shutaiteki kaigai kyōhō undō no shisō to jissen.* Tokyo: Miraisha.

———. [1955] 1993. "Chaeil Choson'in undong ǔi chonhan e taehayo." In Kyongsik Pak, ed., *Chōsen mondai shiryō sōsho,* vol. 9, 610–29. Tokyo: Ajia Mondai Kenkyūjo.

Han Gwanghi. 2002. *Waga Chōsen Sōren no tsumi to batsu.* Tokyo: Bungei Shunjū.

Han Sokkyu. 2007. *Nihon kara "Kita" ni kaetta hito no monogatari.* Tokyo: Shinkansha.

Handlin, Oscar. 1973. *The Uprooted.* 2nd ed. Boston: Little, Brown.

Handō Kazutoshi. 2006. *Shōwashi: Sengohen 1945–1989.* Tokyo: Heibonsha.

Han-san ikka no Shimon Ōnatsu Kyohi o Sasaerukai Jimukyoku. 1985. "Kazoku de shimon ōnatsu o kyohi." In "Hataraku Nakama no Bukkuretto" Kyōdō Henshū Iinkai, ed., *Shimon ōnatsu kyohi!*, 52–54. Tokyo: Shinchiheisha.

Harajiri Hideki. 1989. *Zainichi Chōsenjin no seikatsu sekai.* Tokyo: Kōbundō.

———. 1997. *Nihon teijū Korian no nichijō to seikatsu.* Tokyo: Akashi Shoten.

———. 1998. *"Zainichi" to shite no Korian.* Tokyo: Kōdansha.

Hardacre, Helen. 1984. *The Religion of Japan's Korean Minority: The Preservation of Ethnic Identity.* Berkeley: Institute of East Asian Studies, University of California.

Hatada Isao. 1969. *Nihonjin no Chōsenkan.* Tokyo: Keisō Shobō.

Heidegger, Martin. 2006 [1927]. *Sein und Zeit.* Tübingen, Germany: Niemeyer.

Henshūbu. 1995. "Media ni arawareta Zainichi Korian." *Sai* 15:13–14.

Hester, Jeffry T. 2000. "Kids between Nations." In Sonia Ryang, ed., *Koreans in Japan: Critical Voices from the Margin,* 175–96. London: Routledge.

Hicks, George. 1998. *Japan's Hidden Apartheid: The Korean Minority and the Japanese.* Aldershot, U.K.: Ashgate.

Higuchi Yūichi. 1978. "Zainichi Chōsenjin buraku no seiritsu to tenkai." In Yūsaku Ozawa, ed., *Kindai minshū no kiroku,* vol. 10, 549–64. Tokyo: Shinjinbutsu Ōraisha.

———. 1979. "Zainichi Chōsenjin sensaisha 239,320 nin." *Zainichi Chōsenjinshi kenkyū* 4:42–51.

———. 1995. "Chōsenjin Nihon tokōsha no shusshin kaisō." *Zainichi Chōsenjinshi kenkyū* 25:53–61.

Hirabayashi Hisae. 1978. "8.15 kaihōgo no Zainichi Chōsenjin no seikatsu." *Zainichi Chōsenjinshi kenkyū* 2:1–16.

Hirata Yukie. 2004. "Manazasumono to shite no Nihon josei kan(kō)kyaku." In Yoshitaka Mōri, ed., *Nisshiki Kanryū,* 51–82. Tokyo: Serika Shobō.

Hirschman, Albert O. 1970. *Exit, Voice, and Loyalty: Responses to Decline in Firms, Organizations, and States.* Cambridge, Mass.: Harvard University Press.

Hoerder, Dirk. 2002. *Cultures in Contact: World Migrations in the Second Millennium.* Durham, N.C.: Duke University Press.

Hōmu Kenshūjo, ed. [1955] 1975. *Zainichi Chōsenjin shogū no suii to genjō.* Tokyo: Kōhokusha.

Honda Yasuharu 1992. *Watashitachi no omoni.* Tokyo: Shinchōsha.

Hong Sangjin. 1982. "Zainichi Chōsenjin minzoku kyōiku no genjō." In Kōbe Gakusei—Seinen Sentā, ed., *Zainichi Chōsenjin no minzoku kyōiku,* 64–89. Kōbe: Kōbe Gakusei—Seinen Sentā.

Hong Sŭng-jik and Pae-bo Han. [1977] 1979. "Zainichi dōhō no jittai chōsa." *Zainichi Chōsenjinshi kenkyū* 4:87–147.

Hong Yansin and Tomoko Nakajima. 1980. "Nihon no gakkō ni kodomo a kayowaseteiru Zainichi Chōsenjin fubo no kyōikukan ni taisuru chōsa." *Zainichi Chōsenjinshi kenkyū* 7:93–139.

Hoshino Osami. 2005. *Jichitai no henkaku to Zainichi Korian*. Tokyo: Akashi Shoten.

Hugh of St. Victor. [1120s] 1961. *The Didascalicon of Hugh of St. Victor: A Medieval Guide to the Arts*. Translated by Jerome Taylor. New York: Columbia University Press.

Hwang Mingi. 1993. *Yatsura ga naku mae ni*. Tokyo: Chikuma Shobō.

Hwang Yonchi. 2007. *Kioku no kasō*. Tokyo: Kage Shobō.

Hyōgo-ken Gakumubu Shakaika. [1937] 1982. "Chōsenjin no seikatsu jōtai." In Kyongsik Pak, ed., *Chōsen mondai shiryō sōsho*, vol. 3. Tokyo: Ajia Mondai Kenkyūjo.

Hyon Kwansu. 1983. *Minzoku no shiten*. Tokyo: Dōjidaisha.

Hyon Sunhye. 2007. *Watashi no sokoku wa sekai desu*. Tokyo: Iwanami Shoten.

Iinuma Jirō. [1973] 1983. *Mienai hitobito: Zainichi Chōsenjin*. Expanded ed. Tokyo: Nihon Kirisutokyōdan Shuppankyoku.

———. [1969] 1984. "'Tanminzoku kokkakan' dakkyaku o: Zainichi Chōsenjin no daisan no michi." In Jirō Iinuma, ed., *Shichijūmannin no kiseki*, 261–63. Tokyo: Bakushūsha.

———. 1989. "Zainichi Chōsen-Kankokujin 'shōgaisha' to jinken." *Kikan mintō* 8:132–41.

Iio Kenshi. 1993. *Wonman: Nihonjin no wasuremono*. Tokyo: Kagyūsha.

Ijichi Noriko. 1994. *Zainichi Chōsenjin no namae*. Tokyo: Akashi Shoten.

———. 2000. *Seikatsu sekai no sōzō to jissen*. Tokyo: Ochanomizu Shobō.

Ijūin Shizuka. 1991–2000. *Kaikyō*. 3 vols. Tokyo: Shinchōsha.

Ino Ryōsuke, ed. 2006. *Bessatsu Takarajima: Kenkanryū no shinjitsu*. Tokyo: Takarajimasha.

Ishida Saeko. 2007. "Kanryū būmu no samazamana kataritetachi." In Saeko Ishida, Kan Kimura, and Chie Yamanaka, eds., *Posuto Kanryū no media shakaigaku*, 1–32. Kyoto: Mineruva Shobō.

Ishizaka Kōichi. 1993. *Kindai Nihon no shakaishugi to Chōsen*. Tokyo: Shakai Hyōronsha.

Isogai Jirō. 1979. *Shigen no hikari—Zainichi Chōsenjin bungakuron*. Tokyo: Sōkisha.

Iwabuchi, Koichi. 2000. "Political Correctness, Postcoloniality, and the Self-Representation of 'Koreanness' in Japan." In Sonia Ryang, ed., *Koreans in Japan: Critical Voices from the Margin*, 55–73. London: Routledge.

Iwai Yoshio. [1984] 1989. *Omoni no uta*. Tokyo: Chikuma Shobō.

Iwamoto Mitsuo. 2000. *Nihonjin ni naritai Zainichi Kankokujin*. Tokyo: Asahi Sonorama.

Iwamoto Nobuyuki. 1960. "Kikokusha no ukeire wa kō no jō." In Zainichi Chōsenjin Kikoku Kyōryūkai, ed., *Sokoku ni kaetta hitobito*, 8–24. Tokyo: Zainichi Chōsenjin Kikoku Kyōryūkai.

Iwamura Toshio. 1972. *Zainichi Chōsenjin to Nihon rōdōsha kaikyū*. Tokyo: Azekura Shobō.

Iwata Tamaki. 2001. *Kiri hareru hi made*. Tokyo: Banseisha.

Izumi Seiichi. 1966. *Saishūtō*. Tokyo: Tokyo Daigaku Shuppankai.

Johnson, Mark. 1993. *Moral Imagination: Implications of Cognitive Science for Ethics*. Chicago: University of Chicago Press.

Jon Chonjon. 1984. *On to han to kokoku to*. Tokyo: Nihon Editā Sukūru Shuppanbu.

Jon Gunju. 2005. "Nihon Kyōsantō oyobi Nihon Shakaitō no taiō." In Sōji Takasaki and Junjin Pak, eds., *Kikoku undō to wa nandattanoka*, 212–34. Tokyo: Heibonsha.

Kaikō Takeshi. 1959. *Nihon sanmon opera*. Tokyo: Bungei Shunjūsha.

Kamishima Jirō. 1982. *Jiba no seijigaku*. Tokyo: Iwanami Shoten.

Kan Jon-hon. 1998. "Zainichi dōhō no minzoku ishiki." In Dopyon Mun, ed., *Zainichi Chōsenjin no rekishi to tenbō*, 185–206. Osaka: Osaka Keizai Hōka Daigaku Shuppanbu.

Kanagawa-ken Jichi Sōgō Kenkyū Sentā Kenkyūbu. 1984. *Kanagawa-ken no Kankoku—Chōsenjin*. Tokyo: Kōjinsha.

Kanagawa-kennai Zaijū Gaikokujin Jittai Chōsa Iinkai. 1986. *Nihon no naka no Kankoku—Chōsenjin, Chūgokujin*. Tokyo: Akashi Shoten.

Kanai Yasuo. 1997. *13 no yureru omoi*. Tokyo: Bakushūsha.

Kaneko Hiroshi. 1996. *Dare no tamedemonaku*. Tokyo: San'ichi Shobō.

Kanemoto J. Noritsugu. 2007. *Food Lovers*. Tokyo: Āton.

Kanemura Yoshiaki. [2000] 2004. *Zainichi damashii*. Tokyo: Kōdansha.

Kaneshiro Kazuki. 2000. *Go*. Tokyo: Kōdansha.

———. 2001. *Revorūshon No. 3*. Tokyo: Kōdansha.

———. 2007. *Eigahen*. Tokyo: Shūeisa.

Kang Chol. [1987] 1994. *Zainichi Chōsenjin no jinken to Nihon no hōritsu*. 2nd ed. Tokyo: Yūzankaku.

Kang Hibong. 2001. *The Korean World in Japan*. Tokyo: Rakushokan.

Kang Je'on. 1977a. "Henshū o oete." *Kikan sanzenri* 12:256.

———. 1977b. "Sokoku, rekishi, Zainichi dōhō." *Kikan sanzenri* 12:28–41.

———. 1979. "Zainichi Chōsenjin mondai no bunken." *Kikan sanzenri* 18:51–59.

———. 1980. "Sengo 36 nenme no Zainichi Chōsenjin." *Kikan sanzenri* 24:26–37.

Kang Je'on and Donhun Kim. 1989. *Zainichi Kankoku Chōsenjin—rekishi to tenbō*. Tokyo: Rōdō Keizaisha.

Kang Sangjung. 1994. "Tenkeiki no 'Zainichi' to sanseiken." *Kikan seikyū* 20:36–43.

———. 2004. *Zainichi*. Tokyo: Kōdansha.

———. 2005. *Zainichi futatsu no "sokoku" e no omoi*. Tokyo: Kōdansha.

———. 2008. "Ai no sakuhō." *Aera*, 24 March.

Kang Tongjin. 1984. *Nihon genronkai to Chōsen 1910—1945*. Tokyo: Hōsei Daigaku Shuppankyoku.

Kangaerukai. 1971. "Zentai shūkai." *Mukuge* 1:1–2.

Kashiwazaki, Chikako. 2000. "The Politics of Legal Status." In Sonia Ryang, ed., *Koreans in Japan: Critical Voices from the Margin*, 13–31. London: Routledge.

Kawamura Minato. 1999. *Umaretara sokoga furusato*. Tokyo: Heibonsha.

———. [1986] 2000. "*Yoidorebune" no seishun*. Tokyo: Inpakuto Shuppankai.

———. 2003. *Kankoku, Chōsen, Zainichi o yomu*. Tokyo: Inpakuto Shuppansha.

———. 2005. "Hen'yō suru 'Zainichi.'" In Sadami Suzuki, ed., *Nihon bungeishi*, vol. 8, 219–25. Tokyo: Kawade Shobō Shinsha.

Kawase Junji. 1978. "Zainichi Chōsenjin to engo gyōsei." In Masuo Yoshioka, ed., *Zainichi Chōsenjin to shakai hoshō*, 63–108. Tokyo: Shakai Hyōronsha.

Kawata Hiroshi. 2005. *Uchi naru sokoku e*. Tokyo: Hara Shobō.

Kayama Mitsurō. [1941] 1978. "Naisen ittai zuisōroku." In Yūsaku Ozawa, ed., *Kindai minshū no kiroku*, vol. 10, 357–61. Tokyo: Shinjinbutsu Ōraisha.

Khazanov, Anatoly. 1995. *After the USSR: Ethnicity, Nationalism, and Politics in the Commonwealth of Independent States*. Madison: University of Wisconsin Press.

Kim Chanjung. 1977. *Sokoku o shiranai sedai*. Tokyo: Tabata Shoten.

———. 1979. *Ame no dōkoku*. Tokyo: Tabata Shoten.

———. 1980. *Hi no dōkoku*. Tokyo: Tabata Shoten.

———. 1983. *Kokoku kara no kyori*. Tokyo: Tabata Shoten.

———. 1988. *Kanpū renrakusen*. Tokyo: Asahi Shoten.

———. 2004a. *Zainichi, gekidō no hyakunen*. Tokyo: Asahi Shinbunsha.

———. 2004b. *Chōsen Sōren*. Tokyo: Shinchōsha.

———. 2007. *Zainichi giyūhei kikansezu*. Tokyo: Iwanami Shoten.

Kim Chanjung and Sonhi Ban. 1977. *Kaze no dōkoku*. Tokyo: Tabata Shoten.

Kim Chansen. 1982. *Watashi no Ikaino*. Tokyo: Fūbaisha.

Kim Chonghoe. 1957. "Amerika no Minami Chōsen ni taisuru shokuminchi-teki reizokuka to 'enjo' seisaku no honshitsu." *Chōsen kenkyū* 1:7–44.

Kim Chongmi. 2002. *Shigamakko toketa*. Tokyo: Nihon Hōsō Shuppan Kyōkai.

Kim Chonmi. 1998. "Shinryaku no kyōdōtai to teikō no kyōdōtai." *Horumon bunka* 8:41–56.

Kim Chung-myong. [2000] 2006. "Migiwa no tami." In Jirō Isogai and Kazuo Kuroko, eds., *"Zainichi" bungaku zenshū*, vol. 13, 5–266. Tokyo: Bensei Shuppan.

Kim Dalsu. 1977. *Waga ariran no uta*. Tokyo: Chūō Kōronsha.

———. 1981. "Waga bungaku e no michi." In Dalsu Kim and Je'on Kang, eds., *Shuki = Zainichi Chōsenjin*, 15–27. Tokyo: Ryūkei Shosha.

———. 1990. *Toraijin to torai bunka*. Tokyo: Kawade Shobō Shinsha.

———. 1998. *Waga bungaku to seikatsu*. Tokyo: Seikyū Bunkasha.

———. [1954] 2006. "Genkainada." In Jirō Isogai and Kazuo Kuroko, eds., *"Zainichi" bungaku zenshū*, vol. 1, 165–412. Tokyo: Bensei Shuppan.

Kim Hanil. 2005. *Chōsen kōkō no seishun*. Tokyo: Kōbunsha.

Kim Hiro [Kin Kirō]. 1968. *Kin Kirō mondai shiryōshū*, vol. 1. Tokyo: Kin Kirō Kōhan Taisaku Iinkai.

———. 1989. *Ware ikitari*. Tokyo: Shinchōsha.

Kim Hiro Bengodan. 1972. *Kin Kirō mondai shiryōshū*, vol. 8. Tokyo: Kin Kirō Kōhan Taisaku Iinkai.

Kim Hyandoja. 1988. *Ikaino rojiura tōryanse*. Nagoya: Fūbaisha.

Kim Hyonpyo. 1978. *Aru kōnichi undōka no kiseki*. Edited by Masuo Ōmura and Tomoki Nanri. Tokyo: Ryūkei Shosha.

Kim Ilmen. 1978. *Chōsenjin ga naze "Nihonmei" o nanorunoka*. Tokyo: San'ichi Shobō.

Kim, Jackie J. 2005. *Hidden Treasures: Lives of First-Generation Korean Women in Japan*. Lanham, Md.: Rowman & Littlefield.

Kim Kyonbu. 1998. "Zainichi Chōsenjin no jinken." In Dopyon Mun, ed., *Zainichi Chōsenjin no rekishi to tenbō*, 178–84. Osaka: Osaka Keizai Hōka Daigaku Shuppanbu.

Kim Kyongdok. [1995] 2005. *Zainichi Korian no aidentiti to hōteki ichi*. New ed. Tokyo: Akashi Shoten.

———. 2006. "Wagako no minzoku kyōiku." In Kyongdok Kim, ed., *Wagaya no minzoku kyōiku*, 11–19. Tokyo: Shinkansha.

Kim Kyonghae. 1982. "4.24 kyōiku tōsō—Kōbe." In Kōbe Gakusei—Seinen Sentā, ed., *Zainichi Chōsenjin no minzoku kyōiku*, 4–39. Kōbe: Kōbe Gakusei—Seinen Sentā.

Kim Masumi. [1997] 2004. "Moeru Sōka." In Masumi Kim, *Nason no sora*, 97–184. Tokyo: Sōfūkan.

Kim Munson. 1991. *Hōrōden: Shōwashi no naka no Zainichi*. Tokyo: Sairyūsha.

Kim, Richard E. 1970. *Lost Names*. Seoul: Sisayongo-sa.

Kim Sang-hyŏn. 1969. *Chaeil Han'gug'in*. Seoul: Tangok Haksul Yŏn'guwŏn.

Kim Sangwon. 2004. "Kikoku dōhō to Chōsen Sōren." In Tōhoku Ajia Mondai Kenkyūjo, ed., *Zainichi Chōsenjin wa naze kikoku shitanoka*, 50–71. Tokyo: Gendai Jinbunsha.

Kim Saryan [Kin Shiryō]. [1941] 1973. "Mushi." In Kin Shiryō Zenshū Henshū Iinkai, ed., *Kin Shiryō zenshū*, 5–23. Tokyo: Kawade Shobō Shinsha.

———. [1940] 2006. "Hikari no naka ni." In Jirō Isogai and Kazuo Kuroko, eds., *"Zainichi" bungaku zenshū*, vol. 11, 5–29. Tokyo: Benseisha.

Kim Sijong. 2004. *Waga sei to shi*. Tokyo: Iwanami Shoten.

———. 2005. *Kim Sijong shishūsen: Kyōgai no shi*. Tokyo: Fujiwara Shoten.

Kim Sokpom. 1979. "'Zainichi' to wa nanika." *Kikan sanzenri* 18:26–36.

———. 1981. *"Zainichi" no shisō*. Tokyo: Chikuma Shobō.

———. 1983–97. *Kazantō*. 7 vols. Tokyo: Bungei Shunjū.

———. 1990. *Kokoku kō*. Tokyo: Iwanami Shoten.

———. 1993. *Tenkō to shinnichiha*. Tokyo: Iwanami Shoten.

———. 1996. *Chi no kage*. Tokyo: Shūeisha.

———. 1998. "Ima, 'Zainichi' ni totte 'kokuseki' to wa nanika." *Sekai* 653:131–42.

―――. [1981] 2001. *Zainichi no shisō*. New ed. Tokyo: Kōdansha.

―――. 2002. *Kyojitsu*. Tokyo: Kōdansha.

―――. 2004. *Kokkyō o koerumono*. Tokyo: Bungei Shunjū.

―――. [1974] 2005a. "1945 nen natsu." In Sokpom Kim, *Kim Sokpom sakuhinshū I*, 243–436. Tokyo: Heibonsha.

―――. [1974] 2005b. "Tojō." In Sokpom Kim, *Kim Sokpom sakuhinshū II*, 5–39. Tokyo: Heibonsha.

Kim Sokpom and Sijong Kim. 2001. *Naze kakitsuzuketekitaka, naze chinmokushitekitaka*. Ed. Gyongsu Mun. Tokyo: Heibonsha.

Kim So-un. 1983. *Ten no hate ni ikurutomo*. Tokyo: Shinchōsha.

Kim T'ae-gi. 1997. *Sengo Nihon seiji to Zainichi Chōsenjin mondai*. Tokyo: Keisō Shobō.

Kim Temyong. 2004. *Mainoriti no kenri to fuhenteki jinken gainen no kenkyū*. Tokyo: Transview.

Kim Teseng. 1985. *Nagune densetsu*. Tokyo: Kirokusha.

Kim Teyon. 1999. *Aidentiti—poritikusu o koete*. Kyoto: Sekai Shisōsha.

Kim Wonjo. 1984. *Hyōdo no rakudo*. Tokyo: Aki Shobō.

Kim Yondal. 1990. *Zainichi Chōsenjin no kika*. Tokyo: Akashi Shoten.

―――. 1992. *Nitchō kokkō jūritsu to Zainichi Chōsenjin no kokuseki*. Tokyo: Akashi Shoten.

―――. 2002. *Kim Yondal chosakushū*, vol. 1, ed. Noriko Ijichi. Tokyo: Akashi Shoten.

―――. 2003a. *Kim Yondal chosakushū*, vol. 2, ed. Kyonghae Kim. Tokyo: Akashi Shoten.

―――. 2003b. *Kim Yondal chosakushū*, vol. 3, ed. Yūichi Hida. Tokyo: Akashi Shoten.

Kim Yong. 2006. "Kawariyuku Chōsen gakkō." In Kyongdok Kim, ed., *Wagaya no minzoku kyōiku*, 79–84. Tokyo: Shinkansha.

Kim Yunjon. 2007. *Tabunka kyōsei kyōiku to aidentiti*. Tokyo: Akashi Shoten.

Kimura Kenji. 1997. "Senzenki Zainichi Chōsenjin no teijū katei." *Zainichi Chōsenjinshi kenkyū* 27:114–29.

Kin Kakuei. [1966] 2004. "Kogoeru kuchi." In Kakuei Kin, *Kogoeru kuchi*, 11–103. Tokyo: Kurein.

―――. 2006a. "Manazashi no kabe." In Kakuei Kin, *Tsuchi no kanashimi*, 229–94. Tokyo: Kurein.

―――. 2006b. "Ippiki no hitsuji." In Kakuei Kin, *Tsuchi no kanashimi*, 547–54. Tokyo: Kurein.

Kin Shōichi. 1971. "Senkō yo, shikkari sarase." In Katsumi Satō, ed., *Zainichi Chōsenjin no shomondai*, 33–39. Tokyo: Dōseisha.

Kinoshita Junji. [1961] 1962. "Kuchibue ga fuyu no sora ni . . . " In Junji Kinoshita, *Kuchibue ga fuyu no sora ni . . . : Kinoshita Junji sakuhinshū IV*, 307–76. Tokyo: Miraisha.

Kishida Yumi. 1999. "Zainichi Kankoku—Chōsenjin kyōiku ni okeru minzoku to kokka ni kansuru ichikōsatsu." *Zainichi Chōsenjinshi kenkyū* 29:59–68.

Ko Chunsok. 1985. *Zainichi Chōsenjin kakumei undōshi*. Tokyo: Tsuge Shobō.

Kō Eiri. 2000. *Garasu no tō*. Tokyo: Shisō no Kagakusha.

Ko Samyon. [1976] n.d. "Ikirukoto to manabukoto." In Nihon no Gakkō ni Zaiseki suru Chōsenjin Jidōseito no Kyōiku o Kangaerukai Shiryō Sentā Henshūbu, eds., "*Honmyō to kyōiku*" *kōenshū*, 3–12. Osaka: Nihon no Gakkō ni Zaiseki suru Chōsenjin Jidōseito no Kyōiku o Kangaerukai.

———. [1974] 1986. *Ikirukoto no imi*. Tokyo: Chikuma Shobō.

———. [1997] 2004. *Yami o hamu*. 2 vols. Tokyo: Kadokawa Shoten.

Ko Son-hwi. 1996. *Zainichi Saishūtō shusshinsha no seikatsu katei*. Tokyo: Shinkansha.

Ko Yon-i. 1998. "*Minzoku*" *de arukoto*. Tokyo: Shakai Hyōronsha.

Koh Chung, Hesung, ed. 2007. *Diasupora to shite no Korian*. Translated by Chikako Kashiwazaki. Tokyo: Shinkansha.

Kon Sun-i. 1993. "Shakai to shōgaisha to Zainichi to." *Uri saenghwa* 10:54–58.

Kondo, Atsushi. 2001. "Citizenship Rights for Aliens in Japan." In Atsushi Kondo, ed., *Citizenship in a Global World: Comparing Citizenship Rights for Aliens*, 8–30. Houndmills, U.K.: Palgrave.

Kōtō—Zainichi Chōsenjin no Rekishi o Kirokusurukai, ed. 1995. *Tokyo no Korian—taun*. Tokyo: Kinohanasha.

Kroeger, Brooke. 2003. *Passing: When People Can't Be Who They Are*. New York: Public Affairs.

Kure Tomofusa. 2007. *Kenzen naru seishin*. Tokyo: Futabasha.

Kuroda Fukumi. [1988] 1995. *Souru mai hāto*. Tokyo: Kōdansha.

Kurokawa Yōji. 2006. *Zainichi Chōsenjin—Kankokujin to Nihon no seishin iryō*. Tokyo: Hihyōsha.

Kwak Kihwan. 2006. *Sabetsu to teikō no genshōgaku*. Tokyo: Shinsensha.

Kyō Nobuko. 1987. *Goku futsū no Zainichi Kankokujin*. Tokyo: Asahi Shinbunsha.

———. 1990. *Watashi no ekkyō ressun*. Tokyo: Asahi Shinbunsha.

———. 2000. *Kikyō nōto*. Tokyo: Sakuhinsha.

———. 2002. *Anjūshinai watashitachi no bunka*. Tokyo: Shōbunsha.

Kyoto Daigaku Kyōikugakubu Hikaku Kyōikugaku Kenkyūshitsu. 1990. *Zainichi Kankoku—Chōsenjin no minzoku kyōiku ishiki*. Tokyo: Akashi Shoten.

Langford, Paul. 1989. *Englishness Identified: Manners and Character, 1650–1850*. Oxford: Oxford University Press.

Larkin, Philip. [1971] 1988. "This Be the Verse." In Philip Larkin, *Collected Poems*, ed. Anthony Thwaite, 180. London: Marvell Press.

Lee Bong Ou. 2007. *Patchigi!teki*. Tokyo: Iwanami Shoten.

Lee, Boongeun. 2005. *Zainichi issei*. Tokyo: Ritorumoa.

Lee Changsoo. 1981. "The Politics of Repatriation." In Changsoo Lee and George De Vos, eds., *Koreans in Japan: Ethnic Conflict and Accommodation*, 91–109. Berkeley: University of California Press.

Lee Chong Hwa. 1998. *Tsubuyaki no seiji shisō.* Tokyo: Seidosha.

Lee Chongja. 1994. *Furimukeba Nihon.* Tokyo: Kawade Shobō Shinsha.

Lee Hoesung [Yi Hoe-sŏng/Ri Kaisei]. 1971. *Kin Kirō mondai shiryōshū,* vol. 7, 27–40. Tokyo: Kin Kirō Kōhan Taisaku Iinkai.

———. 1974. *Kita de are Minami de are waga sokoku.* Tokyo: Kawade Shobō Shinsha.

———. 1975. *Tsuihō to jiyū.* Tokyo: Shinchōsha.

———. 1975–79. *Mihatenu yume.* 5 vols. Tokyo: Kōdansha.

———. 1983. *Saharin e no tabi.* Tokyo: Kōdansha.

———. 1996. *Shisha to seisha no ichi.* Tokyo: Bungei Shunjū.

———. 1998. "Kankoku kokuseki shutoku no ki." *Shinchō* 95(7):294–317.

———. 1999. "'Mukokusekisha' no yuku michi." *Sekai* 657:257–69.

———. 2002. *Kanōsei to shite no "Zainichi."* Tokyo: Kōdansha.

———. [1997] 2005a. "Ikitsumodoritsu." In Hoesung Lee, *Shiki,* 19–59. Tokyo: Shinchōsha.

———. 2005b. *Chijō seikatsusha.* 2 vols. Tokyo: Kōdansha.

Lee Hoesung [Yi Hoe-sŏng/Ri Kaisei] and Naoki Mizuno, eds. 1991. *"Ariran no uta" oboegaki.* Tokyo: Iwanami Shoten.

Lee Seijaku. 1997. *Zainichi Kankokujin sansei no mune no uchi.* Tokyo: Sōshisha.

Lee Sun Ae. 2000. *Nisei no kigen to "sengo shisō."* Tokyo: Heibonsha.

Lee Yangji [Yi Yang-ji]. 1981. "Sanchō no ritsudō no naka e." In Dalsu Kim and Je'on Kang, eds., *Shuki = Zainichi Chōsenjin,* 149–76. Tokyo: Ryūkei Shosha.

———. 1985. *Koku.* Tokyo: Kōdansha.

———. 1993. *Yi Yangji zenshū.* Tokyo: Kōdansha..

Lee Younghwa. 1997. *Kita Chōsen Nihonjintsumatachi e no chinkonka.* Tokyo: Za Masada.

———. [1995] 1999. *Chōsen Sōren to shūyōjo kyōwakoku.* Tokyo: Shōgakkan.

Lenin, V. I. [1902] 1988. *What Is To Be Done?* Harmondsworth, U.K.: Penguin.

Lie, John. 1991. "War, Absolution, and Amnesia: The Decline of War Responsibility in Postwar Japan." *Peace & Change* 16:302–15.

———. 1995. "The Transformation of Sexual Work in Twentieth-Century Korea," *Gender & Society* 9:310–27.

———. 1998. *Han Unbound: The Political Economy of South Korea.* Stanford, Calif.: Stanford University Press.

———. 2001. *Multiethnic Japan.* Cambridge, Mass.: Harvard University Press.

———. 2004a. "The Black-Asian Conflict?" In George Fredrickson and Nancy Foner, eds., *Not Just Black and White,* 301–14. New York: Russell Sage Foundation.

———. 2004b. *Modern Peoplehood.* Cambridge, Mass.: Harvard University Press.

Maekawa Keiji. 1981. *Kankoku—Chōsenjin: Zainichi o ikiru.* Tokyo: Sōkisha.

Marrus, Michael R. 1985. *The Unwanted: European Refugees in the Twentieth Century.* New York: Oxford University Press.

Marshall, T. H. [1950] 1992. "Citizenship and Social Class." In T. H. Marshall and Tom Bottomore, *Citizenship and Social Class,* 1–51. London: Pluto.

Matsuda Toshihiko. 1995. *Senzenki no Zainichi Chōsenjin to sanseiken.* Tokyo: Akashi Shoten.

McCann, David R. 1979. "Arirang: The National Folksong of Korea." In David R. McCann, John Middleton, and Edward J. Schultz, eds., *Studies on Korea in Transition,* 43–56. Honolulu: Center for Korean Studies, University of Hawaii.

McNeill, William H. 1986. *Polyethnicity and National Unity in World History.* Toronto: University of Toronto Press.

Milosz, Czeslaw. [1955] 1981. *The Captive Mind.* Translated by Jane Zielonko. New York: Vintage.

Mita Munesuke. 1996. *Gendai shakai no riron.* Tokyo: Iwanami Shoten.

Mitchell, Richard H. 1967. *The Korean Minority in Japan.* Berkeley: University of California Press.

Miyata Hiroto, ed. 1977. *65 mannin—Zainichi Chōsenjin.* Tokyo: Suzusawa Shoten.

Miyata Setsuko. 1985. *Chōsen minshū to "kōminka" seisaku.* Tokyo: Miraisha.

———. 1992. "Sōshi kaimei no jitchi katei." In Setsuko Miyata, Yondal Kim, and T'ae-ho Yang, *Sōshi kaimei,* 77–122. Tokyo: Akashi Shoten.

Miyatsuka Toshio. 1993. "Gappei jigyō no aratana tenkai." In Motoi Tamaki and Toshio Watanabe, eds., *Kita Chōsen,* 109–34. Tokyo: Saimaru Shuppankai.

———. 1999. *Nihon yakiniku monogatari.* Tokyo: Ōta Shuppan.

———. 2006. "Zainichi sangyō to Zainichi manē." In Ryōsuke Ino, ed., *Bessatsu Takarajima: Kenkanryū no shinjitsu,* 96–100. Tokyo: Takarajimasha.

Miyauchi Hiroshi. 1999. "Watashi wa anatagata no koto o dō yobeba yoinodarōka?" *Korian mainoriti kenkyū* 3:5–28.

Mōri Yoshitaka. 2004. "'Fuyu no sonata' to nōdōteki fan no bunka jissen." In Yoshitaka Mōri, ed., *Nisshiki Kanryū,* 7–50. Tokyo: Serika Shobō.

Morita Susumu and Aki Sagawa, eds. 2005. *Zainichi Korian shi senshū 1916 nen—2004 nen.* Tokyo: Doyō Bijutsusha Shuppan Hanbai.

Morris, Mark. 2007. "Passing: Paradoxes of Alterity in *The Broken Commandment.*" In Rachel Hutchinson and Mark Williams, eds., *Representing the Other in Modern Japanese Literature: A Critical Approach,* 127–44. London: Routledge.

Morris-Suzuki, Tessa. 1998. *Re-inventing Japan: Time, Space, Nation.* Armonk, N.Y.: M. E. Sharpe.

———. 2007. *Exodus to North Korea: Shadows from Japan's Cold War.* Lanham, Md.: Rowman & Littlefield.

Mun Gyong-su. 2007. *Zainichi Chōsenjin mondai no kigen.* Tokyo: Kurein.

Mun Il, ed. 1929. *Yŏnghwa sosŏl "Arirang."* Seoul: Pangmun Sŏgwan.

Myrdal, Gunnar. [1944] 1962. *An American Dilemma: The Negro Problem and Modern Democracy.* 20th anniversary ed. New York: Harper & Row.

Naitō Seichū. 1989. *Nihonkai chiiki no Zainichi Chōsenjin.* Tokyo: Taga Shuppan.

Nakahara Ryōji. 1993. *Zainichi Kankoku—Chōsenjin no shūshoku sabetsu to kokuseki jōkō.* Tokyo: Akashi Shoten.

Nakamura Fukuharu. 2001. *Kim Sokpom to "Kazantō."* Tokyo: Dōjidaisha.

Nakane Takayuki. 2004. *"Chōsen" hyōshō no bunkashi.* Tokyo: Shin'yōsha.

Nakao Hiroshi. 1997. *Q & A Zainichi Kankoku—Chōsenjin mondai no kisochishiki.* Tokyo: Akashi Shoten.

Nan Bujin. 2006. *Bungaku no shokuminchishugi.* Kyoto: Sekai Shisōsha.

Nihon no Gakkō ni Zaiseki suru Chōsenjin Jidōseito no Kyōiku o Kangaerukai Shiryō Sentā Henshūbu, eds. n.d. *Zainichi Chōsenjin Jidōseito no Kyōiku o Kangaerutame no Shiryō.* Osaka: Nihon no Gakkō ni Zaiseki suru Chōsenjin Jidōseito no Kyōiku o Kangaerukai.

Nihon Shakaitō Chōsen Mondai Taisaku Tokubetsu Iinkai, ed. 1970. *Sokoku o erabu jiyū.* Tokyo: Shakai Shinpō.

Nishimura Hideki. 2004. *Osaka de tatakatta Chōsen Sensō.* Tokyo: Iwanami Shoten.

Nishinarita Yutaka. 1997. *Zainichi Chōsenjin no "sekai" to "teikoku" kokka.* Tokyo: Tokyo Daigaku Shuppankai.

Nixon, Rob. 1992. *London Calling: V. S. Naipaul, Postcolonial Mandarin.* New York: Oxford University Press.

Noguchi Minoru [Chan Hyokuchu]. [1944] 2001. *Iwamoto shiganhei.* Ed. Yutaka Shirakawa. Tokyo: Yumani Shobō.

Noiriel, Gérard. 1988. *Le creuset français: Histoire de l'immigration XIXᵉ–XXᵉ siècles.* Paris: Seuil.

Nomura Kōsuke. [1943] 1982. "Naisen kyōwa to kyōiku," *Kyōwa kyōiku kenkyū.* In Kyongsik Pak, ed., *Chōsen mondai shiryō sōsho,* vol. 4. Tokyo: Ajia Mondai Kenkyūjo.

Nomura Susumu. 1996. *Korian sekai no tabi.* Tokyo: Kōdansha.

Nozaki Rokusuke. 1994. *Ri Chin'u nōto.* Tokyo: San'ichi Shobō.

O Gyusan. 1992. *Zainichi Chōsenjin kigyō katsudō keiseishi.* Tokyo: Yūzankaku.

O Rimjun. 1971. *Zainichi Chōsenjin.* Tokyo: Ushio Shuppansha.

O Sonfa. 1999. *Watashi wa ikanishite "Nihon shinto" to nattaka.* Tokyo: PHP Kenkyūjo.

Oda Makoto. 1978. *"Kita Chōsen" no hitobito.* Tokyo: Ushio Shuppansha.

Oguma Eiji. 1998. *"Nihonjin" no kyōkai.* Tokyo: Shin'yōsha.

———. 2002. *"Minshu" to "aikoku."* Tokyo: Shin'yōsha.

Ogura Kizō. 2005. *Kanryū inpakuto.* Tokyo: Kōdansha.

Ohnuki-Tierney, Emiko. 2002. *Kamikaze, Cherry Blossoms, and Nationalisms: The Militarization of Aesthetics in Japanese History.* Chicago: University of Chicago Press.

Oka Yuriko. 1993. *Shiroi michi o yuku tabi*. Kyoto: Jinbun Shoin.

Ōmura Masuo. 2003. *Chōsen kindai bungaku to Nihon*. Tokyo: Ryokuin Shobō.

Ōnuma Yasuaki. [1986] 1993. *Tan'ichi minzokushakai no shinwa o koete*. New ed. Tokyo: Tōshindō.

———. 2004. *Zainichi Kankoku—Chōsenjin no kokuseki to jinken*. Tokyo: Tōshindō.

Osaka-fu Gakumubu Shakaika. [1934] 1982. "Zaihan Chōsenjin no seikatsu jōtai." In Kyongsik Pak, ed., *Chōsen mondai shiryō sōsho*, vol. 3. Tokyo: Ajia Mondai Kenkyūjo.

Osaka-shi Shakaibu Chōsaka. [1925] 1975. "Chōsenjin rōdōsha mondai." In Kyongsik Pak, ed., *Zainichi Chōsenjin kankei shiryō shūsei*, vol. 1, 339–96. Tokyo: San'ichi Shobō.

Ōsawa Masachi. 1996. "Nēshon to esunishiti." In Shun Inoue, Chizuko Ueno, Masachi Ōsawa, Munesuke Mita, and Shun'ya Yoshimi, eds., *Iwanami kōza gendai shakaigaku*, vol. 24, 27–66. Tokyo: Iwanami Shoten.

Ōtsuki Takahiro. 2006. "Yū Miri." In Ryōsuke Ino, ed., *Bessatsu Takarajima*, 60–63. Tokyo: Takarajimasha.

Ozawa Yūsaku. 1973. *Zainichi Chōsenjin kyōikuron*. Tokyo: Aki Shobō.

———. 1978. "Herubeki rekishi no tsūro nite." In Yūsaku Ozawa, ed., *Kindai minshū no kiroku*, vol. 10, 7–64. Tokyo: Shinjinbutsu Ōraisha.

Pak Cheil. 1957. *Zainichi Chōsenjin ni kansuru sōgō chōsa kenkyū*. Tokyo: Shinkigensha.

Pak Chonmyon. 1995. "Chōsen hantō no tōitsu to Zainichi Chōsenjin." In Chonmin Pak, ed., *Zainichi Chōsenjin: Rekishi, genjō, tenbō*, 319–33. Tokyo: Akashi Shoten.

Pak Hwami. 2000. "'Okottekurete arigatō." *Horumon bunka* 9:11–31.

Pak Il. 1998. "Ikite, aishite, soshite shinda." *Horumon bunka* 8:140–61.

———. 1999. "*Zainichi*" *to iu ikikata*. Tokyo: Kōdansha.

———. 2005a. "*Zainichi Korian*"*tte nandennen?* Tokyo: Kōdansha.

———. 2005b. "Zainichi Korian no keizai jijō." In Fujiwara Shoten Henshūbu, ed., *Rekishi no naka no "Zainichi*," 267–86. Tokyo: Fujiwara Shoten.

Pak Kyongnam. 1992. *Inochisae wasurenakya*. Tokyo: Iwanami Shoten.

Pak Kyongsik. 1965. *Chōsenjin kyōsei renkō no kiroku*. Tokyo: Miraisha.

———. 1973. *Nihon teikokushugi no Chōsen shihai*. 2 vols. Tokyo: Aoki Shoten.

———. 1975. "Zainichi Chōsenjin undōshi," part 1. *Kikan sanzenri* 1:194–213.

———. 1979. *Zainichi Chōsenjin undōshi*. Tokyo: San'ichi Shobō.

———. 1981. *Zainichi Chōsenjin*. Tokyo: San'ichi Shobō.

———. 1992. *Zainichi Chōsenjin, kyōsei renkō, minzoku mondai*. Tokyo: San'ichi Shobō.

Pak Kyongsik, ed. 1983a. *Chōsen mondai shiryō sōsho*, vol. 9. Tokyo: Ajia Mondai Kenkyūjo.

———. 1983b. *Chōsen mondai shiryō sōsho*, vol. 10. Tokyo: Ajia Mondai Kenkyūjo.

———. 1983c. *Chōsen mondai shiryō sōsho*, vol. 5. Tokyo: Ajia Mondai Kenkyūjo.

Pak Sangdok. 1982. *Zainichi Chōsenjin no kyōiku*. New ed. Tokyo: Ariesu Shobō.

Pak Sil. 1990. "'Kika' sha no ushirometasa o norikoe." In Minzokumei o Torimodosukai, ed., *Minzokumei o torimodoshita Nihonseki Chōsenjin*, 9–17. Tokyo: Akashi Shoten.

Pak Sunam. 1970. "'Fanon Is a Brother': An Interview with Pak Sunam." *AMPO* 6:45–59.

Pak Sunam, ed. 1979. *Ri Chin'u zenshokanshū*. Tokyo: Shinjinbutsu Ōraisha.

Pe Ginban. 2000. "Kwanho no yukue." *Horumon bunka* 9:51–66.

Ramazani, Jahan. 2001. *The Hybrid Muse: Postcolonial Poetry in English*. Chicago: University of Chicago Press.

Reed, Ishmael. 1989. "America's 'Black Only' Ethnicity." In Werner Sollors, ed., *The Invention of Ethnicity*, 226–29. New York: Oxford University Press.

Ri Chek. 2003. *Gekishin! Chōsen Sōren to uchimaku*. Tokyo: Shōgakkan.

Ri Kenji. 2007. *Chōsen kindai bungaku to nashonarizumu*. Tokyo: Sakuhinsha.

Ri Sihyon. 1995. "Waga Chōsen Sōren no 'tsumi to batsu.'" *Bessatsu Takarajima* 221:10–31.

Ri Tōjun. 1956. *Nihon ni iru Chōsen no kodomo*. Tokyo: Shunjūsha.

Ri Yuhwan. 1971. *Zainichi Kankokujin 60 man*. Tokyo: Yōyōsha.

Riesman, David, and Evelyn Thompson Riesman. [1967] 1976. *Conversations in Japan: Modernization, Politics, and Culture*. Chicago: University of Chicago Press.

Riley, Denise. 2005. *Impersonal Passion: Language as Affect*. Durham, N.C.: Duke University Press.

Rōdōsha Ruporutāju Shūdan, ed. 1959. *Nihonjin no mita Zainichi Chōsenjin*. Tokyo: Nihon Kikanshi Tsūshinsha.

Ryang, Sonia. 1997. *North Koreans in Japan: Language, Ideology, and Identity*. Boulder, Colo.: Westview Press.

———. 2002. "Dead-End in a Korean Ghetto: Reading a Complex Identity in Gen Getsu's Akutagawa-Winning Novel *Where the Shadows Reside*." *Japanese Studies* 22:5–18.

———. 2003. "The Great Kanto Earthquake and the Massacre of Koreans in 1923: Notes on Japan's Modern National Sovereignty." *Anthropological Quarterly* 76:731–48.

Ryang, Sonia, and John Lie, eds. 2008. *Diaspora without Homeland: Being Korean in Japan*. Berkeley: Global, Area, and International Archive/University of California Press.

Ryōchikai, ed. 1997. *100 nin no Zainichi Korian*. Tokyo: Sangokan.

Ryu, Catherine. 2007. "Beyond Language: Embracing the Figure of 'the Other' in Yi Yang-ji's *Yuhi*." In Rachel Hutchinson and Mark Williams, eds., *Rep-*

resenting the Other in Modern Japanese Literature: A Critical Approach, 312–31. London: Routledge.

Sagisawa Megumu. 1994. *Kenari mo hana, sakura mo hana*. Tokyo: Shinchōsha.

———. 1997. "Hontō no natsu." In Megumu Sagisawa, *Kimi wa kono kuni o sukika*, 7–109. Tokyo: Shinchōsha.

———. [2001] 2004. "Meganegoshi no sora." In Megumu Sagisawa, *Byūtifuru nēmu*, 7–112. Tokyo: Shinchōsha.

———. [2002] 2005. *Watashi no hanashi*. Tokyo: Kawade Shobō Shinsha.

Saitō Hiroko. 1994. *Kankokukei Nihonjin*. Tokyo: Sairyūsha.

Sakanaka Hidenori. 2005a. "Zainichi Kankoku—Chōsenjin seisakuron no kiketsu." In Fujiwara Shoten Henshūbu, ed., *Rekishi no naka no "Zainichi*," 173–87. Tokyo: Fujiwara Shoten.

———. 2005b. *Nyūkan senki*. Tokyo: Kōdansha.

Sasaki Nobuaki. 1986. "1920 nendai ni okeru Zaihan Chōsenjin no rōdō seikatsu katei." In Kaoru Sugihara and Kingo Tamai, eds., *Taishō Osaka suramu*, 161–212. Tokyo: Shinhyōron.

Sasaki Ryūji. 2004. "Kikoku undō no rekishiteki kankyō o tou." In Tōhoku Ajia Mondai Kenkyūjo, ed., *Zainichi Chōsenjin wa naze kikoku shitanoka*, 114–60. Tokyo: Gendai Jinbunsha.

Sasaki Teru. 2006. *Nihon no kokuseki seido to Koriakei Nihonjin*. Tokyo: Akashi Shoten.

Satō Hisashi. 2005. "Kikokusha no sonogo." In Sōji Takasaki and Junjin Pak, eds., *Kikoku undō to wa nandattanoka*, 93–120. Tokyo: Heibonsha.

Satō Katsumi. 1971. "Tōmen suru Zainichi Chōsenjin mondai to Nihonjin." In Katsumi Satō, ed., *Zainichi Chōsenjin no shomondai*, 7–32. Tokyo: Dōseisha.

———. 1977. "Nozomareru jiritsushita kankei." *Kikan sanzenri* 12:48–53.

Satō Toshiki. 2000. *Fubyōtō shakai Nihon*. Tokyo: Chūō Kōron Shinsha.

Schmid, André. 2002. *Korea between Empires, 1895–1919*. New York: Columbia University Press.

Scholem, Gershom. [1977] 1980. *From Berlin to Jerusalem: Memories of My Youth*. Translated by Harry Zohn. New York: Schocken.

Seidel, Michael. 1986. *Exile and the Narrative Imagination*. New Haven, Conn.: Yale University Press.

Seki Takashi. 1962. *Rakuen no yume yaburete*. Tokyo: Zenbōsha.

Sekikawa Natsuo. 1984a. *Kaikyō o koeta hōmuran*. Tokyo: Futabasha.

———. 1984b. *Seoul no renshū mondai*. Tokyo: Jōhō Sentā Shuppankyoku.

———. 1992. *Taikutsu na meikyū*. Tokyo: Shinchōsha.

Shaw, Martin. 2000. *Theory of the Global State: Globality as Unfinished Revolution*. Cambridge: Cambridge University Press.

Shigeyama Sadako. 2006. *Zainichi shura no uta*. Tokyo: Kōdansha.

Shin, Gi-Wook. 2006. *Ethnic Nationalism in Korea: Genealogy, Politics, and Legacy*. Stanford, Calif.: Stanford University Press.

Shin Sugok. 2003. *Kikoku shūshū*. Tokyo: Kaihō Shuppansha.

————. 2006. *Setchan no gochisō*. Tokyo: NHK Shuppan.

Shirai Miyuki, ed. 2007. *Nihon kokuseki o torimasuka?* Tokyo: Shinkansha.

Shōya Reiko and Tōru Nakayama. 1997. *Kōrei Zainichi Kankoku—Chōsenjin*. Tokyo: Ochanomizu Shobō.

Silone, Ignazio. 1949. [Untitled.] In Richard Crossman, ed., *The God That Failed*, 76–114. New York: Harper & Brothers.

Sin Yong-ha. 1987. *Han'guk kŭndae sahoe sasangsa yŏn'gu*. Seoul: Iljisa.

So, Jon'u. 1993. "Watashi no taikenteki chiiki katsudāron." *Kikan seikyū* 15:35–41.

Son Puja. 2007. *Aisurutoki kiseki wa tsukurareru*. Tokyo: San'ichi Shobō.

Steedman, Carolyn Kay. [1986] 1987. *Landscape for a Good Woman: A Story of Two Lives*. New Brunswick, N.J.: Rutgers University Press.

Sternhell, Zeev. 1998. *The Founding Myths of Israel*. Princeton, N.J.: Princeton University Press.

Sugihara Tōru. 1998. *Ekkyō suru tami: Kindai Osaka no Chōsenjinshi kenkyū*. Tokyo: Shinkansha.

Sugiura Minpei. [1969] 2003. "Kaisetsu." In Sueko Yasumoto, *Nianchan*, 292–307. Fukuoka: Nishi Nihon Shinbunsha.

Suh Kyung Sik. 1988. *Nagaku kibishii michinori—Suh kyōdai—gokuchū no sei*. Tokyo: Kage Shobō.

————. [1995] 1998. *Kodomo no namida*. Tokyo: Shōgakkan.

————. 2002. *Han nanmin no ichi kara*. Tokyo: Kage Shobō.

Suh Kyung Sik, ed. 1981. *Suh kyōdai gokuchū kara no tegami*. Tokyo: Iwanami Shoten.

Suh Sung. 1994. *Gokuchū 19 nen*. Tokyo: Iwanami Shoten.

Sung Mija. 1990. *Kabukichō chinjara kōshinkyoku*. Tokyo: Tokuma Shoten.

Suzuki Michihiko. 2007. *Ekkyō no toki*. Tokyo: Shūeisha.

Tabori, Paul. 1972. *The Anatomy of Exile: A Semantic and Historical Study*. London: Harrap.

Tachihara Masaaki. 1983. *Nihon no bi o motomete*. Tokyo: Kadokawa Shoten.

Taguchi Jun'ichi. 1984. "Iminzoku—ibunka no mondai to masukomi." In Eiichi Isomura and Yasunori Fukuoka, eds., *Masukomi to sabetsugo mondai*, 159–77. Tokyo: Akashi Shoten.

Tai, Eika. 2004. "'Korean Japanese': A New Identity Option for Resident Koreans in Japan." *Critical Asian Studies* 36:355–82.

Takai Yūichi. 1991. *Tachihara Seishū*. Tokyo: Shinchōsha.

Takasaki Sōji. 2005. "Kikoku mondai no keika to haikei." In Sōji Takasaki and Junjin Pak, eds., *Kikoku undō to wa nandattanoka*, 18–53. Tokyo: Heibonsha.

Takayanagi Toshio. 1995. "1950–60 nendai no Zainichi Chōsenjin to Nihon no seron." *Kikan seikyū* 22:53–59.

————. 1999–2000. "Eiga 'umi o wataru yūjō' to Kita Chōsen kokuku jigyō." *Zainichi Chōsenjinshi kenkyū* 29:44–58; 30:131–52.

————. 2002. "'Chōsen Bungei' ni miru sengo Zainichi Chōsenjin bungaku no shutsuritsu." In Minato Kawamura, ed., *Bungakushi o yomikaesu*, vol. 5, 56–66. Tokyo: Inpakuto Shuppankai.

Takeda Seiji. 1983. *"Zainichi" to iu konkyo*. Tokyo: Kokubunsha.

Takenoshita Hirohisa. 1996. "Esunikku aidentiti no kattō to hen'yō." *Kaihō shakaigaku kenkyū* 10.

Tamaki Motoi. 1995. "Chōsen Sōren wa nani o yattekitanoka." *Bessatsu takarajima* 221:32–47.

Tanabe Seiko. [1965] 2004. "Watashi no Osaka hakkei." In Seiko Tanabe, *Tanabe Seiko zenshū*, vol. 1, 7–184. Tokyo: Shūeisha.

Tei Taikin [Chung Dae-Gyun]. 1995. *Kankoku no imēji*. Tokyo: Chūō Kōronsha.

———. 2001. *Zainichi Kankokujin no shūen*. Tokyo: Bungei Shunjū.

———. 2006. *Zainichi no taerarenai karusa*. Tokyo: Chūō Kōronsha.

Tei Tetsu. 1982. *Mindan konjaku—Zainichi Kankokujin no minshuka undō*. Tokyo: Keishūshinsha.

Terao Gorō. 1959. *38 dosen no kita*. Tokyo: Shin Nihon Shuppansha.

———. 1961. *Chōsen—sono kita to minami*. Tokyo: Shin Nihon Shuppansha.

———. 1965. *Chōsen nyūmon*. Tokyo: Shin Nihon Shuppansha.

Terasawa Masaharu. 2002. "1990 nendai Nihon to Kankoku no sōgo ninshiki." In Sun-e Pak and Reiko Tsuchiya, eds., *Nihon taishū bunka to Nikkan kankei*, 141–56. Tokyo: Sangensha.

Terazawa Masako. 1990. "Nihon shakai no heisasei to bunka." In Gyōzaisei Sōgō Kenkyūjo, ed., *Gaikokujin rōdōsha no jinken*, 63–68. Tokyo: Ōtsuki Shoten.

Tonomura Masaru. 2004. *Zainichi Chōsenjin no rekishigakuteki kenkyū*. Tokyo: Ryokuin Shobō.

Torpey, John. 2000. *The Invention of the Passport*. Cambridge: Cambridge University Press.

Totsuka Hideo. 1977. "Nihon teikokushugi no hōkai to 'inyū Chōsenjin' rōdōsha." In Mikio Sumiya, ed., *Nihon rōshikankeishi*, 189–261. Tokyo: Tokyo Daigaku Shuppankai.

Tsubouchi Hirokiyo. 1998. *Boshū to iu na no kyōsei renkō*. Tokyo: Sairyūsha.

Tsuge Yoshiharu. [1967] 1995. "Ri-san ikka." In Yoshiharu Tsuge, *Akai hana*, 19–30. Tokyo: Shōgakkan.

Tsuka Kōhei. 1990. *Musume ni kataru sokoku*. Tokyo: Kōbunsha.

"Turning Rapanese." 2007. *Monocle* 1 (3):98–101.

Uchiyama Kazuo. 1982. *Zainichi Chōsenjin to kyōiku*. Tokyo: San'ichi Shobō.

Ueda Takahiko. 1995. *Zainichi Kankokujin to teiryoku*. Tokyo: Nisshin Hōdō.

Un Jongi. 1978. *Okasareru jinken*. Tokyo: Chōsen Sei'nensha.

———. 1983. *Zoku—okasareru jinken*. Tokyo: Chōsen Sei'nensha.

Underwood, William. 2006. "Names, Bones and Unpaid Wages: Seeking Redress for Korean Forced Labor." 2 parts. *Japan Focus*. http://www.japanfocus.org/products/topdf/2219; http://www.japanfocus.org/products/ topdf/2225 (retrieved 7/7/07).

Unno Fukuju. 1993. "Chōsen no rōmu dōin." In Shinobu Ōe et al., eds., *Kindai Nihon to shokuminchi*, vol. 5, 103–30. Tokyo: Iwanami Shoten.

Uri Hakkyo o Tsuzuru Kai, ed. 2001. *Chōsen gakkōtte donna toko?* Tokyo: Shakai Hyōronsha.

Utsumi Aiko. 1982. *Chōsenjin BC kyū senhan no kiroku*. Tokyo: Keisō Shobō.

Wada Haruki. 1985. "Kita no tomo e, Mirami no tomo e." *Shisō* 734:2–22.

———. 1989. "Rosiaryō kyokutō no Chōsenjin 1863–1937." *Shakai kagaku kenkyū* 40.

———. 1992. *Kin Nissei to Manshū kōnichi sensō*. Tokyo: Heibonsha.

Wagatsuma, Hiroshi. 1981. "Problems of Self-Identity among Korean Youth in Japan." In Changsoo Lee and George De Vos, eds., *Koreans in Japan: Ethnic Conflict and Accommodation*, 304–33. Berkeley: University of California Press.

Wagner, Edward W. 1951. *The Korean Minority in Japan 1904—1950*. New York: Institute of Pacific Relations.

Wakita Ken'ichi. 2004. *Chōsen Sensō to Suita—Hirakata jiken*. Tokyo: Akashi Shoten.

Wales, Nym, and San Kim. 1941. *Song of Ariran: A Korean Communist in the Chinese Revolution*. New York: John Day.

Walzer, Michael. 1985. *Exodus and Revolution*. New York: Basic.

Watanabe Kazutami. 2003. *"Tasha" to shite no Chōsen*. Tokyo: Iwanami Shoten.

Watanabe Masao. 2004. *Kaikyū! Shakai ninshiki no gai'nen sōchi*. Tokyo: Sairyūsha.

Watanabe Osamu, ed., 1996. *Gendai Nihon Shakairon*. Tokyo: Rōdō Junpōsha.

"Watashi ni totte 'Zainichi' to wa." 1980. *Kikan sanzenri* 24:104–15.

Weiner, Michael A. 1989. *The Origins of the Korean Community in Japan, 1910–1923*. Atlantic Highlands, N.J.: Humanities Press International.

———. 1994. *Race and Migration in Imperial Japan*. London: Routledge.

Wender, Melissa L. 2005. *Lamentation as History: Narratives by Koreans in Japan, 1965—2000*. Stanford, Calif.: Stanford University Press.

Williams, Gareth D. 1994. *Banished Voices: Readings in Ovid's Exile Poetry*. Cambridge: Cambridge University Press.

Won Sonjin. 1986. *Nihon no naka no Chōsen mondai*. Tokyo: Gendai Shokan.

Woolf, Virginia. 1928. *Orlando*. London: Hogarth Press.

Yamada Terumi. 1986. "Zainichi Chōsenjin mondai wa wareware Nihonjin no mondai de aru." In Akira Satō and Terumi Yamada, eds., *Zainichi Chōsenjin*, 3–19. Tokyo: Akashi Shoten.

Yamagishi Shigeru. 2002. *Kantō daishinsai to Chōsenjin gyakusatsu*. Tokyo: Waseda Shuppan.

Yamamoto Tetsumi. 1995. *Hokori: Ningen Harimoto Isao*. Tokyo: Kōdansha.

Yamamura Masaaki. [1971] 1975. *Inochi moetsukirutomo*. New ed. Tokyo: Daiwa Shuppan.

Yamasaki Masazumi. 2003. *Sengo "Zainichi" bungakuron*. Tokyo: Yōyōsha.

Yamano Sharin. 2005. *Kenkanryū*. Tokyo: Fuyūsha.

———. 2006. *Zainichi no chizu*. Tokyo: Kaiōsha.

Yamauchi Masayuki and Minzoku Mondai Kenkyūkai, eds., 1991. *Nyūmon sekai no minzoku mondai*. Tokyo: Nihon Keizai Shinbunsha.

Yan Sogiru. [1981] 1987. *Takushī kyōsōkyoku*. Tokyo: Chikuma Shobō.

———. 1990. *Yoru no kawa o watare*. Tokyo: Chikuma Shobō.

———. 1995. *Shura o ikiru*. Tokyo: Kōdansha.

———. 1998. *Chi to hone*. Tokyo: Gentōsha.

———. 1999. *Ajiateki shintai*. Tokyo: Heibonsha.

———. 2001. *Tamashii no nagareyuku hate*. Tokyo: Kōbunsha.

———. 2006. *Mirai e no kioku*. Tokyo: Āton.

———. 2007. *Cinema, cinema, cinema*. Tokyo: Kōbunsha.

Yang Aisun. 2004. *Zainichi Chōsenjin shakai ni okeru saishi girei*. Kyoto: Kōyō Shobō.

Yang Tae-hoon. 2007. *Boku wa Zainichi 'shin' issei*. Tokyo: Heibonsha.

Yang Yonhu. 1982. "4.24 kyōiku tōsō—Osaka." In Kōbe Gakusei—Seinen Sentā, ed., *Zainichi Chōsenjin no minzoku kyōiku*, 40–62. Kōbe: Kōbe Gakusei—Seinen Sentā.

———. 1994. *Sengo Osaka no Chōsenjin undō, 1945–1965*. Tokyo: Miraisha.

Yasumoto Sueko. [1958] 2003. *Nianchan*. Fukuoka: Nishi Nihon Shinbunsha.

Ye Te-won. 1982. *Sabetsu to kanshi no naka de*. Tokyo: Tokuma Shoten.

Yi Chinmi. 2006. "Akkerakan to Kankokujin to shite." In Kyongdok Kim, ed., *Wagaya no minzoku kyōiku*, 32–42. Tokyo: Shinkansha.

Yi Jon'yan. 1985. "Zainichi Chōsenjin to kika." In Yongon Kim and Jon'yan Yi, eds., *Zainichi Kankoku—Chōsenjin*, 43–56. Tokyo: San'ichi Shobō.

Yi Kisun. 1995. *Zerohan*. Tokyo: Kōdansha.

———. 2000. "Korekara no Zainichi dōhō keizaijin no arikata to UG bijinesukurabu no kadai." In UG Bijinesukurabu, ed., *"Zainichi" kara "zaichikyū" e*, 10–26. Osaka: UG Bijinesukurabu.

———. 2006. "Minzoku kyōiku yori ningen kyōiku." In Kyongdok Kim, ed., *Wagaya no minzoku kyōiku*, 115–20. Tokyo: Shinkansha.

Yi Sinhi. 1976. "Henshū o oete." *Kikan sanzenri* 8:222.

———. 1981. "Henshū o oete." *Kikan sanzenri* 28:256.

Yi Unjik. 1967–68. *Dakuryū*. 3 vols. Tokyo: Shinkō Shobō.

Yomota Inuhiko. 1984. *Warera ga "tasha" naru Kankoku*. Tokyo: Riburopōto.

———. 2007 *Nihon eiga to sengo no shinwa*. Tokyo: Iwanami Shoten.

Yoneyama, Lisa. 1999. *Hiroshima Traces: Time, Space, and the Dialectics of Memory*. Berkeley: University of California Press.

Yoon Keun Cha. 1987. *Ishitsu to no kyōzon*. Tokyo: Iwanami Shoten.

———. 1990. *Kozetsu no rekishi ishiki*. Tokyo: Iwanami Shoten.

———. 1992. *"Zainichi" o ikirutowa*. Tokyo: Iwanami Shoten.

———. 1994. *Minzoku gensō no sashitsu*. Tokyo: Iwanami Shoten.

———. 1997. *Nihon kokuminron.* Tokyo: Chikuma Shobō.

Yoshioka Masuo. 1978. "Zainichi Chōsenjin to kokumin kenkō hoken seido." In Masuo Yoshioka, ed., *Zainichi Chōsenjin to shakai hoshō,* 29–61. Tokyo: Shakai Hyōronsha.

———. 1980a. "Zainichi Chōsenjin to nenkin seido." In Masuo Yoshioka, ed., *Zainichi Chōsenjin no seikatsu to jinken,* 51–107. Tokyo: Shakai Hyōronsha.

———. 1980b. "Zainichi Chōsenjin to seikatsu hogo." In Masuo Yoshioka, ed., *Zainichi Chōsenjin no seikatsu to jinken,* 173–250. Tokyo: Shakai Hyōronsha.

———. 1981. "Zainichi gaikokujin to kokumin nenkin." In Masuo Yoshioka, ed., *Zainichi Chōsenjin to jūminken undō,* 139–94. Tokyo: Shakai Hyōronsha.

Yū Miri. 1997. *Mizube no yurikago.* Tokyo: Kadokawa Shoten.

———. 1998. *Gōrudorasshu.* Tokyo: Shinchōsha.

———. [1995] 1999. *Jisatsu.* Tokyo: Bungei shunjū.

———. 2001. *Kotoba wa shizuka ni odoru.* Tokyo: Shinchōsha.

———. [1994] 2002. *Ishi ni oyogu sakana.* Tokyo: Shinchōsha.

———. 2004. *8 gatsu no hate.* Tokyo: Shinchōsha.

———. 2007a. *Yamanotesen uchimawari.* Tokyo: Kawade Shobō Shinsha.

———. 2007b. *Yū Miri fukō zenkiroku.* Tokyo: Shinchōsha.

Yun In-jin. 2004. *K'orian diasŭp'ora.* Seoul: Koryo Taehakkyo Ch'ulp'anbu.

Zai Nihon Daikanminkoku Kyoryū Mindan Chūō Honbu. 1978. *Ken'eki undō no susume.* Tokyo: Zai Nihon Daikanminkoku Kyoryū Mindan Chūō Honbu.

———. 1979. *Seikatsuken o kachitorō.* Tokyo: Zai Nihon Daikanminkoku Kyoryū Mindan Chūō Honbu.

Zainichi Bungei Mintō. 1990. "90 nendai o warera no te ni." *Zainichi bungei mintō* 10:6–7.

Zainichi Chōsen Kagaku Gijutsu Kyōkai. [1951] 1978. "Zainichi Chōsenjin no seikatsu jittai." In Yūsaku Ozawa, ed., *Kindai minshū no kiroku,* vol. 10, 272–311. Tokyo: Shinjinbutsu Ōraisha.

Zainichi Chōsenjin dantai jūyō shiryōshū: 1948 nen—1952 nen. 1975. Tokyo: Kōhokusha.

Zainichi Chōsenjin kanri jūyō bunshoshū. 1978. Tokyo: Kōhokusha.

Zainichi Chōsenjin Kenri Yōgo Iinkai, ed. 1996. *Zainichi Chōsenjin jinken hakusho.* Tokyo: Chōsen Sei'nensha.

Zainichi Chōsenjin no Jinken o Mamorukai, ed. 1963. *Zainichi Chōsenjin wa riyū naki ni sasshō sareteiru.* Tokyo: Zainichi Chōsenjin no Jinken o Mamorukai Shuppankyoku.

———. 1964. *Zainichi Chōsenjin no hōteki ichi.* Tokyo: Zainichi Chōsenjin no Jinken o Mamorukai Shuppankyoku.

———. 1977. *Zainichi Chōsenjin no kihonteki jinken.* Tokyo: Nigatsusha.

Zainichi Hokusenkei Chōsenjin gakkō no kyōkasho no jittai ni tsuite. 1967. n.p.

Zainichi Kankoku—Chōsenjin no Kokumin Nenkin o Motomeru Kai, ed. 1981. *Kokuseki sabetsu e no chōsen*. Tokyo: Zainichi Kankoku—Chōsenjin no Kokumin Nenkin o Motomeru Kai.

Zainichi Kankoku Seinen Dōmei Chūō Honbu, ed. 1970. *Zainichi Kankokujin no rekishi to genjitsu*. Tokyo: Yōyōsha.

Zainichi Kōrai Rōdōsha Renmei. 1992. *Zainichi Chōsenjin no shūrō jittai chōsa*. Tokyo: Shinkansha.

"Zainichi nisei no seikatsu to iken." 1976. *Kikan sanzenri* 8:46–57.

Index

Chong Chi-yong, 180
Chong Jaejung, 7, 71
Chongryun. *See* Zainichi Chōsenjin
  Sōrengōkai
Chongryun Korean, 70
"Chonhā e no michi" (Arai), ix, 162
Chon In: "Kika," 86
Chon Jan: "Nihonjin to koi o shite," 88
Chon Sunpak: "Tonsha no bannin,"
  35–36
Chon Wolson, 126
Chōren. *See* Zainichi Chōsenjin
  Renmei
Chōsen (Korea), viii, 81
Chōsen bungei (journal), 112
Chōsōren. *See* Zainichi Chōsenjin
  Sōrengōkai
Cho Yong-p'il, 110
Christianity, 64, 100, 102, 130
Chung Daekyun. *See* Tei Taikin
Citizenship, 68, 153; and ethnicity, 85,
  86–87; ethnic Koreans, viii, 37, 144;
  Japanese, 134, 144, 145; social, 80–81
Civic participation, 129
Cold War, xi, 29, 39, 68, 90–91,
  107–8, 140, 180, 189
Colonialism, xi, 3, 5, 6, 34, 60, 86,
  172, 186; and racism, 146–47
Comic books, 133. *See also* Manga
Communism, communists, 38, 42–43,
  66, 68, 69–70, 100
Communist Party (Japan), 30, 39, 40,
  41, 66
Community of Resident South
  Koreans in Japan. *See* Zainichi
  Daikanminkoku Kyoryū Mindan
Conscripts, 3, 5
Constitution (Japanese), 74, 100
Conviviality, ethnic, 164–65
Corporation, 14
Costumes: ethnic, 131
Criminality, 6, 38, 109
Culture: Japanese, 124–25, 129;
  national, 15

Dance halls, 72
Deportation, 35, 68

*Dialectical and Historical Material-
  ism* (Stalin), 43
Diaspora: identity in, viii, 115,
  116–17; nationalism and, 169–82
Dictatorship: South Korean, 49, 71,
  104, 149
Discrimination, 5, 32, 52, 61, 75,
  77, 80, 94–95, 100, 111, 129, 151;
  employment, 73–74, 122, 153;
  racial, 4, 8, 23, 38
Disrecognition, 102–3, 125, 150, 165;
  impacts of, 80–84, 91, 92
Dissidents, 116
Domestic violence, 83
Dostoevsky, Fydor: influence of, 63, 64

Earthquakes: Great Kantō, 4, 5
Economic growth, 29, 32; in Japan, 47,
  72; in South Korea, 179
Economies, 8, 30, 38, 134
Education, 9, 78, 120, 153; assimila-
  tion and, 76–77; discrimination
  and, 8, 75; ethnic, 40, 42
Emperor Akihito (Japan): Korean
  ancestry of, 134
Employment, 35, 72–73; discrimina-
  tion, 8, 23, 38, 73–74, 122, 129, 153
English identity, 177
Ennin, 168
Enterprises: family-owned, 73
Esperanto, 100
Essentialism, 89–90
Ethnicity, 20, 28, 75, 152, 159; assert-
  ing, 110–11; and identity, 8–9, 67,
  95–96, 106, 123, 144; naturalization
  and, 86–87
Ethno-political organizations, 39–40,
  131, 189–90. *See also by name*
Europe: Koreans in, 175
Exclusion, 38, 39, 89; systematic,
  75–76
Exile(s), 33, 64: defining, 58–59;
  intellectuals as, 59–60; Kim
  Sokpom on, 48–51; Lee Hoesung
  on, 55–57; Lee Yangji on, 51–55;
  social role of, 57–58
Expatriates, 60